Introduction to Multiregional
Mathematical Demography

A WILEY-INTERSCIENCE PUBLICATION

JOHN WILEY & SONS
New York · London · Sydney · Toronto

Introduction to Multiregional Mathematical Demography

ANDREI ROGERS

Library of Congress Cataloging in Publication Data

Rogers, Andrei.
      Introduction to multiregional mathematical
demography.

      "A Wiley-Interscience publication."
      Bibliography: p.
      Includes index.
      1. Demography—Mathematical models. 2. Migration,
Internal—Mathematical models. 3. Population
forecasting—Mathematical models. I. Title.

HB885.R568 301.32′01′51 74–34027
ISBN 0-471-73035-1

Printed in the United States of America

10 9 8 7 6 5 4 3 2 1

To Tip and Alice

_____

PREFACE

———————

This book is an exposition of some of the mathematics of multiregional population systems. It is designed for the reader who is familiar with the mathematics of single-region demographic analysis and is primarily intended to be a reference work for mathematically inclined demographers, sociologists, geographers, economists, and regional planners. However, it also may be used as a text for a graduate course in mathematical demography. In an effort to make the book relatively self-contained, and to introduce the reader to the notation gradually, I have included a review of single-region mathematical demography. To simplify the exposition I have, without loss of generality, developed the numerical illustrations mostly around two-region population systems. However, to demonstrate the broad applicability of the theory to multiregional population systems, I also have included a few numerical results obtained with data on five-region and nine-region population systems.

Those faced with the prospect of writing a technical book about a vast subject must decide what to include and what to exclude in their exposition. Space and time limitations have led me to omit topics that others may feel should have been addressed in a study of multiregional mathematical demography. In defense, I would argue that the multiregional generalization of topics not included in this text frequently will be straightforward and obvious to the reader who is familiar with the appropriate single-region formulation and has grasped the fundamental concepts described in this book. My particular interests revolve around the analysis of migration and its contribution to projections of the growth and distribution of multi-regional population systems. Having discovered that classical mathematical demography does not provide methods and techniques for carrying out this analysis, I set out to develop such an extension. This study is the product of that effort.

This book is the last of a trilogy dealing with the analysis of multiregional population growth and change, and its contents reflect my involvement in three separate periods of demographic research during the past decade. The work reported here has its origins in a population and migration study I conducted in 1965 for the California State Development Plan, when I was a member of the research staff of the Center for Planning and Development Research at the University of California at Berkeley. The results of those early efforts to introduce an interregional dimension to the demographer's classical single-region cohort survival model of population growth were summarized in my monograph *Matrix Analysis of Interregional Population Growth and Distribution* (Berkeley: University of California Press, 1968). In 1969 I had another opportunity to focus on demographic analysis when, as a member of a consultant team organized by Planning and Development Collaborative and supported by the U.S. Agency for International Development, I spent six months developing a population projection system for Brazil's Federal Department of Housing and Urbanism in Rio de Janeiro. That experience contributed to the demographic sections of my text *Matrix Methods in Urban and Regional Analysis* (San Francisco: Holden-Day, 1971), and it was in Brazil that I first attempted to define the concept of a multiregional life table and to infer migration flows from place of residence by place of birth census data. Finally, in 1971 a two-year grant from the Ford and Rockefeller Foundations enabled me to study the modeling of regional demographic and economic growth, further consolidating and extending my earlier work in multiregional mathematical demography. I wish to express here my deep appreciation to the many individuals and institutions who collectively made the three experiences possible.

Many of the results reported in this book originally appeared in preliminary form in *The Journal of Mathematical Sociology, Environment and Planning*, and *Demography*. I am grateful to the publishers for permission to draw on some of the material contained in those papers. Specifically, Chapter 3 is a much altered version of "The multiregional life table," *The Journal of Mathematical Sociology* (3:1, 1973, 127–137), and the first part of "The mathematics of multiregional demographic growth," *Environment and Planning* (**5**:1, 1973, 3–29, Pion, London). Early summary versions of Chapters 4 and 5 also appear in the latter paper. Parts of Chapter 4 were published as "The multiregional net maternity function and multiregional stable growth," *Demography* (**11**:3, 1974, 473–481). Chapter 6 includes some of the results reported in "Estimation of interregional migration streams from place-of-birth-by-residence data," *Demography* (**8**:2, 1971, 185–194, co-authored with B. von Rabenau), and in "Estimating internal migration from incomplete data using model multiregional life tables," *Demography* (**10**:2, 1973, 277–287).

The influences and assistance of several individuals are reflected in this study. Foremost is that of Nathan Keyfitz, whose outstanding book *Introduction to the Mathematics of Population* (Reading, Mass.: Addison-Wesley, 1968) taught me mathematical demography. My intellectual debt to him will be apparent to anyone who reads both that book and this one. Also of major importance have been the help and counsel of my student Jacques Ledent, who during the two years he served as my research assistant refined the details of several of the models described in this study and in the process identified and corrected a number of errors in my original formulations. His probing questions and valuable insights repeatedly have forced me to clarify my own thinking and to revise some of my ideas. He and Richard Raquillet very expertly carried out most of the data processing and computer programming that produced the numerical results set out in this book. Other students with major contributions in this regard were Burkhard von Rabenau, mentioned previously, Richard Walz, who operationalized and modified the single-region computer programs of Keyfitz and Flieger (1971) that were used to develop the numerical results set out in Chapter 2; and Frans Willekens, who computed the numerical model life tables and stable populations analyzed in Chapters 2 and 6. In-Won Lee and Dan Santini also carried out substantial amounts of programming and data processing chores with good cheer, for which I am grateful. Finally, my thanks go to Colleen Ernst and Mary Malooly for typing a difficult manuscript cheerfully and accurately.

ANDREI ROGERS

*The Technological Institute
Northwestern University
Evanston, Illinois
September 1974*

CONTENTS

Introduction to Multiregional
Mathematical Demography

CHAPTER
ONE

_____

Introduction

Mathematical demography is concerned with the mathematical description of human populations, particularly their structure with regard to age and sex, and the components of change, such as births and deaths, which occur over time to alter that structure. Accordingly, mathematical demographers have focused their attention on population *stocks* and on population *events*. The principal purpose of this book is to extend that focus to include the *flows* that interconnect and weld several regional populations into a multiregional population system. *Multiregional mathematical demography*, therefore, is concerned with the mathematical description of the evolution of human populations over time *and* space. The trifold focus of such models then is on (1) the *stocks* of human population groups at different points in time and locations in space, (2) the vital *events* that occur among these populations, and (3) the *flows* of members of such populations across the spatial borders that delineate the constituent regions of the multiregional population system.

Mathematical demographers traditionally have dealt with single-region populations that are assumed to be undisturbed by, or "closed" to, migration. Thus, for example, Keyfitz's (1968) text *Introduction to the Mathematics*

1

of Population devotes fewer than two of 450 pages to the mathematics of multiregional populations that experience, or are "open" to, internal migration. Another much used reference book, published by the United Nations (1967), is *Methods of Estimating Basic Demographic Measures from Incomplete Data*; this work totally ignores multiregional population systems.[1] Yet many of the major problems associated with national population growth and development revolve around the differential impacts of migration between rural-urban communities, city-suburban areas, and depressed-expanding subregions of national economies.

This book develops a multiregional generalization of classical single-region mathematical demography. Our exposition of the mathematics of multiregional demographic growth parallels in several important respects Keyfitz's (1968) presentation of the single-region theory. To facilitate cross-referencing with that text, we adopt his notation, modifying it slightly where necessary.

The single-region life table and the stationary population it describes are central concepts in the mathematics of single-region population systems. Thus Keyfitz (1968) devotes the first chapter of his book to its exposition. He applies the survivorship proportions of the life table to population projection in Chapter 2, and in Chapter 3 he analyzes the intrinsic rate of growth and the ultimate stable distribution to which a particular population projection is heading. He includes a brief discussion of model life tables in Chapter 4 and devotes Chapters 5, 6, and 7 to an exposition of the continuous model.

We begin this book with a brief review of single-region mathematical demography. We then follow Keyfitz's sequence by first introducing the notion of a *multiregional* life table, which we believe will become a central concept in the mathematics of multiregional population systems. Next we show how such a table provides the regional survivorship and outmigration proportions that are the basis of multiregional population projection, demonstrating that as in the single-region case, the multiregional population projection can be studied in continuous form as an integral equation or in discrete form as a set of linear first-order difference equations. In both the continuous and the discrete formulations, we consider the theory of multi-regional stable population growth and examine relations under stability.

---

[1] Methods of estimating net migration are considered in a more recent United Nations publication (United Nations, 1970). However, the focus on net rather than place-to-place flows turns this effort into a fundamentally single-region approach.

We follow this with a discussion of model multiregional life tables and stable populations and conclude by illustrating their use in procedures that estimate basic demographic measures from incomplete data.

An important ingredient of effective strategies to understand and resolve complex problems of a mathematical nature is a powerful notational system. In extending the principal results of single-region population mathematics to multiregional population systems, we generalize conventional notation as set out, for example, in Keyfitz (1968), although we do not distinguish notationally between continuous and discrete functions. The regional dimension is introduced by means of a system of four subscripts, three of which refer to regions of residence at several successive exact ages. As in the single-region theory, the argument of a variable usually refers to age, and the right superscript, also enclosed in parentheses, refers to time. The left superscript defines the width of the age interval and is omitted when that interval is taken to be 5 years wide. A dot in place of a subscript is an indication that the variable has been summed over all regions included in the range of that subscript. The dot is omitted when the context of the discussion makes clear the meaning of the variable without it.

By way of illustration, consider the notation for the stationary life table population at exact age x. Conventional notation for the discrete form of this variable is l_y, and $l(y)$ usually designates its continuous analog. In the multiregional situation, we introduce a subscript k to denote the *current* region of residence and another, j, to denote a *future* region of residence, adding a third, i say, to designate a *previous* region of residence. Thus

$$_{ix}^{h}l_{kj}(y)$$

denotes the number of persons in the stationary population of region k at exact age y who were residents of region i at exact age x and will be living in region j at exact age $y + h$. For a unit age interval of 5 years, the i-born stationary life table population of region j at exact age $x + 5$ may be denoted by

$$\sum_{k=1}^{m} {}_{i0}^{5}l_{kj}(x) = {}_{i0}^{5}l_{.j}(x) = {}_{i0}l_{j}(x + 5),$$

which in turn leads to the definition of the following two related sets of probabilities:

$$p_{ij}(x) = \frac{{}_{.0}l_{ij}(x)}{{}_{0}l_{i}(x)} = \frac{l_{ij}(x)}{l_{i}(x)}$$

and

$$_{io}p_j(x) = \frac{_{io}l_j(x)}{l_i(0)}.$$

The former probabilities, which describe migration from region i to region j during a unit age interval, are used to generate a multiregional life table. The latter probabilities refer to migration from region of birth to region of residence and are used in the definition of the continuous model of multi-regional demographic growth developed in Chapter 4. Both are set out in matrix form as $P(x)$, the former in italic type, the latter in boldface. (Although we have attempted as much as possible to avoid assigning two different meanings to the same symbol, we have not been entirely successful, and there remain a few instances of the same symbol appearing in different places to designate different quantities, notably $P(x)$ and $M(x)$ in Chapters 3 and 4.)

CHAPTER TWO

Review of Single-Region
Mathematical Demography

The life table and the continuous and discrete models of population growth form the methodological core of classical deterministic single-region mathematical demography. The life table was developed first, appearing in the seventeenth century in the work of the Englishman John Graunt (1662), who first used such a table to study the population of London. The continuous model of population growth was formulated much later and first appears in the work of Alfred Lotka (1907) and Sharpe and Lotka (1911). The discrete counterpart of the continuous model has its origins in papers by Bernardelli (1941) and Lewis (1942), and a definitive exposition of it appears in a pair of papers by Leslie (1945, 1948).

More recently, important new developments in single-region mathematical demography have been stimulated by the need to produce population projections in countries possessing only incomplete and inadequate data (United Nations, 1955 and 1967; Coale and Demeny, 1966). These efforts generally have revolved around the notion of model life tables and stable populations and their use to infer mortality and fertility patterns in regions that lack reliable vital statistics.

By outlining the four principal areas of mathematical demography just listed, this chapter sets the background against which the contents of the rest of this book may be interpreted and digested.

2.1 THE LIFE TABLE

The life table is a device for exhibiting the mortality history of an artificial population, called a *cohort*, as it gradually decreases in size until all its members have died. Normally it is assumed that the age-specific mortality experience to which this cohort is exposed remains constant and that the cohort is undisturbed by migration. Consequently, changes in the cohort's membership can occur only in the form of a decrease due to deaths.

All the columns in a life table originate from a set of probabilities of dying within each interval of age $q(x)$. Life tables that deal with age intervals of a year are frequently referred to as *complete* life tables, whereas those using longer intervals are called *abridged* life tables. However, we ignore this somewhat spurious distinction and for convenience, without loss of generality, deal only with 5-year age intervals in this chapter.

2.1.1 Elementary Life Table Functions

Let $l(0)$ denote a group or *cohort* of babies born at a given instant in time. Typically, $l(0)$, called the *radix*, is set equal to some arbitrary constant such as 100,000. When subjected to the age-specific mortality of an observed population, the cohort decreases in size until the last individual dies. In this interpretation, $l(x)$ denotes the expected number of individuals in the original cohort who survive to exact age x. If, however, the radix is set equal to unity, $l(x)$ becomes the probability that an individual member of the cohort will live to exact age x.

The number of deaths experienced by the cohort in the age interval $(x, x + dt)$ is $l(x) - l(x + dt)$, and the number exposed to death is $l(x)\, dt$. Hence we conclude that

$$\frac{l(x) - l(x + dt)}{l(x)\, dt}$$

is the age-specific death rate. Defining the instantaneous *force of mortality* $\mu(x)$ to be limiting value of this death rate when the age interval becomes very small, we have

$$\mu(x) = \lim_{dt \to 0} \frac{l(x) - l(x + dt)}{l(x)\, dt}$$

$$= -\frac{1}{l(x)} \left[\lim_{dt \to 0} \frac{[l(x + dt) - l(x)]}{dt} \right]$$

$$= -\frac{1}{l(x)} \frac{d}{dx} l(x),$$

whence

$$\mu(x) = -\frac{d}{dx} \ln l(x), \tag{2.1}$$

where $\ln l(x)$ denotes the natural logarithm of $l(x)$.

Given the definition of $\mu(x)$ in (2.1), we may find $l(x)$ by integrating the differential equation

$$\mu(x)\, dx = -d \ln l(x)$$

to obtain

$$l(x) = C \exp\left[-\int_0^x \mu(t)\, dt \right].$$

Setting $x = 0$, we find that $C = l(0)$.

Since the probability that an individual at age x will live an additional h years is

$$\text{Pr(alive at } x + h | \text{alive at } x) = \frac{\text{Pr(alive at } x + h \text{ and at } x)}{\text{Pr(alive at } x)}$$

$$= \frac{\text{Pr(alive at } x + h)}{\text{Pr(alive at } x)}$$

$$= \frac{l(x + h)}{l(x)} = {}^h p(x), \text{ say,}$$

we have the result

$$^h p(x) = \frac{\exp[-\int_0^{x+h} \mu(t)\, dt]}{\exp[-\int_0^x \mu(t)\, dt]} = \exp\left[-\int_x^{x+h} \mu(t)\, dt \right]. \tag{2.2}$$

In the remainder of this chapter $h = 5$ and therefore is omitted.

Denoting the complement of $p(x)$ by $q(x)$, we observe that this *probability of dying within the next 5 years* after exact age x may be defined as

$$q(x) = 1 - p(x) = 1 - \frac{l(x + 5)}{l(x)} = \frac{l(x) - l(x + 5)}{l(x)}. \tag{2.3}$$

The number of individuals in the cohort who die in the age interval $(x, x + dx)$ is $l(x) - l(x + dx)$, or $l(x)\mu(x)\,dx$. Integrating this quantity over an interval of 5 years, we obtain the decrement due to deaths:

$$d(x) = \int_0^5 l(x + t)\mu(x + t)\,dt, \tag{2.4}$$

which when subtracted from the discrete version of $l(x)$ yields $l(x + 5)$:[1]

$$l(x + 5) = l(x) - d(x). \tag{2.5}$$

We may give the set of $l(x)$ values yet another interpretation: that of an age distribution of individuals alive at a given moment in a stationary population whose total annual births exactly equal total annual deaths. If this population is undisturbed by migration, the number of persons alive between the ages x and $x + dx$ is $l(x)\,dx$, between ages x and $x + 5$ it is

$$L(x) = \int_0^5 l(x + t)\,dt, \tag{2.6}$$

and between ages $x + 5$ and $x + 10$ it is

$$L(x + 5) = \int_0^5 l(x + 5 + t)\,dt.$$

Hence we may define the proportion of those in age group x to $x + 4$ surviving into age group $x + 5$ to $x + 9$ as

$$s(x) = \frac{L(x + 5)}{L(x)}. \tag{2.7}$$

---

[1] A notational distinction is usually made in the literature to distinguish continuous functions from their discrete counterparts, expressing age as an argument in the former and as a subscript in the latter. We have found this form of notation most inconvenient in multiregional mathematical demography and therefore have adopted the same notation for both the continuous and discrete life table functions, leaving it to the reader to establish, from the context, which of the two classes of functions is being described.

Using (2.4) and (2.6), we may define

$$m(x) = \frac{d(x)}{L(x)} = \frac{\int_0^5 l(x+t)\mu(x+t)\,dt}{\int_0^5 l(x+t)\,dt} \tag{2.8}$$

to be the annual age-specific death rate in the synthetically constructed life table stationary population. We need to distinguish this rate from the corresponding annual age-specific death rate in the observed population:

$$M(x) = \frac{D(x)}{K(x)} = \frac{\int_0^5 k(x+t)\mu(x+t)\,dt}{\int_0^5 k(x+t)\,dt}, \tag{2.9}$$

where $D(x)$ stands for the observed annual number of deaths in the age interval $(x, x+5)$, and $K(x)$ denotes the average population in that age group during the year that was "exposed" to the corresponding risk of dying. Normally, the midyear population is used as an approximation of $K(x)$.

Returning to our earlier interpretation of $l(x)$ as a cohort, we observe that $L(x)$ in such instances represents the total *person-years* lived by the cohort between ages x and $x+5$. The expected total number of person-years $T(x)$ remaining to the $l(x)$ survivors of $l(0)$ births may be found by integrating from x to the maximum age to which any individual can live, ω:

$$T(x) = \int_0^{\omega-x} l(x+t)\,dt = L(x) + L(x+5) + \cdots, \tag{2.10}$$

and for each of the $l(x)$ individuals, the average expectation of life at age x will be

$$e(x) = \frac{T(x)}{l(x)}. \tag{2.11}$$

2.1.2   Estimating the Age-Specific Probabilities of Dying

Each of the $d(x)$ persons in the cohort population who dies during the next 5 years has lived x complete years plus some portion of the last 5-year interval of life. Using $a(x)$ to denote the average number of years lived in the 5-year interval by those who ultimately die in it, we may decompose the total person-years lived by the cohort in the age-interval into years lived by those who survive the interval and years lived by those who die in the interval:

$$L(x) = 5l(x+5) + a(x)\,d(x), \tag{2.12}$$

whence

$$a(x) = \frac{L(x) - 5l(x + 5)}{d(x)}. \tag{2.13}$$

Recalling (2.5), we easily may establish that as a consequence of (2.13),

$$q(x) = \frac{5m(x)}{1 + [5 - a(x)]m(x)}. \tag{2.14}$$

The problem of estimating $q(x)$ therefore is one of obtaining values for $a(x)$ and $m(x)$, for $x = 0, 5, 10, \ldots$ Normally it is assumed that $m(x)$ is equal to the observed death rate $M(x)$ and that deaths are uniformly distributed over age and time, with the result that $a(x) = \frac{5}{2}$, whence

$$q(x) = \frac{5M(x)}{1 + \frac{5}{2}M(x)}. \tag{2.15}$$

Note that this implies a linear numerical approximation for the integration of $l(x)$ over the 5-year interval in (2.6).

2.1.3 Life Table Computations

Numerical values of elementary life table functions generally are set out in tabulations called *life tables*. Life table computations normally are initiated with the application of an estimated set of age-specific probabilities of dying $q(x)$ in sequence to a hypothetical cohort of births $l(0)$, to determine the survivors at each exact age of life $l(x)$:

$$l(x + 5) = l(x)[1 - q(x)] = l(x)p(x). \tag{2.16}$$

Table 2.1 is a life table that was calculated using the schedule of mortality prevailing in 1968 among females in the United States. In constructing this life table, it was assumed that deaths were uniformly distributed over age and time within each 5-year interval and that $m(x) = M(x)$. Using the $q(x)$ obtained with (2.15) and a radix of 100,000 for $l(0)$, the columns of the life table were obtained by applying in the appropriate sequence the formulas developed in the previous sections. From (2.3) and (2.5) we have

$$q(x) = \frac{d(x)}{l(x)},$$

Table 2.1 Single-Region Life Table: United States Females, 1968

Age, x	$q(x)$	$l(x)$	$d(x)$	$L(x)$	$m(x)$	$s(x)$	$T(x)$	$e(x)$
0	0.021427	100,000	2,143	494,643	0.004332	0.988264	7,436,654	74.37
5	0.001834	97,857	179	488,838	0.000367	0.998329	6,942,011	70.94
10	0.001508	97,678	147	488,021	0.000302	0.997742	6,453,173	66.07
15	0.003010	97,531	294	486,919	0.000603	0.996664	5,965,152	61.16
20	0.003662	97,237	356	485,295	0.000734	0.996010	5,478,233	56.34
25	0.004319	96,881	418	483,358	0.000866	0.994821	4,992,938	51.54
30	0.006044	96,462	583	480,855	0.001212	0.992309	4,509,580	46.75
35	0.009349	95,880	896	477,157	0.001879	0.988267	4,028,725	42.02
40	0.014140	94,983	1,343	471,558	0.002848	0.982253	3,551,568	37.39
45	0.021405	93,640	2,004	463,189	0.004327	0.973719	3,080,010	32.89
50	0.031265	91,636	2,865	451,016	0.006352	0.962069	2,616,821	28.56
55	0.044813	88,771	3,978	433,908	0.009168	0.944908	2,165,805	24.40
60	0.065854	84,793	5,584	410,004	0.013619	0.916220	1,731,897	20.43
65	0.102969	79,209	8,156	375,654	0.021712	0.873784	1,321,893	16.69
70	0.152131	71,053	10,809	328,240	0.032931	0.800900	946,240	13.32
75	0.254497	60,243	15,332	262,888	0.058321	0.693757	617,999	10.26
80	0.375655	44,912	16,871	182,380	0.092506	0.947098	355,112	7.91
85+	1.0	28,040	28,040	172,732	0.162335	—	172,732	6.16

13

whence

$$d(x) = l(x)q(x). \tag{2.17}$$

Thus, for example, in Table 2.1,

$$d(15) = l(15)q(15)$$
$$= 97,531(0.003010) = 294.$$

Having found $d(x)$, we may proceed to find $l(x + 5)$ by using (2.5). Again referring to Table 2.1 for an illustration, we note that

$$l(20) = l(15) - d(15)$$
$$= 97,531 - 294 = 97,237.$$

Applying (2.17) and (2.5) recursively, we complete the columns headed by $l(x)$ and $d(x)$ in Table 2.1 and derive the values $L(x)$, as defined by (2.12), which may be reexpressed as

$$L(x) = \tfrac{5}{2}[l(x) + l(x + 5)]. \tag{2.18}$$

Thus, for example, in Table 2.1, we note that 97,237 of 97,531 women at age 15 survived to age 20. If the $97,531 - 97,237 = 294$ deaths were distributed uniformly over the 5-year interval, the 294 women who died lived an average of 2.5 years each, or $\tfrac{5}{2}(294) = 735$ person-years. The 97,237 who survived lived a full 5 years each, or $5(97, 237) = 486,185$ person-years. Hence the total number of person-years lived by this cohort, during the 5-year interval, was

$$L(15) = \tfrac{5}{2}(294) + 5(97,237)$$
$$= 735 + 486,185$$
$$= 486,920,$$

or, equivalently, using (2.18),

$$L(15) = \tfrac{5}{2}[l(15) + l(20)]$$
$$= \tfrac{5}{2}(97,531 + 97,237)$$
$$= 486,920.$$

The discrepancy with the life table value of 486,919 is due to rounding.

The remainder of the life table now may be constructed by applying the definitions of $s(x)$, $m(x)$, $T(x)$, and $e(x)$ set out in (2.7), (2.8), (2.10), and (2.11), respectively.

In Table 2.1, $m(x) = M(x)$ for all ages. This is a consequence of our assumptions and implies that $k(x)$ and $l(x)$ have the same curve. However, if allowance is made for the difference between the observed age distribution and the synthetically created stationary one in the life table, $k(x)$ and $l(x)$ do not follow the same curve and $m(x) \neq M(x)$. This occurs, for example, in the iterative life table construction methods proposed by Keyfitz (1970), wherein the calculations ultimately lead to a life table that reproduces exactly the age-specific mortality rates that are its basis, subject to an allowance made for the difference between the distribution of population and deaths within age groups in the observed empirical population and in the stationary population of the life table.

2.1.4   The Terminal Age Interval in the Life Table

The terminal age interval in a life table is a half-open interval: z years and over. For this interval $q(z)$ is set to unity, and the values $M(z)$, $q(z)$, $l(z)$, $d(z)$, $L(z)$, $m(z)$, $T(z)$, and $e(z)$ all refer to the interval age z and over. Since the length of the interval is infinite, $l(z + 5)$ is not available and (2.18) cannot be used to obtain $L(z)$. We must therefore adopt a slightly different approach.

Since

$$m(x) = \frac{d(x)}{L(x)},$$

$$L(x) = \frac{d(x)}{m(x)},$$

and setting $x = z$,

$$L(z) = \frac{d(z)}{m(z)}.$$

Each of the $l(z)$ people at age z will ultimately die. Hence $d(z) = l(z)$, and

$$L(z) = \frac{l(z)}{m(z)} = \frac{l(z)}{M(z)}, \qquad \text{if} \quad m(x) = M(x). \tag{2.19}$$

By definition,

$$T(z) = L(z); \tag{2.20}$$

consequently

$$e(z) = \frac{T(z)}{l(z)} = \frac{L(z)}{l(z)} = \frac{1}{m(z)}.$$
(2.21)

2.1.5 An Alternative Method for Estimating Age-Specific Probabilities of Dying

We have seen that the normal method for constructing a single-region life table begins with the estimation of the probability of dying within each interval of age $q(x)$, using the corresponding observed annual age-specific death rate. An alternative method of life table construction relies on census information alone. If a closed population has been enumerated at two points in time—5 years apart, say—observed survivorship proportions can be computed and equated to their life table counterparts. We begin by noting that purely as a consequence of our definitions,

$$q(x) = 1 - p(x) = 1 - \frac{s(x)}{1 + p(x + 5) - s(x)},$$
(2.22)

where

$$s(x) = \frac{L(x + 5)}{L(x)}.$$

Setting $s(x)$ equal to the observed survivorship proportions, we obtain the set of $q(x)$ with which to compute the life table.

In the latter method one must begin with the last age group, 85 years and over, say, and work backward to find $q(80)$ and, ultimately, $q(0)$. Since the last age interval is open-ended, we assume that $q(85) = 1.0$ and derive

$$s(80) = \frac{L(85)}{L(80)} = \frac{l(85)/m(85)}{\frac{5}{2}[l(80) + l(85)]} = \frac{p(80)/m(85)}{\frac{5}{2}[1 + p(80)]},$$

since $L(85) = l(85)/m(85)$, whence[2]

$$p(80) = \frac{\frac{5}{2}m(85)s(80)}{1 - \frac{5}{2}m(85)s(80)}$$
(2.23)

[2] To obtain $q(80)$ given $s(80)$, we need an estimate of $m(85)$. Since $m(85) = 1/e(85)$, an equivalent but more convenient procedure is to specify a value for $e(85)$ instead.

and

$$q(80) = 1 - p(80) = 1 - \frac{\frac{5}{2}m(85)s(80)}{1 - \frac{5}{2}m(85)s(80)}. \tag{2.24}$$

For a numerical illustration of the foregoing formulas, consider the data presented in Table 2.1. For example, recall that $m(15) = M(15) = 0.000603$, whence, by (2.15),

$$q(15) = \frac{5(0.000603)}{1 + \frac{5}{2}(0.000603)} = 0.003010.$$

Alternatively, we could use (2.22) to find the same result by recalling that $s(15) = 0.996664$ and $q(20) = 0.003662$, whence

$$q(15) = 1 - \frac{0.996664}{1 + (1 - 0.003662) - 0.996664} = 0.003010.$$

For the next-to-last age group we have, using (2.24),

$$q(80) = 1 - \frac{\frac{5}{2}(0.162335)(0.947098)}{1 - \frac{5}{2}(0.162335)(0.947098)} = 0.375655.$$

Age misreporting, the impacts of internal migration, and census enumeration errors often lead to observed survivorship proportions that misrepresent the underlying mortality patterns. Consequently demographers usually adopt the conventional method of estimating $q(x)$ on the basis of vital statistics data, whenever such data are reliable and easily available. Since many developing countries lack such data, however, the alternative method (see Section 2.4) is sometimes used to arrive at crude estimates of mortality schedules, which subsequently may be adjusted or smoothed in various ways.

For future reference, let us summarize and label the two alternative estimation methods as follows:

OPTION 1

Given the vector $\{\hat{\mathbf{m}}(x)\}$ find $\{\mathbf{q}(x)\}$ such that $\{\mathbf{m}(x)\} = \{\hat{\mathbf{m}}(x)\}$.   (2.25)

OPTION 2

Given the vector $\{\hat{\mathbf{s}}(x)\}$ find $\{\mathbf{q}(x)\}$ such that $\{\mathbf{s}(x)\} = \{\hat{\mathbf{s}}(x)\}$.   (2.26)

2.2   THE CONTINUOUS MODEL OF DEMOGRAPHIC GROWTH

The principal contribution of the continuous model of demographic growth lies in its ability to trace through the ultimate consequences of applying a particular regime of fixed age-specific rates of fertility and mortality to a population of a single sex. It is, therefore, a natural generalization of the life table stationary population whose births are equal to deaths. When births are not found to equal deaths, but instead are assumed to occur according to rates that are forever fixed, we obtain the more interesting model of a stable population due to Lotka. In this model the births of a current generation are associated with those of the preceding generation to define several important constants that describe the ultimate growth and composition of such a population.

2.2.1   The Renewal Equation and Stable Growth

The continuous single-sex model of single-region mathematical demography is expressed as an integral equation. Beginning with $B(t)$, the density of female births at time t, we note that the number of women aged x to $x + dx$ at time t were born since time zero and are the survivors of those born x years ago, $B(t - x)p(x)\, dx$, where $x \leq t$. At time t these women give birth to

$$B(t - x)p(x)m(x)\, dx \qquad (2.27)$$

female children per year. Here $p(x)$ denotes the probability of surviving to age x, and $m(x)\, dx$ is the annual rate of female childbearing among women aged x to $x + dx$.

Integrating (2.27) over all x and adding $G(t)$ to include births to women already alive at time zero gives the fundamental Lotka integral equation

$$B(t) = G(t) + \int_0^t B(t - x)p(x)m(x)\, dx, \qquad (2.28)$$

where (Keyfitz, 1968, p. 97)

$$G(t) = \int_{\alpha - t}^{\beta - t} k(x + t)m(x + t)\, dx = \int_{\alpha - t}^{\beta - t} k(x) \frac{p(x + t)}{p(x)} m(x + t)\, dx, \quad (2.29)$$

and $k(x)\,dx$ denotes the number of women aged x to $x + dx$ at time zero. For $t \geq \beta$, $G(t)$ is zero; hence

$$B(t) = \int_0^t B(t - x)p(x)m(x)\,dx, \qquad \text{for} \quad t \geq \beta. \tag{2.30}$$

On replacing $B(t)$ and $B(t - x)$ by Qe^{rt} and $Qe^{r(t-x)}$, respectively, and noting that $m(x)$ is nonzero only in the childbearing ages $\alpha \leq x \leq \beta$, we find the *characteristic equation*

$$\Psi(r) = \int_\alpha^\beta e^{-rx}p(x)m(x)\,dx = \int_\alpha^\beta e^{-rx}\Phi(x)\,dx = 1, \tag{2.31}$$

where the product $p(x)m(x)$, denoted by $\Phi(x)$, is commonly known as the *net maternity function*. To solve the integral equation in (2.31), we need to determine that value of r for which $\Psi(r)$ is unity.

The terms inside the integral in (2.31) are always nonnegative, and e^{-rx} is a decreasing function of r. Consequently $\Psi(r)$ must be a decreasing function of r, which guarantees the existence of a real root. Differentiating $\Psi(r)$ with respect to r, we observe that the first derivative is always negative for all real values of r. Hence $\Psi(r)$ is a monotonically decreasing function. Thus there can only be one real value of r for which $\Psi(r)$ is unity.

The complex roots of (2.31) occur in complex conjugate pairs. Suppose that $u + iv$ is a complex root of (2.31). Then using DeMoivre's theorem,

$$\int_\alpha^\beta e^{-ux}[\cos(vx) - i\sin(vx)]\Phi(x)\,dx = 1.$$

Separating the real and imaginary parts, we have

$$\int_\alpha^\beta e^{-ux}\cos(vx)\Phi(x)\,dx = 1, \tag{2.32}$$

and since there is no imaginary term on the right-hand side,

$$\int_\alpha^\beta e^{-ux}\sin(vx)\Phi(x)\,dx = 0. \tag{2.33}$$

Consequently $u - iv$ must also be a root of (2.31).

It is easily demonstrated that the real root r must be larger than the value of u in any complex root $u \pm iv$. Since $\cos(vx)$ must be less than unity for some values of x in (2.32),

$$\int_\alpha^\beta e^{-ux}\Phi(x)\,dx > 1.$$

But

$$\int_{\alpha}^{\beta} e^{-r_1 x}\Phi(x)\,dx = 1.$$

Therefore $r_1 > u$.

For any r_k that is a root of (2.31),

$$B(t) = Q_k e^{r_k t}$$

is a solution and, assuming distinct roots, so is the general solution

$$B(t) = \sum_{k=1}^{\infty} Q_k e^{r_k t} \tag{2.34}$$

$$= Q_1 e^{r_1 t} + \sum_{k=2}^{\infty} Q_k e^{u_k t}[\cos(v_k t) + i\sin(v_k t)]. \tag{2.35}$$

For sufficiently large values of t, all terms beyond the first in (2.35) become negligibly small relative to the first, because $r_1 > u_k$ for all $k > 1$. Hence ultimately we have

$$B(t) \doteq Q_1 e^{r_1 t}. \tag{2.36}$$

Finally, consider the problem of evaluating the Q_k to fit a given initial condition defined by $G(t)$. We begin by taking Laplace transforms of both sides of (2.28), after denoting $p(x)m(x)$ by $\Phi(x)$ the net maternity function:

$$B^*(r) = G^*(r) + B^*(r)\Phi^*(r),$$

where

$$B^*(r) = \int_0^{\infty} e^{-rt}B(t)\,dt,$$

$$G^*(r) = \int_0^{\infty} e^{-rt}G(t)\,dt,$$

and

$$\Phi^*(r) = \int_0^{\infty} e^{-rt}\Phi(t)\,dt.$$

It follows that

$$B^*(r) = \frac{G^*(r)}{1 - \Phi^*(r)},$$

the right-hand side of which may be expanded as follows:

$$B^*(r) = \frac{G^*(r)}{1 - \Phi^*(r)} = \sum_{k=1}^{\infty} \frac{Q_k}{r - r_k},$$ (2.37)

subject to conditions normally satisfied in demographic analysis. Inverting the terms of the expansion in (2.37), we obtain (2.34) once again. Applying the usual procedure for determining the coefficients of partial fractions, we have

$$Q_k = \lim_{r \to r_k} \frac{(r - r_k)G^*(r)}{1 - \Phi^*(r)} = \frac{G^*(r)}{-d\Phi^*(r)/dr}\bigg|_{r=r_k},$$

whence

$$Q_k = \frac{\int_0^\beta e^{-r_k t} G(t)\,dt}{\int_\alpha^\beta x e^{-r_k x} p(x)m(x)\,dx}.$$ (2.38)

For the maximal root, this relationship may be expressed more conveniently as

$$Q = \frac{V}{A},$$ (2.39)

where

$$V = \int_0^\beta e^{-rt} G(t)\,dt$$ (2.40)

is called the *total reproductive value* of a (single-sex) population and

$$A = \frac{\int_\alpha^\beta x e^{-rx} p(x)m(x)\,dx}{\int_\alpha^\beta e^{-rx} p(x)m(x)\,dx} = \int_\alpha^\beta x e^{-rx} p(x)m(x)\,dx$$ (2.41)

is the *mean age of childbearing in the stable population.*

2.2.2 Numerical Solution of the Characteristic Equation

The conventional numerical solution of (2.31) is carried out using an expression in which the integral

$$\int_0^5 e^{-r(x+t)} p(x+t)m(x+t)\,dt, \qquad x = \alpha, \ldots, \beta - 5$$

is evaluated as the product of $e^{-r(x+2.5)}$, $L(x)/l(0)$, and $F(x)$, where $F(x)$ is the observed birthrate among women aged x to $x + 4$ at last birthday. Thus normally $\Psi(r)$ is approximated by

$$\sum_{x=\alpha}^{\beta-5} e^{-r(x+2.5)} \frac{L(x)}{l(0)} F(x), \qquad (2.42)$$

the summation being taken over childbearing ages x which are multiples of 5. Consequently, assuming that the childbearing ages lie between $\alpha = 10$ and $\beta = 50$, (2.31) may be solved numerically by determining that value of r for which

$$e^{-12.5r} \frac{L(10)}{l(0)} F(10) + e^{-17.5r} \frac{L(15)}{l(0)} F(15) + \cdots + e^{-47.5r} \frac{L(45)}{l(0)} F(45) = 1.$$
$$(2.43)$$

Several iterative methods have been proposed to find the r that satisfies (2.43). Of these, the method of *functional iteration* described by Keyfitz (1968, p. 111) is one of the most efficient. To apply that method, we begin by multiplying both sides of (2.43) by $e^{27.5r}$ and choose an arbitrary initial value for r, with which we evaluate the resulting expression on the left-hand side of the equals sign. Taking 1/27.5 of the natural logarithm of this quantity, we obtain an improved approximation of r with which we once again evaluate the same expression and continue to seek improved approximations until two consecutive approximations differ by less than a small prescribed amount.

Applying the method of functional iteration to the life table data in Table 2.1 and the fertility data in Table 2.2, we get $r = 0.005715$. The same calculations carried out with comparable 1958 data yield an r of 0.020649, indicating a considerable decline in fertility, since mortality remained relatively unchanged during the decade $[e_{1958}(0) = 73.03]$.

Given a numerical approximation of r, we may apply the following expressions to evaluate V and A (Keyfitz, 1968, pp. 264, 134):

$$V = \tfrac{5}{2} \sum_{x=0}^{\beta-5} K(x)F(x) + 5 \sum_{x=0}^{\beta-5} \sum_{t=5}^{\beta-x-5} e^{-rt} K(x) \frac{L(x+t)}{L(x)} F(x+t) \quad (2.44)$$

and

$$A = \sum_{x=\alpha}^{\beta-5} (x + 2.5)e^{-r(x+2.5)} \frac{L(x)}{l(0)} F(x), \qquad (2.45)$$

Table 2.2 Net Maternity Function and Relations Under Stability: United States Females, 1968

Age, x	Stationary Population, $L(x)/l(0)$	Birthrate $F(x)$	Net Maternity Function $\Phi(x)$	Moments of Net Maternity Function	
				First	Second
10	4.88021	0.00048	0.00233	0.02910	0.36375
15	4.86919	0.03195	0.15559	2.72285	47.64992
20	4.85295	0.08119	0.39403	8.86558	199.47549
25	4.83358	0.06805	0.32891	9.04506	248.73927
30	4.80855	0.03615	0.17381	5.64875	183.58452
35	4.77157	0.01730	0.08256	3.09617	116.10641
40	4.71558	0.00472	0.02227	0.94648	40.22527
45	4.63189	0.00030	0.00138	0.06553	3.11262
Total		0.24014	1.16088	30.41953	839.25725

Reproduction rates
  Gross reproduction rate $\qquad GRR = 1.201$
  Net reproduction rate $\qquad R(0) = 1.161$
Stationary population
  Mean age of childbearing $\qquad \mu = 26.204$
  Variance of age of childbearing $\qquad \sigma^2 = 36.307$
Stable population[a]
  Intrinsic rate of growth
    Method of functional iteration $\qquad r = 0.00572$
    Method of normal fit $\qquad r = 0.00572$
  Intrinsic birthrate $\qquad b = 0.01669$
  Intrinsic death rate $\qquad d = 0.01097$
  Mean age of childbearing $\qquad A = 25.998$
  Total reproductive value $\qquad V = 50,916,901$
  Stable births $\qquad Q = 1,958,470$
  Mean age $\qquad a = 36.225$
  Mean length of generation $\qquad T = 26.100$
  Stable age composition
    0–14 $\qquad 0.2354$
    15–64 $\qquad 0.6211$
    65+ $\qquad 0.1435$
    $\qquad \overline{1.0000}$

[a] Computed using the numerical value of the intrinsic rate of growth as given by the method of functional iteration ($r = 0.005715$).

using data with an interval width of 5 years. Dividing (2.44) by (2.45) yields a numerical approximation of Q.

2.2.3   The Net Maternity Function

Net maternity functions of various countries at different points in time have exhibited a regularity that demographers have tried to capture by means of curve fitting. Lotka himself proposed its representation by a normal probability function, and Keyfitz (1968, Chapter 6) has compared the fits of the normal curve with those provided by alternative probability functions. Such a view of the net maternity function leads naturally to an examination of its moments:

$$R(n) = \int_{\alpha}^{\beta} x^n \Phi(x)\, dx, \qquad n = 0, 1, 2, \ldots .$$

The first three moments are of principal interest because they define, respectively, the *net reproduction rate* $R(0)$, the *mean age of childbearing* in the stationary life table population μ, and the corresponding variance σ^2, where

$$R(0) = \int_{\alpha}^{\beta} p(x)m(x)\, dx = \Psi(0), \tag{2.46}$$

$$\mu = \frac{\int_{\alpha}^{\beta} x p(x)m(x)\, dx}{\int_{\alpha}^{\beta} p(x)m(x)\, dx} = \frac{R(1)}{R(0)} \tag{2.47}$$

$$\sigma^2 = \frac{\int_{\alpha}^{\beta} (x - \mu)^2 p(x)m(x)\, dx}{\int_{\alpha}^{\beta} p(x)m(x)\, dx} = \frac{R(2)}{R(0)} - \mu^2. \tag{2.48}$$

The net reproduction rate gives the number of (girl) children expected to be born to a (girl) baby now born, if the current schedule of fertility and mortality is maintained. A related measure, which however does not consider the effects of mortality, is the *gross reproduction rate*

$$GRR = \int_{\alpha}^{\beta} m(x)\, dx.$$

Table 2.2 presents the net maternity function for United States females in 1968. Observe that

$$GRR = 5 \sum_{x=10}^{45} F(x) = 1.201$$

$$R(0) = \sum_{x=10}^{45} \frac{L(x)}{l(0)} F(x) = 1.161,$$

$$\mu = \frac{\sum_{x=10}^{45}(x + 2.5)L(x)F(x)}{\sum_{x=10}^{45}L(x)F(x)} = \frac{30.41953}{1.16088} = 26.204,$$

$$\sigma^2 = \frac{839.25725}{1.16088} - (26.20388)^2 = 36.307.$$

Lotka showed how these three parameters may be used to obtain a numerical approximation of r, the intrinsic rate of growth. He divided both sides of (2.31) by $R(0)$, expanded the exponential inside the integral up to the term in r^2, and taking logarithms of both sides, obtained

$$\ln\left[\int_\alpha^\beta \left(1 - rx + \frac{r^2 x^2}{2}\right) \frac{p(x)m(x)}{R(0)} dx\right] = -\ln R(0),$$

or, more compactly,

$$\ln\left(1 - r\frac{R(1)}{R(0)} + \frac{r^2}{2}\frac{R(2)}{R(0)}\right) = -\ln R(0).$$

Applying the expansion formula $\ln(1 + a) = a - a^2/2 + \cdots +$, and retaining only quantities up to terms in r^2, gives

$$-r\mu + \frac{r^2\sigma^2}{2} = -\ln R(0)$$

or

$$\tfrac{1}{2}\sigma^2 r^2 - \mu r + \ln R(0) = 0. \tag{2.49}$$

Solving the quadratic equation in (2.49), we have as the solution for the real root

$$r = \frac{\mu - \sqrt{\mu^2 - 2\sigma^2 \ln R(0)}}{\sigma^2} \tag{2.50}$$

or, alternatively,

$$r = \frac{\ln R(0)}{\mu - r\sigma^2/2}, \tag{2.51}$$

in which the r on the left-hand side may be viewed as an improved approximation of the r used in the numerical evaluation of the right-hand side. We
start with r set to some arbitrary value, say $r = 0$, and obtain an improved
approximation by means of (2.51). Repeating this procedure until two consecutive approximations of r differ by less than a small amount, we obtain our
estimate of r. Keyfitz and Flieger (1970) refer to this iterative solution method
as the *method of normal fit*. Its application to the data in Table 2.2 yields an
r of 0.005716.

2.2.4   Relations Under Stability

The age composition of a population that is undisturbed by migration is
determined by the regime of fertility and mortality to which it has been
subject. If this regime has remained unchanged for a long enough period,
the initial age composition of the population is "forgotten" in that its influence on the current age composition disappears entirely. Such a *stable
population* is characterized by a proportionally fixed age composition and
increases at a constant intrinsic rate of growth r.

Let $c(x, t)$ denote the proportional age composition of a female population
at time t. The number at age x at time $t—k(x, t)$, say—are survivors of
$B(t - x)$ births x years ago, whence

$$k(x, t) = B(t - x)p(x).$$

Integrating this quantity over all ages of life, we obtain the total female
population. Thus the proportion of this population which is at age x at time
t is of density

$$c(x, t) = \frac{k(x, t)}{\int_0^\omega k(x, t)\, dx} = \frac{B(t - x)p(x)}{\int_0^\omega B(t - x)p(x)\, dx}. \tag{2.52}$$

If $c(x, t)\, dx$ is the proportion of females aged x to $x + dx$ at time t, the
consolidated or "crude" death rate at time t of this population is

$$d(t) = \int_0^\omega c(x, t)\mu(x)\, dx; \tag{2.53}$$

analogously, its crude birthrate at time t is

$$b(t) = \int_\alpha^\beta c(x, t)m(x)\, dx, \tag{2.54}$$

which also may be found by setting $x = 0$ in the numerator of (2.52)

$$b(t) = c(0, t) = \frac{B(t)}{\int_0^\omega B(t - x)p(x)\,dx}. \tag{2.55}$$

Recall that at stability $B(t) = Qe^{rt}$. Substituting this into (2.52) and (2.55), we have a stable population with the proportional age composition

$$c(x, t) = \frac{Qe^{r(t-x)}p(x)}{\int_0^\omega Qe^{r(t-x)}p(x)\,dx} = \frac{e^{-rx}p(x)}{\int_0^\omega e^{-rx}p(x)\,dx} = c(x), \tag{2.56}$$

and birthrate

$$b(t) = \frac{Qe^{rt}}{\int_0^\omega Qe^{r(t-x)}p(x)\,dx} = \frac{1}{\int_0^\omega e^{-rx}p(x)\,dx} = b, \tag{2.57}$$

whence

$$c(x) = be^{-rx}p(x). \tag{2.58}$$

Since under stability t has disappeared from the expressions for $c(x, t)$ and $b(t)$, these quantities are independent of time and may be denoted simply as $c(x)$ and b, respectively. We call $c(x)$ the *stable age composition* and b the *intrinsic birthrate*. The *intrinsic death rate* d may be found by subtracting the intrinsic rate of growth from the intrinsic birthrate:

$$d = b - r. \tag{2.59}$$

The total stable female population $K(t)$ increases exponentially:

$$K(t) = \int_0^\omega B(t - x)p(x)\,dx = \int_0^\omega Qe^{r(t-x)}p(x)\,dx = \left(\frac{Q}{b}\right)e^{rt} = Ye^{rt}, \tag{2.60}$$

with each generation being a multiple e^{rt} of the one before.[3] Since the net reproduction rate $R(0)$ is a measure of the level of intergenerational increase, we conclude that

$$e^{rT} = R(0), \tag{2.61}$$

where T is the *mean length of generation*. Taking natural logarithms of both sides and simplifying, we find

$$T = \frac{1}{r}\ln R(0). \tag{2.62}$$

[3] The constant term Y in (2.60) is known as the *stable equivalent* (Keyfitz, 1969). Its interpretation is discussed in Section 2.3.4.

The mean age of the stable population is

$$a = \frac{\int_0^\omega xe^{-rx}p(x)\,dx}{\int_0^\omega e^{-rx}p(x)\,dx} = \int_0^\omega x\,c(x)\,dx. \tag{2.63}$$

Finally, consider the numerical descriptions of relations under stability set out in Table 2.2. Using data for United States females in 1968, we find for $r = 0.005715$

$$b = \frac{1}{\sum_{x=0}^{85} e^{-r(x+2.5)}\,L(x)/l(0)} = 0.01669$$

$$d = b - r = 0.01097$$

$$T = \frac{1}{r}\ln(1.16088) = 26.100$$

$$a = \frac{\sum_{x=0}^{85}(x+2.5)e^{-r(x+2.5)}L(x)}{\sum_{x=0}^{85} e^{-r(x+2.5)}L(x)} = 36.225$$

$$Q = 1{,}958{,}470,$$

whence

$$K(2008) \doteq e^{50r}\frac{Q}{b} = 156{,}145{,}691,$$

the projection of the total population in the year 2008 when only the first term in (2.35) is used. To obtain the proportions of the stable population that are in various age groups, we define

$$C(x) = \int_x^{x+5} c(a)\,da = b\int_x^{x+5} e^{-ra}p(a)\,da, \tag{2.64}$$

and evaluate it numerically for each 5-year age group as

$$C(x) = be^{-r(x+2.5)}\frac{L(x)}{l(0)} = \frac{e^{-r(x+2.5)}L(x)}{\sum_{x=0}^{z} e^{-r(x+2.5)}L(x)}.$$

2.3 THE DISCRETE MODEL OF DEMOGRAPHIC GROWTH

The discrete formulation of Lotka's model expresses the process of population projection by means of a matrix operation in which a population age distribution, set out as a vector, is multiplied by a projection matrix that survives that population forward through time. Drawing on the mathematical theory of nonnegative matrices, one may examine the properties of this projection process and establish results analogous to those found by solving the integral renewal equation of the continuous model.

2.3.1 Survivorship

Consider a cohort of babies who were born not at a moment in time, but whose births were uniformly spread out over a unit time interval of 5 years, ending at $t = 0$. Suppose that these births occurred at a rate of B per year, so that $B\, dt$ babies were born between time t and $t + dt$ ($-5 \le t \le 0$). The expected number of these babies who survive to the end of the 5-year interval, that is, to $t = 0$, is then $Bl(-t)\, dt$, and the expected total number of survivors of this cohort at the end of the 5 years will be $\int_{-5}^{0} Bl(-t)\, dt$.[4] Setting $u = -t$ we have $B \int_{0}^{5} l(u)\, du$, or, more compactly, $BL(0)$. Analogously, the expected number of survivors x years after the end of the initial 5-year period will be $BL(x)$, and at the end of $x + 5$ years will be $BL(x + 5)$, where $x = 0, 5, 10, \ldots$ and $L(x) = \int_{0}^{5} l(x + u)\, du$.

An observed population x to $x + 4$ years of age at midyear, $K(x)$, may be viewed as the survivors of 5 years of $B = K(x)/L(x)$ annual births that took place some time ago. Assuming no migration, the preceding argument indicates that the expected number of survivors of five consecutive years of B annual births living to be $x + 5$ to $x + 9$ years of age at last birthday is $K(x + 5) = BL(x + 5) = [K(x)/L(x)]L(x + 5)$ or, equivalently,

$$K(x + 5) = K(x)s(x), \tag{2.65}$$

where

$$s(x) = \frac{L(x + 5)}{L(x)}.$$

Equation 2.65 can also be derived from the continuous model. The expected number of survivors t years from now among $k(x)\, dx$ persons of age x to $x + dx$ alive today is

$$k(x)\frac{l(x + t)}{l(x)}\, dx.$$

---

[4] In this section, we adopt a radix of unity for $l(0)$. Therefore $l(x)$ is interpreted as the probability that an individual baby will live to exact age x, and the life table function $l(x)$ discussed in Section 2.1 corresponds to $100,000\, l(x)$ in this section's notation, except where explicitly stated to the contrary.

But today ($t = 0$) we can only observe the number of people between ages x and $x + 5$, say

$$K^{(0)}(x) = \int_0^5 k(x + u)\, du,$$

and of these,

$$K^{(1)}(x + 5) = \int_0^5 k(x + u)\, \frac{l(x + 5 + u)}{l(x + u)}\, du \qquad (2.66)$$

will be alive after 5 years. It is common practice to substitute

$$\frac{\int_0^5 k(x + u)\, du \int_0^5 l(x + 5 + u)\, du}{\int_0^5 l(x + u)\, du} = \frac{K^{(0)}(x)L(x + 5)}{L(x)} \qquad (2.67)$$

for the right-hand side of the equality in (2.66). This simplification is valid only if $k(x)$ and $l(x)$ have the same curve within the age group. Accepting such an approximation and substituting it into (2.66), yields

$$K^{(1)}(x + 5) = K^{(0)}(x)\, \frac{L(x + 5)}{L(x)} = K^{(0)}(x)s(x),$$

as in (2.65), or in general

$$K^{(t+1)}(x + 5) = K^{(t)}(x)s(x), \qquad x = 0, 5, \ldots, z - 5, \qquad (2.68)$$

where t is measured in 5-year unit intervals.

When applied to all age groups, the projection process described in (2.68) may be expressed compactly in matrix form. Collecting all the $K^{(t)}(x)$, for $x = 0, 5, 10, \ldots, z$ into the vector $\{\mathbf{K}^{(t)}\}$:

$$\{\mathbf{K}^{(t)}\} = \left\{ \begin{array}{c} K^{(t)}(0) \\ K^{(t)}(5) \\ K^{(t)}(10) \\ \vdots \\ K^{(t)}(z) \end{array} \right\}$$

we have

$$\{\mathbf{K}^{(t+1)}\} = \mathbf{S}\{\mathbf{K}^{(t)}\}, \qquad (2.69)$$

where

$$
S = \begin{bmatrix}
0 & 0 & 0 & \cdots & 0 \\[6pt]
\dfrac{L(5)}{L(0)} & 0 & 0 & \cdots & 0 \\[10pt]
0 & \dfrac{L(10)}{L(5)} & 0 & \cdots & 0 \\[10pt]
\vdots & & \ddots & \cdots & \vdots \\[6pt]
0 & 0 & \cdots & \dfrac{L(z)}{L(z-5)} & 0
\end{bmatrix}.
\qquad (2.70)
$$

2.3.2   Fertility

Equation 2.69 may be used to project a population disaggregated by age 5 years forward. However, such a projection will contain only the survivors of the initial population. To obtain a complete projection, one must make an allowance for the expected number of babies born during those 5 years *that survive to the end of the 5-year interval.* Suppose that these births took place uniformly over the 5-year interval, and let $B(x)$ denote the number of live female babies born during a calendar year to women aged x to $x + 4$ at last birthday. The *annual* age-specific birthrate then may be defined as

$$
F(x) = \frac{B(x)}{K(x)} \qquad (2.71)
$$

for all x in the childbearing ages. To obtain the number of babies born during the projection period, we apply the foregoing annual age-specific birthrates to the average number of women in the corresponding age groups that were exposed to the probability of having a baby. A commonly used approximation is the arithmetic mean of the initial and final populations in each of the respective age groups. For example,

$$
\left[\frac{K^{(t)}(x) + K^{(t+1)}(x)}{2} \right] 5F(x) \qquad (2.72)
$$

is the contribution of women aged x to $x + 4$ to the total number of births during the 5-year interval $(t, t + 1)$. Recalling that $K^{(t+1)}(x) = s(x - 5)$

$K^{(t)}(x - 5)$, we may rewrite (2.72) as

$$\tfrac{5}{2}[K^{(t)}(x) + s(x - 5)K^{(t)}(x - 5)]F(x), \tag{2.73}$$

for $x = \alpha, \alpha + 5, \ldots, \beta - 5$, where α and β are multiples of 5 and delimit the childbearing ages. Summing (2.73) over all the childbearing age groups, we obtain the total number of births over the 5 years

$$\tfrac{5}{2} \sum_{x=\alpha}^{\beta-5} [K^{(t)}(x) + s(x - 5)K^{(t)}(x - 5)]F(x). \tag{2.74}$$

On the assumption that births were uniformly distributed over the 5 years, we may take $\tfrac{1}{5}$ of (2.74) to be equal to the annual rate of births B and proceed to find the survivors at the end of the 5-year period. This quantity, derived in the first paragraph of Section 2.3.1, is simply $BL(0)$. Thus we have

$$K^{(t+1)}(0) = \frac{L(0)}{2} \left\{ \sum_{x=\alpha}^{\beta-5} [K^{(t)}(x) + s(x - 5)K^{(t)}(x - 5)] \right\} F(x). \tag{2.75}$$

Equation 2.75, after some rearrangement of terms, may be expressed in matrix form as the multiplication of the vector $\{K^{(t)}\}$ by a matrix $\mathbf{B}$ that has zeros everywhere except in its first row. To define these positive elements, we need to rearrange the right-hand side of (2.75) in a way such that each term in the summation contains only a single element of the vector $\{K^{(t)}\}$:

$$K^{(t+1)}(0) = \sum_{x=\alpha-5}^{\beta-5} \left\{ \frac{L(0)}{2} [F(x) + s(x)F(x + 5)] \right\} K^{(t)}(x) \tag{2.76}$$

$$= \sum_{x=\alpha-5}^{\beta-5} b(x)K^{(t)}(x), \quad \text{say.}$$

2.3.3 The Projection Matrix

Equations 2.68 and 2.76 project a population that is closed to migration and exposed to a fixed schedule of age-specific fertility and mortality forward over a 5-year interval. The combined application of these two equations in their matrix form may be described by the matrix multiplication $\mathbf{G}\{K^{(t)}\}$, where $\mathbf{G} = \mathbf{S} + \mathbf{B}$, and the positive elements in the first row of $\mathbf{B}$ are the components of the summation enclosed by the curly braces in (2.76).[5] For an arbitrary $l(0)$, the population projection model developed previously may be expressed as

$$\{\mathbf{K}^{(t+1)}\} = \mathbf{G}\{\mathbf{K}^{(t)}\},\tag{2.77}$$

where, if $\alpha = 10$, for example,

$$\mathbf{G} = \begin{bmatrix} 0 & \dfrac{L(0)}{2l(0)}\left[\dfrac{L(10)}{L(5)}F(10)\right] & \dfrac{L(0)}{2l(0)}\left[F(10) + \dfrac{L(15)}{L(10)}F(15)\right] & \cdots & 0 \\[2ex] \dfrac{L(5)}{L(0)} & 0 & 0 & \cdots & 0 \\[2ex] 0 & \dfrac{L(10)}{L(5)} & 0 & \cdots & 0 \\[2ex] \vdots & \vdots & \vdots & \ddots & \vdots \\[2ex] 0 & 0 & 0 & \cdots & 0 \end{bmatrix}.$$

$$\tag{2.78}$$

To illustrate (2.78), consider the female population of the United States in 1968. During that year, for example, 4766 live female births were reported by women 10 to 14 years old at last birthday. Therefore, their age-specific birthrate was

$$F(10) = \frac{4766}{9,991,000} = 0.00048.$$

The survivorship of these babies may be determined by referring to the life table set out in Table 2.1. Thus we find the first positive element in the first row of the $\mathbf{G}$ matrix to be

$$b(5) = \frac{L(0)}{2l(0)}\left[\frac{L(10)}{L(5)}F(10)\right] = \frac{494,643}{200,000}\left(\frac{488,021}{488,838}0.000477\right) = 0.00118.$$

This quantity, along with the remaining positive elements in the first row and the survivorship proportions in the subdiagonal, are set out in Figure 2.1.

The foregoing single-region matrix model may be applied to either sex. For each sex, one can compute an appropriate life table and introduce

---

[5] Recall that the $L(0)$ in (2.76) is $1/100,000$ of the $L(0)$ defined in Section 2.1, because in this section we have set $l(0)$ equal to unity rather than 100,000, as before.

0	0.00118	0.08003	0.27917	0.36843	0.25723	0.13186	0.05434	0.01240	0.00074	0	0	0	0	0	0	0	0
0.98826	0	0	0	0	0	0	0	0	0	0	0	0	0	0	0	0	0
0	0.99833	0	0	0	0	0	0	0	0	0	0	0	0	0	0	0	0
0	0	0.99774	0	0	0	0	0	0	0	0	0	0	0	0	0	0	0
0	0	0	0.99666	0	0	0	0	0	0	0	0	0	0	0	0	0	0
0	0	0	0	0.99601	0	0	0	0	0	0	0	0	0	0	0	0	0
0	0	0	0	0	0.99482	0	0	0	0	0	0	0	0	0	0	0	0
0	0	0	0	0	0	0.99231	0	0	0	0	0	0	0	0	0	0	0
0	0	0	0	0	0	0	0.98827	0	0	0	0	0	0	0	0	0	0
0	0	0	0	0	0	0	0	0.98225	0	0	0	0	0	0	0	0	0
0	0	0	0	0	0	0	0	0	0.97372	0	0	0	0	0	0	0	0
0	0	0	0	0	0	0	0	0	0	0.96207	0	0	0	0	0	0	0
0	0	0	0	0	0	0	0	0	0	0	0.94491	0	0	0	0	0	0
0	0	0	0	0	0	0	0	0	0	0	0	0.91622	0	0	0	0	0
0	0	0	0	0	0	0	0	0	0	0	0	0	0.87378	0	0	0	0
0	0	0	0	0	0	0	0	0	0	0	0	0	0	0.80090	0	0	0
0	0	0	0	0	0	0	0	0	0	0	0	0	0	0	0.69376	0	0
0	0	0	0	0	0	0	0	0	0	0	0	0	0	0	0	0.94710	0

Figure 2.1   The single-region population projection matrix: United States females, 1968.

the age-specific rates of motherhood and fatherhood, respectively, to obtain a separate projection matrix for females and for males.

A separate projection for the two sexes, however, can be satisfactorily carried out in a short-run projection only, since it is clear that neither growth path can be independent of the other indefinitely without producing serious discrepancies. Thus we need to turn to a combined projection model that introduces the interdependencies between the female and male sectors. A commonly used concept for linking the two is the notion of *dominance*, the degree by which births of boys as well as of girls are attributed to a single parent, father or mother.

A matrix population projection model that embodies complete female dominance is perhaps the easiest to fit to available data, for it requires only the childbearing age of a single parent—in this case, the mother. The matrix projection process is defined as before, only now it contains two sets of submatrices: a female survivorship matrix $\mathbf{S}$ and fertility matrix $\mathbf{B}$ and a survivorship matrix $\mathbf{S}'$ for males. Then, assuming complete female dominance,

$$\begin{Bmatrix} \mathbf{K}^{(t+1)} \\ \mathbf{K}^{(t+1)'} \end{Bmatrix} = \begin{bmatrix} \mathbf{B} + \mathbf{S} & 0 \\ s\mathbf{B} & \mathbf{S}' \end{bmatrix} \begin{Bmatrix} \mathbf{K}^{(t)} \\ \mathbf{K}^{(t)'} \end{Bmatrix}, \tag{2.79}$$

where females are listed first, age by age, in the vector $\{\mathbf{K}^{(t)}\}$, and s is $L'(0)/L(0)$ times the ratio of male to female births.

In the model with complete female dominance, the submatrix for females determines the ultimate rate of increase of the population, this rate being independent of the male population and of the female population above the ages of reproduction. By obvious extension, one can develop a model based on complete male dominance, or one founded on mixed dominance. The latter may be expressed as

$$\begin{Bmatrix} \mathbf{K}^{(t+1)} \\ \mathbf{K}^{(t+1)'} \end{Bmatrix} = \begin{bmatrix} (1-v)\mathbf{B} + \mathbf{S} & \dfrac{v}{s}\mathbf{B}' \\ s(1-v)\mathbf{B} & v\mathbf{B}' + \mathbf{S}' \end{bmatrix} \begin{Bmatrix} \mathbf{K}^{(t)} \\ \mathbf{K}^{(t)'} \end{Bmatrix}, \tag{2.80}$$

where v denotes the fraction of males who produce births.

2.3.4   Stable Growth

Having expressed population growth in matrix form, as in (2.77), let us now use repeated multiplication to examine the long-run implications of maintaining current age-specific birth and death rates. For example, observe that

$$\{\mathbf{K}^{(t+2)}\} = \mathbf{G}\{\mathbf{K}^{(t+1)}\} = \mathbf{G}^2\{\mathbf{K}^{(t)}\},$$

and, in general,

$$\{\mathbf{K}^{(t+n)}\} = \mathbf{G}^n\{\mathbf{K}^{(t)}\}. \tag{2.81}$$

The properties of such a projection, as n increases indefinitely, have been studied by Leslie (1945), Lopez (1961), and Keyfitz (1968), among others, and more recently by McFarland (1969), Sykes (1969), and Parlett (1970). This body of theory, commonly referred to as *stable growth theory*, draws on the properties of matrices with nonnegative elements, and, in particular, on the Perron–Frobenius theorem.

The Perron–Frobenius theorem establishes that any nonnegative, indecomposable, primitive square matrix has a unique, real, positive characteristic root λ_1 say, that is larger in absolute value than any other characteristic root of that matrix. Moreover, one can associate with this *dominant characteristic root* a characteristic vector $\{\mathbf{K}_1\}$ that has only positive elements, which for convenience we assume are scaled to sum to unity.

The matrix $\mathbf{G}$ in (2.81) is decomposable. However, we may partition $\mathbf{G}$ into four submatrices, as follows:

$$\mathbf{G} = \begin{bmatrix} \mathbf{W} & \mathbf{0} \\ \mathbf{U} & \mathbf{Z} \end{bmatrix}, \tag{2.82}$$

where the submatrix $\mathbf{W}$ extends horizontally until the highest age of reproduction. The matrix $\mathbf{W}$ is nonnegative and indecomposable, and it is primitive if it contains at least two positive fertility elements in column positions that are relatively prime—for example, two consecutive positive fertility elements (Sykes, 1969; Pollard, 1973). Then, by the Perron–Frobenius theorem, $\mathbf{W}$ has a unique positive characteristic root λ_1 that is larger in absolute value than any other characteristic root. Moreover, if we partition the vector $\{\mathbf{K}^{(t)}\}$, in a manner corresponding to the partitioning of $\mathbf{G}$ (i.e., at the point of the highest age of reproduction β) it is easily established that the submatrices $\mathbf{U}$ and $\mathbf{Z}$, and the age groups beyond the highest age of reproduction never affect the ages younger than β:

$$\{\mathbf{K}^{(t+n)}\} = \mathbf{G}^n\{\mathbf{K}^{(t)}\} = \begin{bmatrix} \mathbf{W}^n & \mathbf{0} \\ h(\mathbf{U}) & \mathbf{Z}^n \end{bmatrix} \begin{Bmatrix} \mathbf{X}^{(t)} \\ \mathbf{D}^{(t)} \end{Bmatrix} = \begin{Bmatrix} \mathbf{X}^{(t+n)} \\ \mathbf{D}^{(t+n)} \end{Bmatrix}. \tag{2.83}$$

Thus without loss of generality we may focus on the submatrix $\mathbf{W}$ for our analysis of the stable growth properties of $\mathbf{G}$. The dominant characteristic roots of both matrices will be the same, and the associated characteristic vector may be found by drawing on the recurrence relationship that is implicit in the characteristic value equation

$$\mathbf{W}\{\mathbf{X}_1\} = \lambda_1\{\mathbf{X}_1\}. \tag{2.84}$$

From this equation and the structure of the matrix $\mathbf{W}$ we have

$$s(x)K_1(x) = \lambda_1 K_1(x + 5),$$

whence

$$K_1(x + 5) = \frac{s(x)K_1(x)}{\lambda_1} = \lambda_1^{-1}\frac{L(x + 5)}{L(x)}K_1(x). \tag{2.85}$$

Thus starting with an arbitrary value for any element of the characteristic vector $\{\mathbf{K}_1\}$, we can find its remaining elements by means of the recurrence relationship expressed in (2.85).

In summary, then, to study the stable growth properties of (2.81), it is sufficient to examine those of

$$\{\mathbf{X}^{(t+n)}\} = \mathbf{W}^n\{\mathbf{X}^{(t)}\}. \tag{2.86}$$

If the characteristic roots of $\mathbf{W}$ are distinct, the associated characteristic vectors are independent. Hence $\mathbf{X}$, the matrix of these vectors side by side, has an inverse, and

$$\mathbf{W} = \mathbf{X}\Lambda\mathbf{X}^{-1}, \tag{2.87}$$

where

$$\Lambda = \begin{bmatrix} \lambda_1 & 0 & 0 & \cdots & 0 \\ 0 & \lambda_2 & 0 & \cdots & 0 \\ \vdots & & \ddots & & \vdots \\ 0 & & \cdots & & \lambda_k \end{bmatrix},$$

that is, a diagonal matrix with diagonal elements that are the characteristic roots of $\mathbf{W}$.

Using (2.87), we establish that

$$\mathbf{W}^n = \mathbf{X}\Lambda^n\mathbf{X}^{-1}$$

and substituting into (2.86), we find

$$\{\mathbf{X}^{(t+n)}\} = \mathbf{X}\boldsymbol{\Lambda}^n\mathbf{X}^{-1}\{\mathbf{X}^{(t)}\}$$
$$= \mathbf{X}\boldsymbol{\Lambda}^n\{\mathbf{Y}\},$$

where $\{\mathbf{Y}\} = \mathbf{X}^{-1}\{\mathbf{X}^{(t)}\}$. Thus

$$\{\mathbf{X}^{(t+n)}\} = [\{\mathbf{X}_1\}\{\mathbf{X}_2\}\cdots\{\mathbf{X}_k\}]\begin{Bmatrix}\lambda_1^{\,n}Y_1\\\lambda_2^{\,n}Y_2\\\vdots\\\lambda_k^{\,n}Y_k\end{Bmatrix}$$

$$= \lambda_1^{\,n}Y_1\{\mathbf{X}_1\} + \lambda_2^{\,n}Y_2\{\mathbf{X}_2\} + \cdots + \lambda_k^{\,n}Y_k\{\mathbf{X}_k\};$$

whence

$$\{\mathbf{X}^{(t+n)}\} = \lambda_1^{\,n}\left[Y_1\{\mathbf{X}_1\} + \left(\frac{\lambda_2}{\lambda_1}\right)^n Y_2\{\mathbf{X}_2\} + \cdots + \left(\frac{\lambda_k}{\lambda_1}\right)^n Y_k\{\mathbf{X}_k\}\right]. \qquad (2.88)$$

Since $\mathbf{W}$ is nonnegative, indecomposable, and primitive,

$$\lambda_1 > |\lambda_j|, \qquad j = 2, 3, \ldots, k;$$

therefore, as n approaches infinity, all terms beyond the first in the square brackets in (2.88) tend to zero. Hence ultimately the projection in (2.86) converges to $\lambda_1^{\,n}Y_1\{\mathbf{X}_1\}$ and consequently that of (2.83) converges to $\lambda_1^{\,n}Y_1\{\mathbf{K}_1\}$, which is called *the stable population*. Note that the principal feature of such a stable population is the unchanging proportional relationship between the elements of its age distribution, that is, *the stable age composition*. Also observe that the stable population does not depend on the initial age distribution $\{\mathbf{K}^{(t)}\}$. This tendency of a population to "forget" its past is called *ergodicity*.[6]

Because the population projection in (2.83) ultimately converges to $\lambda_1^{\,n}Y_1\{\mathbf{K}_1\}$, we conclude that for sufficiently large n it may be closely approximated by this limiting value. Since the elements of $\{\mathbf{K}_1\}$ sum to unity, the total projected population at time $t + n$ is approximately $\lambda_1^{\,n}Y_1$. In light of this, Keyfitz (1969) calls Y_1 the *stable equivalent* of the observed population, which if distributed as the stable age composition would increase at the same

[6] The tendency of a population to forget its initial age distribution has been shown also to occur under conditions somewhat weaker than those just described. Lopez (1961) proved that two populations with different initial age distributions will tend toward the same stable age structure if both are subjected to the same schedules of fertility and mortality, which may be assumed to be changing over time. This property is referred to as *weak ergodicity*.

rate and toward the same population as would, in the long run, the observed population under projection in (2.81). That is, for sufficiently large n,

$$\{\mathbf{K}^{(t+n)}\} = \mathbf{G}^n\{\mathbf{K}^{(t)}\} \doteq \lambda_1{}^n Y_1\{\mathbf{K}_1\}, \qquad (2.89)$$

whence

$$Y = \frac{\{\mathbf{1}'\}\mathbf{G}^n\{\mathbf{K}^{(t)}\}}{\lambda^n}, \qquad (2.90)$$

where $\{\mathbf{1}'\}$ is a row vector of ones, and the unit subscripts have been dropped from Y and λ. Keyfitz (1969) shows that

$$Y = \frac{Q}{b}, \qquad (2.91)$$

where Q is the Q in (2.60) and b is the intrinsic birthrate. He also demonstrates the utility of Y as a simple measure of the favorability of an observed age distribution to reproduction under the current schedule of fertility and mortality, by noting that a high Y relative to the observed population is a sign of a recent decline in fertility and, consequently, of a population that has a relatively higher proportion of potential mothers.

   Table 2.3 illustrates the convergence to stability of the 1968 female population of the United States, projected under the regime of fertility and mortality of that year. Note that the stable equivalent accurately reflects the decline in fertility that preceded 1968. Furthermore, the intrinsic rate of growth, obtained with the discrete model by means of the relationship

$$r_d = \tfrac{1}{5}\ln \lambda, \qquad (2.92)$$

is slightly higher than its counterpart in the continuous model.[7] This is always the case because a given amount of growth can be achieved with a lower rate of growth in continuously compounded systems than in discretely compounded systems. Finally, it is interesting to compare the results in Table 2.3 with those that arise from a similar projection carried out using 1958 data. Such a projection yields the following stable growth parameters:

$$\lambda = 1.10905$$
$$r_d = 0.02070$$
$$b = 0.02734$$
$$d = 0.00664$$
$$Y = 74{,}172{,}787$$

---

[7] In our particular numerical example the difference between r_c and r_d appears only in the sixth decimal place: $r_c = 0.005715$, $r_d = 0.005719$.

**Table 2.3   Population Projection to Stability and Associated Stable Growth Parameters:[a]
United States Females, 1968**

Age, x	1968 Population	1968 Proportion	2018 Population	2018 Proportion	Stable Equivalent Population	Stable Equivalent Proportion
0	8,772,000	0.0858	12,715,009	0.0823	9,552,087	0.0814
5	10,008,000	0.0979	12,335,420	0.0798	9,173,851	0.0782
10	9,991,000	0.0977	11,965,964	0.0774	8,900,325	0.0758
15	9,017,000	0.0882	11,408,676	0.0738	8,629,875	0.0735
20	7,837,000	0.0766	10,858,647	0.0703	8,358,609	0.0712
25	6,453,000	0.0631	10,637,586	0.0688	8,090,554	0.0689
30	5,660,000	0.0553	10,708,632	0.0693	7,821,745	0.0667
35	5,823,000	0.0569	10,507,030	0.0680	7,542,773	0.0643
40	6,299,000	0.0616	9,666,031	0.0625	7,244,121	0.0617
45	6,151,000	0.0601	8,447,681	0.0547	6,914,961	0.0589
50	5,579,000	0.0545	7,998,313	0.0518	6,543,405	0.0558
55	5,120,000	0.0501	8,883,425	0.0575	6,117,734	0.0521
60	4,409,000	0.0431	8,393,788	0.0543	5,617,727	0.0479
65	3,683,000	0.0360	6,956,535	0.0450	5,001,971	0.0426
70	3,117,000	0.0305	5,300,735	0.0343	4,247,427	0.0362
75	2,130,000	0.0208	3,509,639	0.0227	3,305,863	0.0282
80	1,320,000	0.0129	2,146,741	0.0139	2,228,807	0.0190
85+	908,000	0.0089	2,107,939	0.0136	2,051,389	0.0175
Total	102,277,000	1.0000	154,547,790	1.0000	117,343,220	1.0000

[a] Parameters
  $\lambda = 1.02901$
  $r_d = 0.00572$
  $b = 0.01669$
  $d = 0.01097$
  $Y = 117,343,220$

where

$$b = \sum_{x=\alpha}^{\beta-5} C(x)F(x) \qquad \text{and} \qquad d = b - r.$$

The stable equivalent population in this instance is *lower* than the empirical population, indicating an observed population that is relatively unfavorable to reproduction, and the 1968 population is overprojected by more than 400,000 persons, another indication of the decline in fertility during the intervening decade.

2.4   ESTIMATING BASIC DEMOGRAPHIC MEASURES FROM INCOMPLETE DATA

In most developing countries, studies that seek to assess the severity of population-related problems or strive to evaluate the impacts of programs and policies on population trends are seriously impaired by the general absence of reliable data on fertility, mortality, and migration. At the same time, the need for accurate population data in such countries is urgent, for without this information it is virtually impossible to formulate intelligent plans for social and economic development.

To assist developing countries in their quest for better methods of estimating demographic measures from incomplete data, the United Nations published a manual on the subject (United Nations, 1967). The principal feature of the procedures outlined there is the use of *model life tables*, which utilize the regularities exhibited by available mortality data, collected in countries with accurate registration systems, to systematically approximate the mortality schedule in a region lacking such data. These tables are entered with initial crude estimates of survivorship proportions to obtain the expectation of life at birth that best matches the pattern of mortality implied by the observed survivorship schedule. This expectation of life is the parameter that identifies the appropriate model life table.

2.4.1   Model Life Tables

A model single-region life table approximates the mortality schedule of a region that is closed to migration by resorting to the mortality experience of other regions with populations and conditions that may be presumed to be similar to the one being studied. A common method for incorporating the mortality experience of more than one region is by means of regression, and several studies have used this method to develop model life tables for use in situations where accurate observed data are unavailable (Coale and Demeny, 1966; United Nations, 1967). The usual procedure in such studies is to associate the probabilities of dying within each age interval $q(x)$ with the expectation of life at a given age $e(x)$. For example, consider the following regional (Standard Metropolitan Statistical Area) male expectations of life at birth and probabilities of dying within the first 5 years of age:

Region	$e(0)$	$q(0)$
1. San Francisco SMSA	67.62	0.029863
2. Los Angeles SMSA	67.50	0.032562
3. San Diego SMSA	67.44	0.033425
4. Rest of California	67.35	0.032782
5. Rest of the United States	66.74	0.036100

A simple linear regression of the five $q(0)$'s on the associated five $e(0)$'s yields

$$q(0) = 0.42487 - 0.00582e(0), \tag{2.93}$$

and a coefficient of determination (R^2) of 0.84. Thus the probability of dying within the first 5 years of age for males in a region in the United States may be approximated by inserting the appropriate expectation of life at birth into (2.93) and solving for $q(0)$. Comparable equations may be derived for all age groups and the results may be used to compute a model single-region life table.

Single-region model life tables reflect the pronounced regularities that are usually found in observed mortality schedules of human populations. These normally exhibit a pattern of moderately high levels of mortality immediately after birth, followed by a drop to a minimum between ages 10 to 15, increasing slowly until about age 50, and thereafter rising at an increasing rate until the last years of life. Moreover, within each mortality schedule of a given mortality level, the mortality rates experienced at different ages are highly intercorrelated. And if mortality at a particular age in one schedule exceeds that of the same age in another schedule the first schedule is likely to have higher mortality rates at every other age as well.

Table 2.4   "West" Model Single-Region Life Table: Females with $e(0) = 42$

Age, x	$q(x)$	$l(x)$	$d(x)$	$L(x)$	$m(x)$	$s(x)$	$T(x)$	$e(x)$
0	0.2553	100,000	25,526	405,936	0.0629	0.9030	4,200,000	42.00
5	0.0312	74,474	2,321	366,567	0.0063	0.9722	3,794,064	50.95
10	0.0243	72,153	1,756	356,375	0.0049	0.9717	3,427,497	47.50
15	0.0323	70,397	2,276	346,296	0.0066	0.9635	3,071,122	43.63
20	0.0408	68,121	2,779	333,661	0.0083	0.9567	2,724,826	40.00
25	0.0459	65,343	3,000	319,215	0.0094	0.9512	2,391,166	36.59
30	0.0519	62,343	3,236	303,625	0.0107	0.9454	2,071,951	33.23
35	0.0575	59,107	3,397	287,042	0.0118	0.9399	1,768,326	29.92
40	0.0629	55,710	3,504	269,789	0.0130	0.9336	1,481,284	26.59
45	0.0702	52,206	3,666	251,864	0.0146	0.9193	1,211,494	23.21
50	0.0920	48,540	4,464	231,539	0.0193	0.8951	959,631	19.77
55	0.1193	44,076	5,256	207,239	0.0254	0.8556	728,091	16.52
60	0.1729	38,820	6,712	177,319	0.0379	0.7987	520,852	13.42
65	0.2356	32,108	7,563	141,631	0.0534	0.7207	343,533	10.70
70	0.3366	24,545	8,262	102,069	0.0809	0.6125	201,902	8.23
75	0.4642	16,283	7,558	62,518	0.1209	0.3738	99,833	6.13
80+	1.0	8,724	8,724	37,315	0.2338	—	37,315	4.28

Table 2.4 is a specimen model single-region life table for females with an expectation of life at birth of 42 years. This table was derived by interpolation in the set of model life tables developed by Ansley Coale and Paul Demeny and published in the United Nations Manual (1967).[8] The fundamental mortality relationships described in Coale and Demeny (1966), involve the use of simple least-squares linear regressions of $q(x)$ and of log $q(x)$ on $e(10)$ and log $e(10)$, respectively. In constructing the UN model life tables, Coale and Demeny used values of $q(x)$ taken from the simple regressions at points with low life expectancies, the values of $q(x)$ generated by the logarithmic regressions at points with high life expectancies, and the mean values of $q(x)$

---

[8] The model life tables in Coale and Demeny (1966) reflect their observation that the life tables of different geographical regions and nations tend to cluster around four distinct age patterns of mortality. These four families of life tables are identified as the North, East, South, and West life tables, respectively. The UN Manual, however, reproduces only the West family of life tables, and they are the ones we consider throughout this book whenever the subject of model life tables is discussed.

produced by the two regressions at points in between. To terminate their model life tables, Coale and Demeny used a regression equation that associates the last expectation of life $e(80)$ with $l(80)$, the survivors to age 80.

2.4.2 Model Stable Populations

We have seen that a population undisturbed by migration and subject to an unchanging regime of fertility and mortality ultimately assumes an unchanging age composition $c(x)$, increases at a constant rate of growth r, and has constant birth and death rates b and d, respectively. Such a population has been defined as a stable population with an age composition given by

$$c(x) = be^{-rx}p(x), \qquad (2.94)$$

where $p(x)$ is the proportion surviving from birth to exact age x.

Underlying every stable age composition and its associated birthrate and death rate is a combination of a schedule of mortality, as expressed by a life table, and an intrinsic rate of growth. Specifically, given the values of $L(x)$ from a life table and a particular value for r, we may apply the numerical approximation

$$C(x) = be^{-r(x+2.5)}\frac{L(x)}{l(0)}, \qquad (2.95)$$

where

$$b = \frac{1}{\displaystyle\sum_{x=0}^{z} e^{-r(x+2.5)}\frac{L(x)}{l(0)}},$$

to obtain the proportion of the stable population that is x to $x + 4$ years old. The intrinsic death rate follows from the definitional equation: $r = b - d$.

Table 2.5 sets out several parameters associated with the model stable populations that arise from the combination of the mortality schedule defined by the model life table in Table 2.4 with one of several specific values of r. The table presents the proportion within each 5-year age group; the intrinsic rates of birth, death, and natural increase and the gross reproduction rates associated with four alternative mean ages of childbearing.

Although every combination of life table and intrinsic rate of growth implies a particular stable age composition, we should note that more than one fertility schedule can be paired with the life table to produce the same intrinsic rate of growth. A fertility schedule is simply the pattern of age-specific fertility rates for the quinquennial reproductive age groups between the ages α and β. Coale and Demeny (1966, p. 30) observe that in most populations fertility is zero until about age 15, rises to a single peak, and falls smoothly to zero by age 45 to 50. The mean age of the fertility schedule usually lies between 26 and 33 years. They also assert that although variations in the form of the fertility schedule do occur, knowledge of the gross reproduction rate (GRR) and the mean age of the fertility schedule $\bar{m}$ may be combined with a given life table to estimate the intrinsic rate of growth r to within a very small margin of error.

The mean age of the fertility schedule has a strong influence on r, especially in instances of high fertility. In Table 2.5, for example, a $GRR(\bar{m})$ of 3.0 implies an r of 0.025 when $\bar{m} = 27$ years, and only 0.018 when $\bar{m} = 33$ years. Thus for a given value of GRR, a different mean of the fertility schedule implies a different stable age composition. Consequently, with each stable population in Table 2.5, we include gross reproduction rates with mean ages of 27, 29, 31, and 33 years, respectively.

Coale and Demeny's fertility schedules with mean ages of 27, 29, 31, and 33 years are multiples of four basic schedules having these mean ages and a GRR of unity. They were obtained after a careful study of a large collection of national age-specific fertility rates published in the United Nations Demographic Yearbook of 1959. The four basic fertility schedules appear in Figure 2.2.

The stable populations set out in Table 2.5 were derived using (2.95) with r equal to $-0.010, -0.005, 0.000, \ldots, +0.030$. To calculate $GRR(\bar{m})$ for $\bar{m} = 27, 29, 31$, and 33, we observe that in a stable population

$$\int_0^\omega e^{-rx}p(x)m(x)\,dx = \int_0^\omega e^{-rx}p(x)[GRR(\bar{m})m'(x)]\,dx = 1,$$

where $m'(x)$ is the basic fertility schedule with $\bar{m}$ as the mean age and a gross reproduction rate of unity. It follows, therefore, that

$$GRR(\bar{m}) = \frac{1}{\int_0^\omega e^{-rx}p(x)m'(x)\,dx}. \tag{2.96}$$

Each stable population in Table 2.5 is associated with a single intrinsic rate of growth r and a single gross reproduction rate at a given mean age $\bar{m}$. For example, the first model stable population may be specified either

Table 2.5 "West" Model Single-Region Stable Populations: Females with $e(0) = 42$

Intrinsic Rate of Growth, r

Age, x	−0.010	−0.005	0.000	0.005	0.010	0.015	0.020	0.025	0.030
0	0.0703	0.0829	0.0967	0.1114	0.1271	0.1435	0.1605	0.1780	0.1957
5	0.0667	0.0768	0.0873	0.0981	0.1092	0.1202	0.1312	0.1418	0.1521
10	0.0682	0.0765	0.0849	0.0931	0.1010	0.1084	0.1154	0.1217	0.1273
15	0.0697	0.0762	0.0825	0.0882	0.0933	0.0978	0.1014	0.1043	0.1065
20	0.0706	0.0753	0.0794	0.0829	0.0855	0.0874	0.0884	0.0887	0.0883
25	0.0710	0.0739	0.0760	0.0773	0.0778	0.0776	0.0766	0.0749	0.0727
30	0.0710	0.0720	0.0723	0.0717	0.0704	0.0684	0.0659	0.0629	0.0595
35	0.0705	0.0698	0.0683	0.0661	0.0633	0.0600	0.0564	0.0525	0.0484
40	0.0697	0.0673	0.0642	0.0606	0.0566	0.0523	0.0479	0.0435	0.0392
45	0.0684	0.0644	0.0600	0.0552	0.0503	0.0453	0.0405	0.0358	0.0315

50	0.0661	0.0607	0.0551	0.0495	0.0440	0.0387	0.0337	0.0291	0.0249
55	0.0622	0.0557	0.0493	0.0432	0.0374	0.0321	0.0273	0.0230	0.0192
60	0.0559	0.0489	0.0422	0.0361	0.0305	0.0255	0.0211	0.0173	0.0141
65	0.0470	0.0400	0.0337	0.0281	0.0232	0.0189	0.0153	0.0122	0.0097
70	0.0356	0.0296	0.0243	0.0197	0.0159	0.0126	0.0100	0.0078	0.0060
75	0.0229	0.0186	0.0149	0.0118	0.0092	0.0072	0.0055	0.0042	0.0032
80+	0.0144	0.0114	0.0089	0.0069	0.0052	0.0040	0.0030	0.0022	0.0016

Parameters of Stable Populations

Birthrate	0.0169	0.0202	0.0238	0.0278	0.0321	0.0367	0.0416	0.0467	0.0520
Death rate	0.0269	0.0252	0.0238	0.0228	0.0221	0.0217	0.0216	0.0217	0.0220
GRR(27)	1.195	1.368	1.563	1.804	2.035	2.319	2.639	3.002	3.411
GRR(29)	1.195	1.381	1.593	1.836	2.115	2.432	2.794	3.207	3.677
GRR(31)	1.195	1.394	1.625	1.892	2.200	2.554	2.965	3.436	3.977
GRR(33)	1.195	1.409	1.659	1.951	2.292	2.690	3.155	3.696	4.326
Average age	36.70	34.35	32.06	29.87	27.78	25.82	24.00	22.30	20.75

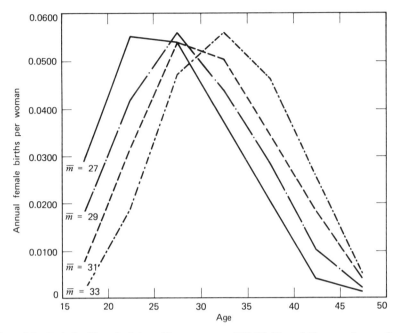

Figure 2.2 Basic fertility schedules with mean ages of 27, 29, 31, and 33 years. *Source.* Coale and Demeny (1966), p. 30.

by its growth rate of -0.010 or by its gross reproduction rate of 1.195 (for all four values of $\bar{m}$). Either of the two summary demographic measures may be used to uniquely identify the particular stable population. Recognizing this, Coale and Demeny (1966) provide two sets of model stable populations: a "growth rate" set, which is entered with the intrinsic rate of growth r, and a "GRR" set, which is entered with a value for $GRR(29)$.

2.4.3 Estimating Basic Demographic Measures Using Model Life Tables and Two Census-Enumerated Age Distributions

The principal reliable sources of demographic data in many developing countries are the decennial censuses of population. These compilations offer indirect measures of fertility, mortality, and migration, for the age distribution of a population manifests the past behavior of these fundamental components of population growth and change. For example, if a population undisturbed by migration is enumerated in two consecutive decennial censuses, and if each census contains tabulations of the population by 5-year age groups, it is a simple matter to compute the proportion of each cohort that survived the decade and proceed with the construction of a life table according to the Option 2 method described in Section 2.1.5.

Two fundamental problems need to be resolved before we can construct a life table from observed survivorship proportions. First, to complete such a life table we must either have available adequate records of births during the decade or be able to estimate infant and child mortality indirectly. Second, the considerable age misreporting and differential omission by age that occurs in such censuses often leads to observed survivorship proportions that are obviously too low or that exceed unity. Both problems can be minimized by the appropriate use of model life tables. Once a model life table has been selected—on the basis of how well it accounts for the observed effects of mortality during the intercensal decade—it can be combined with the data from the two censuses to furnish estimates of birth and death rates during that decade. The death rate can be approximated by applying the age-specific life table death rates to the average of the two census-enumerated age distributions, and the birthrate can be estimated by adding the average annual rate of growth to the estimated death rate.

Columns 1 and 2 of Table 2.6 present counts of the female population of Brazil in 1940 and 1950. Although the censuses were not enumerated exactly 10 years apart, let us assume for convenience that they were; and although the population was not a closed one, let us further assume that the impact of migration was small enough to be ignored.

Column 3 contains the initial estimates of 10-year survivorship proportions, which vary erratically because of age misreporting and our simplifying assumptions. To select a model life table on the basis of a sequence of these proportions, we could simply take the average or median of the set of expectations of life at birth that they imply. Specifically by comparing each $\hat{s}(x)$, with the corresponding $s(x)$ in a set of model life tables, we could associate one life table with each survivorship proportion. Each table would imply a particular level of mortality corresponding to its particular value of the expectation of life at birth, and an average or median value for this index could be used as the parameter with which to select a model life table. For example, Table 2.6 indicates that the ratio of women aged 10 to 14 in the 1950 Brazilian Census to those aged 0 to 4 in the 1940 census is 0.9880, which is an approximation of the survivorship proportion $^{10}s(0) = L(10)/L(0)$ in a life

Table 2.6 Female Population of Brazil, by Age, and Age-Specific Survivorship Proportions: 1940 and 1950

Age at Last Birthday, x	(1) Population in 1940	(2) Population in 1950	(3) Initial Estimates of 10-Year Survivorship Proportions	(4) Estimate of Mortality Level,[a] $\hat{e}(0)$	(5) Model Life Table 10-Year Survivorship Proportions, $e(0) = 45.00$
0	3,182,123	4,135,004	0.9880	68.85	0.9063
5	2,836,100	3,454,677	1.0076	(70.00)	0.9516
10	2,650,507	3,143,863	0.9835	64.90	0.9439
15	2,286,954	2,857,784	0.9191	41.10	0.9309
20	1,972,062	2,606,679	0.8121	21.15	0.9203
25	1,701,699	2,101,959	0.9043	42.90	0.9106
30	1,277,680	1,601,571	0.9123	48.25	0.9007
35	1,151,572	1,538,766	0.8281	31.70	0.8899
40	944,478	1,165,588	0.8193	33.95	0.8713
45	704,699	953,664	0.7321	27.00	0.8377
50	604,179	773,840	—	—	0.7836
55	384,493	515,894	—	—	0.7045
60	350,546	469,733	—	—	0.5987
65	198,268	252,933	—	—	0.4644
70	155,008	196,293	—	—	0.1951
75+	181,731	228,393	—	—	0.0

[a] Average $\hat{e}(0) = 45.0$; Median $\hat{e}(0) = 42.0$.

table representing the schedule of mortality among females during the intercensal decade. Entering the "West" family of model life tables in the UN Manual (1967) with $^{10}\hat{s}(0) = 0.9880$, we find that the associated expectation of life at birth is approximately 68 years. Repeating this procedure with $^{10}\hat{s}(15) = 0.9191$ and $^{10}\hat{s}(45) = 0.7321$, we obtain expectations of life at birth of approximately 41 and 27 years, respectively. An average value of about 45 years seems to be indicated by the data. (The median value is approximately 42 years.) The 10-year survivorship proportions that are associated with a UN model life table for females with an expectation of life at birth of 45 years appear in column 5 of Table 2.6.

The UN Manual suggests an alternative procedure that reduces the effect of age misreporting by examining the survivorship of *cumulated* age groups. In this method, the survivorship proportions are not affected by misreporting *within* the groups whose survival is calculated but are only influenced by age misstatements that transfer persons across an age group. Thus this method takes advantage of the dampening effect of cumulation of age groups on age misreporting.

The computational procedure of the "UN method" requires that the initial population (in our illustration, the 1940 population) be projected forward 10 years by the application of the survivorship proportions of model life tables representing different levels of mortality. Next the several projected populations are cumulated, and the level of mortality that produces a projected population aged x years and over which exactly matches the census enumerated total in the later period (in our case, 1950) is found by interpolation. Similar computations result in a set of values for $e(0)$. The average or median value of $e(0)$ then is adopted as the appropriate parameter with which to select a model life table. The application of such a procedure to the data in Table 2.6 gives an average $e(0)$ of 40.39 years and a median $e(0)$ of 40.04 years.

Yet a third method of determining the appropriate expectation of life at birth with which to select a model life table is offered by the Option 2 method of life table construction outlined in Section 2.1.5. Aggregating to 10-year age groups and equating observed survivorship proportions to their life table equivalents, we may apply the Option 2 life table construction method to find an expectation of life at birth of 52.80 years.[9] We learn in Chapter 6 that this procedure easily can be generalized to the multiregional case.

---

[9] The Option 2 method, it will be recalled, requires an estimate of $e(z)$ as an input. For our Brazilian data, we assumed that $e(70) = 10$.

2.4.4   Estimating Basic Demographic Measures Using Model Stable Populations, a Single Census-Enumerated Age Distribution, and an Observed Growth Rate

The model stable population tables provided in the UN Manual (1967) and the more extensive collection presented in Coale and Demeny (1966) include a broad range of stable age compositions bracketing all those likely to be found in actual populations that are themselves approximately stable and follow patterns of mortality such as those appearing in the model life tables. Thus if an observed population seems to belong to the family of model stable populations, it is possible to match the observed age composition with one in the model tables and to attribute to it the parameters of the model stable population. The relevant features of the observed population that are usually available are its age composition and its average annual rate of growth. The problem of identifying the appropriate model stable population therefore reduces to one of finding a stable population for the given rate of growth that most closely matches the enumerated population in age composition.

In Table 2.7 we illustrate the use of stable population theory to estimate fertility and mortality based on the 1950 census-enumerated female age distribution of Brazil and the observed average rate of growth of that population during the 1940–1950 intercensal period (i.e., $r = 0.0234$). In column 1 we list the cumulative proportion of the total female population up to age x. Once again the principal reason for cumulating the age composition is to dampen the influence of age misreporting. Another reason is the following simple relationship among cumulated stable age compositions (called *ogives*): among stable populations having the same intrinsic rate of growth, those with higher fertility schedules have greater cumulative proportions to every age than those with lower fertility schedules. This property is sometimes useful in detecting patterns of age misreporting (United Nations, 1967, pp. 17–22).

The stability conditions that justify the application of this particular estimation method to Brazil's population are likely to have been satisfied in 1950. The UN Manual, in considering the applicability of the method to Brazil in 1950, concludes that the case for assuming stability is convincing. This conclusion is based on the following factors: the similarity of the 1940 and 1950 age compositions, the essentially identical levels of fertility indicated by 1940 and 1950 census reports on children ever born, the relative

Table 2.7 Derivation of Stable Population Estimates of Mortality Based on Reported 1950 Age Distribution of the Female Population of Brazil and the Rate of Growth ($r = 0.0234$) of that Population During 1940–1950 Intercensal Period

Age, x	(1) $\Sigma(x)$ (Proportion up to Age x) Brazil, 1950, Females	(2) Values of $\Sigma(x)$ in Female Stable Population with $r = 0.0234$ and Levels of Mortality as Indicated					(3) Values of Various Expectations of Life at Birth in Female Stable Populations[a] with $\Sigma(x)$ as in Col. 1 and $r = 0.0234$ $\hat{e}(0)$
		(a) $e(0) = 35.00$	(b) $e(0) = 40.00$	(c) $e(0) = 45.00$	(d) $e(0) = 50.00$	(e) $e(0) = 55.00$	
5	0.1542	—	—	—	0.1587	0.1526	53.70
10	0.2919	—	—	—	0.2920	0.2830	50.05
15	0.4129	—	—	0.4207	0.4083	—	46.25
20	0.5228	—	—	0.5235	0.5099	—	45.25
25	0.6231	—	0.6280	0.6119	—	—	41.50
30	0.7039	0.7208	0.7035	—	—	—	39.90
35	0.7655	—	0.7672	0.7521	—	—	40.55
40	0.8247	0.8352	0.8205	—	—	—	38.55
45	0.8695	0.8778	0.8649	—	—	—	38.20

[a] Average $\hat{e}(0) = 43.8$; median $\hat{e}(0) = 41.5$.

insignificance of international migration, and the apparently constant levels of mortality prior to 1950 that are indicated by reports on proportions of children surviving in the 1950 and 1940 censuses (United Nations, 1967, p. 67).

The procedure for obtaining the values of the various parameters in the female stable populations with $\Sigma(x)$ as shown in column 1 of Table 2.7 and with $r = 0.0234$ is by interpolation among various model stable populations published in the UN Manual (1967). Columns 2a, through 2e provide values of $\Sigma(x)$ corresponding to female stable populations with $r = 0.0234$ and several different levels of mortality. Locating the observed $\Sigma(x)$ for each age among these model populations, we obtain the estimates of the expectation of life at birth that appear in Column 3. The average value of $\hat{e}(0)$ at approximately 44 years is, once again, slightly higher than the corresponding median value.

A simpler but cruder procedure for estimating the expectation of life at birth on the basis of a single census-enumerated age distribution and an observed growth rate is to "create" a second age distribution by multiplying the population in each age group in the first distribution by the observed growth ratio $\lambda = e^{10r}$, and applying one of the three estimation procedures described in Section 2.4.3. For example, the Option 2 method yields an expectation of life at birth of 50.93 years when applied to the data in Table 2.7 (assuming once more that $e(70) = 10$).

Finally, the value of $\bar{m}$ necessary to estimate the female gross reproduction rate (GRR) can be estimated by using the following formula suggested in the UN Manual (1967, p. 24):

$$\bar{m} = 2.25\left[\frac{P(3)}{P(2)}\right] + 23.95, \tag{2.97}$$

where $P(3)$ denotes the average number of children ever born (i.e., *average parity*) to women in the 25 to 29 age group, and $P(2)$ denotes the same index for women in the 20 to 24 age group. Since the ratio $P(3)/P(2)$ for Brazilian females in 1950 was 2.289 according to the 1950 census, we have

$$\bar{m} = 2.25(2.289) + 23.95 = 29.1 = 29, \text{ say,}$$

and interpolating in Table 2.5 with $\bar{m} = 29$, we obtain for $r = 0.0234$ a $GRR(29)$ of 3.075. Consequently, we may infer the age-specific set of female fertility rates $F(x)$ by multiplying the Coale and Demeny basic fertility schedule for $\bar{m} = 29$ by 3.075. This yields

$$F(15) = 0.0553$$
$$F(20) = 0.1291$$
$$F(25) = 0.1722$$
$$F(30) = 0.1353$$
$$F(35) = 0.0861$$
$$F(40) = 0.0307$$
$$F(45) = 0.0061$$

and we now have all the necessary inputs with which to construct a projection matrix and carry out a population projection.

CHAPTER THREE

———————————————

The Multiregional Life Table

The life table and the stationary population it describes are central concepts in single-region mathematical demography. An analogous fundamental role is assumed by the multiregional life table in multiregional mathematical demography. However, the presence of internal migration in a system of regional stationary populations undisturbed by emigration or immigration introduces several new dimensions that do not appear in the single-region formulation. These new dimensions and the development of the concept of a multiregional life table are the central focus of this chapter.

3.1 THE LEXIS DIAGRAM

Because it easily can be demonstrated that our results are equally valid for any finite number of regions, we may without loss of generality focus only on a two-region population system, with the two regions denoted by 1 and 2, respectively. Let δ denote the state of being dead, and consider the age interval $(x, x + h)$. During the interval $(x, x + h)$, an individual in region 1 at age x may migrate continually between 1 and 2 or enter the state of death δ.

57

The individual's movement between these states may be illustrated by a Lexis diagram.

The single-region Lexis diagram, found in the actuarial-demographic literature, is easily generalizable to include the two-region case. We simply draw two separate Lexis diagrams, one directly beneath the other, and connect them via the life lines of the migrants between the two regions, as in Figure 3.1. Note the five classes of life lines, represented by A, B, C, D, and E, respectively. Life line A represents a survivor in region 1 who does not migrate. Life lines B and E refer to individuals in region 1 who die during the unit age interval. Life line C represents an individual who outmigrates from region 1 to region 2 and returns before the end of the age interval. Finally, life line D refers to an individual in region 1 who outmigrates, survives the unit age interval, and *does not* return before the end of the interval.

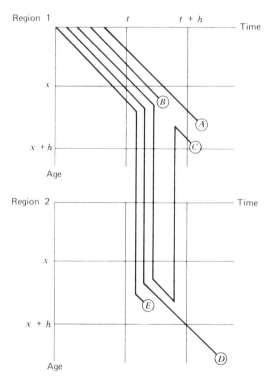

Figure 3.1 Two-region Lexis diagram.

Next we consider the number of person-years lived during the unit age interval of h years by each of these classes of life lines. Let

$^h a_{ii}(x)$ = average number of years lived during the unit interval in region i by persons who were alive at age x in region i and alive at age $x + h$ in region i (life lines A and C),

$^h a_{ij}(x)$ = average number of years lived during the unit interval in region i by persons who were alive at age x in region i and alive at age $x + h$ in region j (life line D),

$^h a_{i\delta}(x)$ = average number of years lived during the unit interval in region i by persons who were alive at age x in region i and who died before age $x + h$ (life lines B and E).

In single-region models it is common practice to set $^h a_{i\delta}(x) = h/2$, for all x, to reflect the assumption of a uniform distribution of deaths over the unit age interval. The same assumption may be made here; however, the appropriate values for $^h a_{ii}(x)$ and $^h a_{ij}(x)$ are not immediately obvious. As a crude approximation, we set $^h a_{ii}(x) = h$ and $^h a_{ij}(x) = ^h a_{i\delta}(x) = h/2$. This assumption seems to be adequate for most numerical calculations, and it greatly simplifies the analytical computations required to calculate a multiregional life table.

By setting $^h a_{ii}(x) = h$, where h is the width of the interval of age, we are in fact assuming that persons who are in region i at both the beginning and the end of the interval never outmigrate during that interval. Thus we are assuming the absence of a multiple transition during a unit interval, such as is exhibited by life line C. Deaths to outmigrants also cannot occur (life line E), since this event is a multiple transition, that is, a move from region i to region j and then to state δ, all within the same unit interval.

A crude test of the importance of such an assumption may be carried out by shortening the width of the unit interval to some fraction of a year, say one-fifth of a year, and carrying out all the normal life table calculations as before. Aggregating the results to form a multiregional life table with a 5-year interval, we may check for the equality of life table and observed outmigration and death rates or survivorship and outmigration proportions, as the case may be. If such equality has not been attained, we may iterate until it occurs. In this manner we can relax our fundamental assumption in that multiple transitions now may occur within the 5-year interval. The details of such an iterative, *micro* method of building up a life table are discussed elsewhere (Ledent and Rogers, 1972; Rogers, 1973) and are not considered further in this book.

3.2 ELEMENTARY MULTIREGIONAL LIFE TABLE FUNCTIONS

The computation of a multiregional life table begins with the estimation of the age-specific outmigration and death probabilities:

$^h p_{ij}(x)$ = probability that an individual in region i at age x will survive and be in region j at age $x + h$,

$^h q_i(x)$ = probability that an individual in region i at age x will die before reaching age $x + h$,

$$^h p_{ii}(x) = 1 - \sum_{\substack{j=1 \\ j \neq i}}^{m} {}^h p_{ij}(x) - {}^h q_i(x), \qquad i, j = 1, 2, \ldots, m.$$

The problem of estimating these age-specific outmigration and death probabilities from observed data on the migration and mortality of a multiregional population system lies in the province of actuarial science and biostatistics (Chiang, 1968). To avoid interrupting the flow of the argument, the discussion of that problem has been relegated to the Appendix at the end of this chapter.

Given estimates of age-specific outmigration and death probabilities for each region, we may proceed to develop a multiregional life table in a manner that is analogous to the procedures used to obtain a single-region life table. Applying the normal single-region life table relationships recursively, we begin our calculations by generating the region-specific survivors at each age for each regional birth cohort. However, this is not enough. To compute complete life table statistics, such as expectations of life by age and regions of residence, we must keep track of the survivorship and migration history of each age-region-specific group of survivors. That is, each $l_i(x)$ must be viewed as a "cohort" for which a separate life table must be constructed. To do this more efficiently, we introduce the following additional definitions and notation:

$_{ix}l_j(y)$ = expected number of survivors alive in region j at age y, among the $l_i(x)$ individuals now alive in region i at age x,

$_{ix}^h l_{jk}(y)$ = expected number of survivors alive in region k at age $y + h$, among the $_{ix}l_j(y)$ individuals now alive in region j at age y and previously living in region i at age x,

${}_{ix}^{h}d_j(y)$ = expected number of deaths between ages y and $y + h$ among the ${}_{ix}l_j(y)$ individuals now alive in region j at age y and previously living in region i at age x.

Using the foregoing notation may define the relationships

$$
\left.
\begin{aligned}
{}_{ix}l_j(x + h) &= {}_{ix}^{h}l_{ij}(x) \\[4pt]
{}_{ix}^{h}l_{jk}(y) &= {}_{ix}l_j(y)\,{}^{h}p_{jk}(y) \\[4pt]
{}_{ix}^{h}d_j(y) &= {}_{ix}l_j(y)\,{}^{h}q_j(y) \\[4pt]
{}_{ix}l_j(y) &= {}_{ix}l_{j\cdot}(y) = \sum_{k=1}^{m} {}_{ix}^{h}l_{jk}(y) + {}_{ix}^{h}d_j(y) \\[4pt]
{}_{ix}l_j(y + h) &= {}_{ix}l_{\cdot j}(y + h) = \sum_{k=1}^{m} {}_{ix}^{h}l_{kj}(y) = \sum_{k=1}^{m} {}_{ix}l_k(y)\,{}^{h}p_{kj}(y).
\end{aligned}
\right\}
\tag{3.1}
$$

The multiregional life table may now be obtained in a manner analogous to the single-region procedure. We begin our cycle of computations with $l_i(x)$ and find ${}_{ix}^{h}l_{ij}(x)$ for all $i, j = 1, 2, \ldots, m$. Next, using ${}_{ix}^{h}l_{ij}(x)$ or, equivalently, ${}_{ix}l_j(x + h)$, we calculate ${}_{ix}^{h}l_{jk}(x + h)$ and ${}_{ix}^{h}d_j(x + h)$, for each $i, j, k = 1, 2, \ldots, m$, and using these, we obtain the corresponding ${}_{ix}^{h}L_{jk}(x + h)$, where

${}_{ix}^{h}L_{jk}(y)$ = total person-years lived in region k, between ages y and $y + h$, by individuals who were alive in region j at age y and previously were living in region i at age x.

$$
= \int_{0}^{h} {}_{ix}^{t}l_{jk}(y)\, dt.
\tag{3.2}
$$

Recalling the various average numbers of years lived during the unit age interval defined earlier, we may obtain numerical values for the necessary person-years lived by means of such linear approximations as

$$
\left.
\begin{aligned}
{}_{ix}^{h}L_{jj}(y) &= \sum_{k=1}^{m} {}^{h}a_{jk}(y)\,{}_{ix}^{h}l_{jk}(y) + {}^{h}a_{j\delta}(y)\,{}_{ix}^{h}d_j(y)
\end{aligned}
\right\}
$$

and
$$
{}_{ix}^{h}L_{jk}(y) = [h - {}^{h}a_{jk}(y)]\,{}_{ix}^{h}l_{jk}(y).
$$
$$\tag{3.3}$$

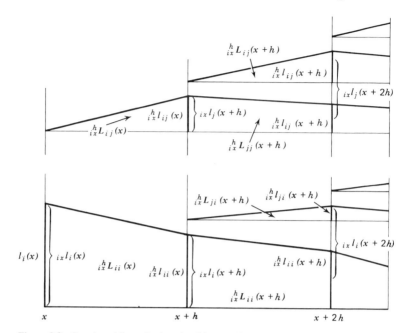

Figure 3.2 Survivorship and migration history of the cohort $l_i(x)$.

Figure 3.2 illustrates some of the important relationships that arise between two regions by tracing graphically the survivorship and migration history of the life table population in region i at age x. Of these people, $_{ix}^{h}l_{ij}(x)$ move to region j during the ensuing unit interval, living $_{ix}^{h}L_{ij}(x)$ person-years in that region by the end of the interval. Others, $_{ix}^{h}l_{ii}(x)$ persons in all, remain and survive in region i, living a total of $^{h}a_{ii}(x)_{ix}^{h}l_{ii}(x)$ person-years in that region during the same interval. Adding these $^{h}a_{ii}(x)_{ix}^{h}l_{ii}(x)$ person-years lived in region i to the $^{h}a_{ij}(x)_{ix}^{h}l_{ij}(x)$ person-years lived *in region i* by those in region i at age x who are in region j at age $x + h$ and to the $^{h}a_{i\delta}(x)_{ix}^{h}d_{i}(x)$ person-years lived in region i by those in region i at age x who die in the unit interval, gives $_{ix}^{h}L_{ii}(x)$. During the following unit interval some of the migrants included in $_{ix}^{h}l_{ij}(x)$ return to region i to live a total of $_{ix}^{h}L_{ji}(x + h)$ person-years there, and they join the survivors of the $_{ix}^{h}l_{ii}(x)$ nonmigrants in region i to form $_{ix}l_{i}(x + 2h)$, the survivors of the original population in region i at age x now in region i at age $x + 2h$.

The remainder of the life table specific to the "cohort" $l_i(x)$ follows directly. First we complete the survivorship and migration history of this group of individuals. The results permit us to compute the total person-years in prospect beyond age x for the "cohort" $l_i(x)$, by region of residence, $_{ix}T_j(x)$, with which the expectation of life beyond age x for the "cohort" $l_i(x)$, by region of residence, may be found by

$$_{ix}e_j(x) = \frac{_{ix}T_j(x)}{l_i(x)}, \tag{3.4}$$

where

$$_{ix}T_j(x) = \sum_{y=x}^{z} \sum_{k=1}^{m} {}_{ix}^{h}L_{kj}(y) = \sum_{y=x}^{z} {}_{ix}^{h}L_{\cdot j}(y), \tag{3.5}$$

z denoting the starting age of the terminal interval. The average expected remaining lifetime beyond age x, of an individual alive at age x in region i, is

$$_{ix}e(x) = \frac{\sum_{j=1}^{m} {}_{ix}T_j(x)}{l_i(x)} = \sum_{j=1}^{m} {}_{ix}e_j(x). \tag{3.6}$$

That is, an individual currently at age x in region i can expect to live a total of $_{ix}e(x)$ years beyond age x, of which $_{ix}e_i(x)$ years will be spent in region i and $_{ix}e_j(x)$ years will be spent in region j, $j = 1, 2, \ldots, m, j \neq i$.

The above-described process for computing a life table specific to the "cohort" $l_i(x)$ may be applied to generate such a life table for each $l_i(y)$, $y = 0, h, 2h, \ldots, z$. The entire process then may be repeated for each $l_j(y), j = 1, 2, 3, \ldots, m, j \neq i$. The mass of information that is the end product of all these computations is *the multiregional life table*.

To terminate the multiregional life table and calculate the various person-years lived by the last and open-ended age group in each region, we may adopt the following straightforward generalization of the single-region procedure. Define the following life table age-specific outmigration and death rates:

$$^{h}m_{ij}(x) = \frac{_{ix}^{h}l_{ij}(x)}{_{ix}^{h}L_{ii}(x)} = \frac{_{ix}^{h}l_{ij}(x)}{_{ix}^{h}L_{\cdot i}(x)} \tag{3.7}$$

and

$$^{h}m_{i\delta}(x) = \frac{_{ix}^{h}d_i(x)}{_{ix}^{h}L_{ii}(x)} = \frac{_{ix}^{h}d_i(x)}{_{ix}^{h}L_{\cdot i}(x)}, \tag{3.8}$$

since $_{ix}^{h}L_{ji}(x) = 0$ and multiple transitions are not permitted. Next equate the terminal regional age-specific life table death rates to their empirical counterparts and assume that individuals in that age group no longer migrate ($p_{ij}(z) = 0$). Then, for example, assuming that $h = 5$ and $z = 85$, we have

$$^{\infty}\hat{m}_{ij}(85) = 0$$

and

$$^{\infty}\hat{m}_{i\delta}(85) = {}^{\infty}M_{i\delta}(85).$$

But

$$^{\infty}m_{i\delta}(85) = \frac{_{i85}^{\infty}d_i(85)}{_{i85}^{\infty}L._i(85)} = \frac{l_i(85)}{_{i85}^{\infty}L._i(85)} = \frac{\sum_{j=1}^{m}{}_{j80}^{5}l_{ji}(80)}{_{i85}^{\infty}L._i(85)}$$

and

$$_{i85}^{\infty}L._i(85) = {}_{i85}^{\infty}L_{ii}(85) = \sum_{j=1}^{m}{}_{j80}^{\infty}L_{ii}(85).$$

Since all residents of a region are assumed to exhibit the same death rate, irrespective of their previous life-residence history, it follows that

$$^{\infty}m_{i\delta}(85) = \frac{\sum_{j=1}^{m}{}_{j80}^{5}l_{ji}(80)}{\sum_{j=1}^{m}{}_{j80}^{\infty}L_{ii}(85)} = \frac{_{j80}^{5}l_{ji}(80)}{_{j80}^{\infty}L_{ii}(85)}, \tag{3.9}$$

whence

$$_{i80}^{\infty}L._i(85) = {}_{i80}^{\infty}L_{ii}(85) = \frac{_{i80}^{5}l_{ii}(80)}{^{\infty}M_{i\delta}(85)} = \frac{_{i80}l._i(85)}{^{\infty}M_{i\delta}(85)} \tag{3.10}$$

$$_{j80}^{\infty}L._i(85) = {}_{j80}^{\infty}L_{ii}(85) = \frac{_{j80}^{5}l_{ji}(80)}{^{\infty}M_{i\delta}(85)} = \frac{_{j80}l._i(85)}{^{\infty}M_{i\delta}(85)} \tag{3.11}$$

and

$$_{i80}^{\infty}L_{ij}(85) = {}_{i80}^{\infty}L_{ji}(85) = 0. \tag{3.12}$$

The fundamental elementary multiregional life table functions may be compactly expressed in matrix form. The definitional relationship

$$_{ix}l_j(y + 5) = \sum_{k=1}^{m}{}_{ix}l_k(y)p_{kj}(y)$$

may be expressed as

$$_x\mathbf{l}(y + 5) = P(y)_x\mathbf{l}(y), \tag{3.13}$$

where the elements in the ith row and jth column of $_x\mathbf{l}(y)$ and $P(y)$ are $_{jx}l_i(y)$ and $p_{ji}(y)$, respectively.

Observe the transposed subscripting in the matrices, and note the Markovian assumption implicit in (3.13). That is, the same $p_{ji}(y)$ probabilities are applied to all residents of region j irrespective of their previous life-residence history.

Let $_{ix}L_j(y)$ denote the total person-years lived in region j, between ages y and $y + 5$ by individuals who were alive in region i at age x [i.e., $_{ix}L_j(y) = _{ix}L._j(x)$]. Assuming a uniform distribution of outmigrations and deaths over the 5-year unit interval of age, we may develop the following multiregional generalization of the single-region formula for $L(y)$:

$$_x\mathbf{L}(y) = \tfrac{5}{2}[_x\mathbf{l}(y) + _x\mathbf{l}(y + 5)] \tag{3.14}$$

$$= \tfrac{5}{2}[\mathbf{I} + P(y)]_x\mathbf{l}(y), \tag{3.15}$$

where the element in the ith row and jth column of $_x\mathbf{L}(y)$ is $_{jx}L_i(y)$.

The remaining elementary multiregional life table functions follow directly with

$$_x\mathbf{e}(x) = _x\mathbf{T}(x)_x\mathbf{l}(x)^{-1}, \tag{3.16}$$

where

$$_x\mathbf{T}(x) = \sum_{y=x}^{z} {_x\mathbf{L}(y)}, \tag{3.17}$$

and the element in the ith row and jth column of $_x\mathbf{e}(x)$ is $_{jx}e_i(x)$. Note that $_x\mathbf{l}(x)$ is a diagonal matrix.

We may terminate the life table with the matrix version of (3.10) and (3.11), namely

$$_{80}\mathbf{L}(85) = {}^{\infty}M(85)^{-1}{}_{80}\mathbf{l}(85), \tag{3.18}$$

where $^{\infty}M(85)$ is a diagonal matrix containing the regional death rates of the terminal age group.

Table 3.1   Two-Region Life Table for Yugoslavian Females, 1961:
Probabilities of Surviving, Outmigrating, and Dying by Exact Age

| Age, | (1) Slovenia | | | (2) Rest of Yugoslavia | | |
x	$p_{11}(x)$	$p_{12}(x)$	$q_1(x)$	$p_{22}(x)$	$p_{21}(x)$	$q_2(x)$
0	0.956075	0.013848	0.030077	0.892412	0.001289	0.106299
5	0.986462	0.011393	0.002145	0.995833	0.000827	0.003340
10	0.991129	0.007393	0.001479	0.996831	0.000785	0.002385
15	0.972027	0.025430	0.002543	0.992312	0.003380	0.004308
20	0.961182	0.035155	0.003664	0.989272	0.004661	0.006067
25	0.969422	0.027246	0.003332	0.989596	0.002519	0.007885
30	0.976509	0.018557	0.004934	0.989539	0.001741	0.008720
35	0.985166	0.008758	0.006075	0.988570	0.001123	0.010307
40	0.985423	0.005026	0.009550	0.984838	0.000910	0.014251
45	0.979646	0.002686	0.017668	0.980281	0.000464	0.019255
50	0.970992	0.003266	0.025742	0.967963	0.000640	0.031397
55	0.957745	0.003079	0.039176	0.952076	0.001003	0.046922
60	0.933122	0.004271	0.062607	0.918191	0.000971	0.080837
65	0.874355	0.004448	0.121198	0.869420	0.000730	0.129850
70	0.783256	0.003903	0.212840	0.785139	0.000347	0.214514
75	0.678322	0.004662	0.317016	0.694256	0.000420	0.305323
80	0.461657	0.002573	0.535769	0.562470	0.000766	0.436764
85+	0.0	0.0	1.0	0.0	0.0	1.0

To provide an empirical application of the concept of the multiregional
life table, a two-region table has been computed for Yugoslavian females
using the mortality and migration data presented in Table 3.A.1 of the
Appendix. For illustrative purposes, we have assumed that the data on
outmigrants refer to moves recorded during the interval January 1, 1961,
through December 31, 1961. Estimates of the relevant average number of
years lived during the unit age interval of 5 years were

$$a_{11}(x) = a_{22}(x) = 5 \quad \text{and} \quad a_{12}(x) = a_{21}(x) = a_{1\delta}(x) = a_{2\delta}(x) = \tfrac{5}{2},$$

where 1 denotes the Republic of Slovenia and 2 refers to the rest of Yugoslavia.

Of the mass of information provided by these calculations, only a few
selected statistics are included in this chapter. These are set out in Tables 3.1

Table 3.2   Two-Region Life Table for Yugoslavian Females, 1961: Survivors, Outmigrants, and Deaths at Exact Ages by Region of Residence

Age, x	(1) Slovenia				(2) Rest of Yugoslavia			
	$l_1(x)$	$_{1x}l_{11}(x)$	$_{1x}l_{12}(x)$	$d_1(x)$	$l_2(x)$	$_{2x}l_{22}(x)$	$_{2x}l_{21}(x)$	$d_2(x)$
0	100,000	95,607	1,385	3,008	100,000	89,241	129	10,630
5	95,736	94,440	1,091	205	90,626	90,248	75	303
10	94,515	93,677	699	140	91,339	91,050	72	218
15	93,748	91,126	2,384	238	91,748	91,043	310	395
20	91,436	87,887	3,214	335	93,427	92,425	435	567
25	88,322	85,622	2,406	294	95,639	94,644	241	754
30	85,862	83,845	1,593	424	97,051	96,035	169	846
35	84,014	82,768	736	510	97,629	96,513	110	1,006
40	82,878	81,670	417	791	97,249	95,774	89	1,386
45	81,758	80,094	220	1,445	96,191	94,294	45	1,852
50	80,138	77,814	262	2,063	94,514	91,486	60	2,967
55	77,875	74,584	240	3,051	91,747	87,350	92	4,305
60	74,676	69,682	319	4,675	87,590	80,425	85	7,081
65	69,767	61,001	310	8,456	80,744	70,200	59	10,485
70	61,060	47,826	238	12,996	70,510	55,360	24	15,125
75	47,850	32,458	223	15,169	55,599	38,600	23	16,976
80	32,481	14,995	84	17,402	38,823	21,837	30	16,956
85+	15,025	0	0	15,025	21,920	0	0	21,920

through 3.5, and their interpretation is largely self-evident. We now highlight a few of the more important statistics.

Many useful probabilities and expectations may be computed using the elements of a multiregional life table. The most obvious are those that relate to probabilities of survivorship and migration and to expectations of life by age, region, and place of birth. For example, to find the probability that a woman now living in Slovenia at age x will be a living resident of the rest of Yugoslavia at age y, we need only to compute the ratio $_{1x}l_2(y)/l_1(x)$. Thus, for example,

$$\frac{_{10}l_2(10)}{l_1(0)} = \frac{_{10}^5l_{22}(5) + _{10}^5l_{12}(5)}{l_1(0)} = \frac{1,379 + 1,089}{100,000} = 0.02468$$

Table 3.3 Two-Region Life Table for Yugoslavian Females, 1961:
Person-Years Lived During Age Interval by Region of Residence

Age, x	(1) Slovenia			(2) Rest of Yugoslavia		
	$_{1x}L_1.(x)$	$_{1x}L_{11}(x)$	$_{1x}L_{12}(x)$	$_{2x}L_2.(x)$	$_{2x}L_{22}(x)$	$_{2x}L_{21}(x)$
0	492,481	489,019	3,462	473,425	473,103	322
5	478,169	475,442	2,727	452,373	452,186	187
10	472,227	470,480	1,747	456,151	455,972	179
15	468,146	462,186	5,960	457,754	456,979	775
20	456,343	448,307	8,036	465,718	464,629	1,089
25	440,876	434,859	6,016	476,311	475,708	602
30	428,253	424,270	3,983	483,137	482,715	422
35	418,796	416,957	1,840	485,628	485,354	274
40	412,410	411,369	1,041	482,778	482,557	221
45	405,180	404,631	549	476,323	476,212	112
50	395,537	394,882	654	465,149	464,998	151
55	381,746	381,147	599	447,975	447,745	230
60	361,692	360,895	797	420,250	420,037	213
65	327,696	326,920	776	377,506	377,359	147
70	272,810	272,214	596	314,738	314,677	61
75	201,327	200,769	558	235,555	235,496	58
80	118,900	118,691	209	151,723	151,649	74
85+	73,792	73,792	0	152,769	152,769	0

is the probability that a baby girl now born in Slovenia will be living at
age 10 in the rest of Yugoslavia, and

$$\frac{_{10}l_1(10)}{l_1(0)} = \frac{_{10}^5l_{11}(5) + _{10}^5l_{21}(5)}{l_1(0)} = \frac{94,313 + 1}{100,000} = 0.94314$$

is the probability that she will be a resident of her place of birth at age 10.
Clearly

$$0.94314 + 0.02468 = 0.96782$$

is the probability that this Slovenian baby girl will live to exact age 10.

Table 3.4   Two-Region Life Table for Yugoslavian Females, 1961:
Expectations of Life by Age and Region of Residence

Age,	(1) Slovenia			(2) Rest of Yugoslavia		
x	$_{1x}e(x)$	$_{1x}e_1(x)$	$_{1x}e_2(x)$	$_{2x}e(x)$	$_{2x}e_2(x)$	$_{2x}e_1(x)$
0	72.57	64.90	7.67	66.25	65.43	0.82
5	69.75	62.75	7.00	68.83	68.00	0.83
10	64.91	58.57	6.34	64.05	63.27	0.78
15	60.00	54.06	5.94	59.20	58.45	0.74
20	55.17	50.53	4.64	54.44	53.88	0.56
25	50.38	47.46	2.92	49.76	49.42	0.34
30	45.56	43.87	1.68	45.13	44.91	0.22
35	40.77	39.87	0.91	40.51	40.36	0.15
40	36.01	35.43	0.58	35.90	35.80	0.11
45	31.33	30.91	0.42	31.39	31.31	0.08
50	26.85	26.50	0.35	26.95	26.89	0.07
55	22.49	22.22	0.27	22.75	22.69	0.05
60	18.31	18.09	0.22	18.74	18.71	0.03
65	14.36	14.21	0.15	15.17	15.15	0.02
70	10.99	10.89	0.10	12.06	12.05	0.01
75	8.28	8.21	0.06	9.68	9.67	0.01
80	5.95	5.92	0.02	7.83	7.83	0.01
85+	4.91	4.91	0.0	6.97	6.97	0.0

A variety of expectations of life are provided by a multiregional life table. Prominent among these are the region-specific ones. For example, a Slovenian baby girl has an expectation of life at birth of 72.57 years, of which 7.67 years, on the average, will be lived in the rest of Yugoslavia. A rest-of-Yugoslavian baby girl, on the other hand, has a life expectancy of only 66.25 years, of which only .82 year, on the average, will be lived in Slovenia. Yet beginning with the age of 50 years, rest-of-Yugoslavian women residents have a longer life expectancy. For example, a 50-year-old female Slovenian resident has a life expectancy of 26.85 years, but a 50-year-old female resident of the rest of Yugoslavia has the slightly higher life expectancy of 26.95 years.

The two-region life table results are consistent with those that arise from a single-region life table computed using the same data base in consolidated

Table 3.5   Two-Region Life Table for Yugoslavian Females, 1961: Outmigration and Death Rates by Age and Region of Residence

Age, x	(1) Slovenia		(2) Rest of Yugoslavia	
	$m_{12}(x)$	$m_{1\delta}(x)$	$m_{21}(x)$	$m_{2\delta}(x)$
0	0.002832	0.006150	0.000272	0.022468
5	0.002294	0.000432	0.000166	0.000669
10	0.001485	0.000297	0.000157	0.000478
15	0.005158	0.000516	0.000679	0.000865
20	0.007170	0.000747	0.000937	0.001220
25	0.005534	0.000677	0.000506	0.001585
30	0.003756	0.000999	0.000350	0.001753
35	0.001765	0.001224	0.000226	0.002073
40	0.001013	0.001924	0.000183	0.002872
45	0.000543	0.003570	0.000094	0.003889
50	0.000663	0.005224	0.000130	0.006382
55	0.000629	0.008004	0.000205	0.009615
60	0.000884	0.012955	0.000203	0.016857
65	0.000949	0.025864	0.000156	0.027784
70	0.000876	0.047742	0.000078	0.048067
75	0.001111	0.075556	0.000099	0.072034
80	0.000704	0.146620	0.000196	0.111814
85+	0.0	0.203611	0.0	0.143486

form. Thus Table 3.6 shows that a single-region life table, calculated in the conventional way (as in Chapter 2) and using the same data, yields a total expectation of life at birth of 66.68 years for a Yugoslavian baby girl. An appropriately weighted aggregation of the corresponding two region-specific values of 72.57 and 66.25 years yields a value of 66.69 years for the same statistic.

Having illustrated an empirical application of the multiregional life table, we now report, for purposes of comparison, a few results that were generated in the course of computing several two-region life tables for United States males and females, using migration and mortality data published by the U.S. Census Bureau and the U.S. Department of Vital Statistics. Crude estimates

Table 3.6 Expectations of Life at Birth by Region of Birth and Residence: Selected Two-Region and One-Region Models

Expectation of Life at Birth by Region of Birth and Residence	(1) Slovenia (2) Rest of Yugoslavia		(1) California (2) Rest of United States				(1) West Virginia (2) Rest of United States			
	1961		1958		1968		1958		1968	
	Males	Females	Males	Females	Males	Females	Males	Females	Males	Females
Two-Region Model										
$_{10}e(0)$	67.02	72.57	67.30	73.86	67.57	75.19	66.75	73.15	66.49	74.39
$_{10}e_1(0)$	59.95	64.90	43.52	48.95	38.57	43.25	25.94	28.06	26.80	29.51
$_{10}e_2(0)$	7.07	7.67	23.77	24.90	29.00	31.93	40.81	45.09	39.69	44.88
$_{20}e(0)$	63.09	66.25	66.70	73.11	66.83	74.41	66.64	73.04	66.78	74.37
$_{20}e_2(0)$	62.19	65.43	61.22	67.36	62.33	69.63	66.44	72.82	66.55	74.11
$_{20}e_1(0)$	0.90	0.82	5.48	5.75	4.50	4.78	0.20	0.22	0.23	0.26
$_{(1+2)0}e(0)^a$	63.36	66.69	66.75	73.17	66.90	74.49	66.64	73.04	66.78	74.37
One-Region Model										
$_{(1+2)0}e(0)^b$	63.33	66.68	66.63	73.03	66.77	74.37	66.63	73.03	66.77	74.37
$_{10}e(0)^b$	66.78	72.59	67.31	74.21	68.13	75.93	66.22	72.45	65.44	74.13
$_{20}e(0)^b$	63.10	66.24	66.57	72.93	66.63	74.22	66.64	73.04	66.78	74.37

[a] Aggregation of two-region results calculated with regional radices set proportional to observed number of births in each region.

[b] Calculated on the assumption that the region was closed to migration.

71

of annual data for the former were obtained by taking one-fifth of the published 5-year migration data. Mortality data are reported annually and were taken for the year approximately midway in the interval (i.e., 1958 and 1968).

Two sets of two-region life tables were calculated for 1958 and again for 1968: one using a division of the United States into the regions of California and the rest of the United States; the other disaggregating the United States into the regions of West Virginia and the rest of the United States. Also included are results for Yugoslavian males. The different expectations of life at birth produced by these computations are set out in Table 3.6.

The results in Table 3.6 indicate, for example, that under the 1958 growth schedule a California-born girl, with a total expectation of life at birth of

Table 3.7   Regional Expectations of Life at Birth by Region of Residence: United States Males and Females, 1958

A. Males

Region of Birth	Region of Residence					
	1	2	3	4	5	Total
1. San Francisco SMSA	32.51	5.50	1.10	5.59	22.92	67.62
2. Los Angeles SMSA	4.11	36.06	1.56	3.62	22.16	67.50
3. San Diego SMSA	3.64	7.67	21.72	2.46	31.95	67.44
4. Rest of California	8.81	7.39	1.27	27.09	22.78	67.35
5. Rest of United States	1.34	2.69	0.58	0.87	61.26	66.74

B. Females

Region of Birth	Region of Residence					
	1	2	3	4	5	Total
1. San Francisco SMSA	35.96	6.61	1.18	6.02	24.22	73.98
2. Los Angeles SMSA	4.77	40.81	1.79	3.82	22.97	74.15
3. San Diego SMSA	4.22	9.05	24.63	2.61	33.26	73.78
4. Rest of California	10.59	9.09	1.37	27.97	24.71	73.73
5. Rest of United States	1.42	2.99	0.55	0.83	67.35	73.14

73.86 years, will, on the average, spend 24.90, or about a third, of those years in the rest of the United States. By way of contrast, the corresponding estimate for West Virginia is 45.09 years, or almost two-thirds, out of a life expectancy of 73.15 years. The data for 1968 show a decline in the level of migration into California and out of West Virginia. The results for males mirror those of females. Finally, the two-region results, when appropriately aggregated, are consistent with their single-region counterparts.

For convenience and ease of exposition, most of the numerical calculations in this book are illustrated with two-region population systems. The procedures are of course equally applicable to multiregional systems in general. To demonstrate this we present, in Table 3.7, sex-specific regional expectations of life at birth by place of residence for the five-region population system comprised of four regions of California and the rest of the United States.

3.3   THE HISTORY OF THE BIRTH COHORT:
THE STATIONARY COHORT POPULATION

The discussion of the multiregional life table thus far has centered on the consequences of applying regional age-specific probabilities of outmigrating and dying to regional "cohorts" at the various ages, $x = 0, 5, \ldots, z$. The initial and only cohorts in the true sense of the term were the birth cohorts, or *radices*, in each region, $l_i(0) = 1, 2, \ldots, m$. Their life history is of special interest because the total expected number of person-years lived by them in each region between exact ages x and $x + 5$, $_{i0}L_j(x) = {_{i0}L_{\cdot j}(x)}$, for $i, j = 1, 2, \ldots, m$, is the principal input to numerical computations carried out with the *continuous* and *discrete* models of multiregional demographic growth described in Chapters 4 and 5, respectively.

Table 3.8 presents the regional survivors of an initial birth cohort of 100,000 babies in Slovenia and of another birth cohort of the same size born at the same instant in the rest of Yugoslavia. Of the 100,000 baby girls born in Slovenia, 3,008 died during their first 5 years of life and 1,385 outmigrated to the rest of Yugoslavia, leaving 95,607 Slovenian-born girls in Slovenia at exact age 5. Thus on the assumption of a uniform distribution of out-migration and deaths, over the unit interval of age, we calculate that Slovenian-born girls lived a total of $\frac{5}{2}(100{,}000 + 95{,}607) = 489{,}019 = {_{10}L_1(0)}$

person-years in Slovenia and a total of $\frac{5}{2}(1,385) = 3,462 = {}_{10}L_2(0)$ person-years in the rest of Yugoslavia while 0 to 4 years old. From this we conclude that if births occur in region 1 at a rate of $l_1(0)$ every year for 5 years, a proportion ${}_{10}L_2(0)/5l_1(0) = 0.006924$ will survive in region 2 to be counted at the end of the first 5-year interval. Such proportions are used in developing the fertility elements of the multiregional projection matrix in the discrete model of multiregional demographic growth. Finally, summing the various columns of person-years lived in Table 3.8 we may find the total person-years lived beyond each age ${}_{i0}T_j(x)$, by region of residence and birth, and the corresponding expectations of remaining life at each age ${}_{i0}e_j(x)$.

As in the single-region model, the entire collection of region-specific survivors ${}_{i0}l_j(x)$, $i, j = 1, 2, \ldots, m$ also may be viewed as a *stationary* multiregional population in which births occur at the uniform annual level of $l_i(0)$ in each region. Since the multiregional population is assumed to be undisturbed by emigration or immigration, ultimately a population with a particular unchanging stationary age-region composition will arise. The total population in region i, for example, will be equal to $T_i(0) = \sum_{j=1}^{m} {}_{j0}T_i(0)$. Of this total population, $L_i(x) = {}_{x}L_{\cdot i}(x)$ individuals will be aged x to $x + 4$ at last birthday. Therefore the proportion that will be x to $x + 4$ years old in this stationary population is $L_i(x)/T_i(0)$. The crude birthrate in region i will be $l_i(0)/T_i(0)$. For example, referring to Table 3.8, we observe that the total stationary population in region 1 is

$$T_1(0) = {}_{10}T_1(0) + {}_{20}T_1(0)$$

$$= \sum_{x=0}^{z} {}_{10}L_1(x) + \sum_{x=0}^{z} {}_{20}L_1(x)$$

$$= \sum_{x=0}^{z} L_1(x)$$

$$= 6{,}571{,}948.$$

Hence the crude stationary birth rate in region 1 would appear to be

$$b_1 = \frac{l_1(0)}{T_1(0)} = \frac{100{,}000}{6{,}571{,}948} = 0.01522, \text{ or } 15.22 \text{ per thousand.}$$

But in computing $T_1(0)$ we have aggregated regional stationary populations that evolved from birth cohorts of equal size! This equality is not likely to have occurred in the empirical population the life table purports to describe. Consequently, we must introduce an appropriate weighting to reflect the size

Table 3.8 Two-Region Life Table for Yugoslavian Females, 1961: Region of Birth Life Table Statistics

Age, x	(1) Slovenia						(2) Rest of Yugoslavia					
	$_{10}l_1(x)$	$_{10}l_2(x)$	$_{10}L_1(x)$	$_{10}L_2(x)$	$_{10}e_1(x)$	$_{10}e_2(x)$	$_{20}l_2(x)$	$_{20}l_1(x)$	$_{20}L_2(x)$	$_{20}L_1(x)$	$_{20}e_2(x)$	$_{20}e_1(x)$
0	100,000	0	489,019	3,462	64.90	7.67	100,000	0	473,103	322	65.43	0.82
5	95,607	1,385	474,804	9,633	61.87	7.87	89,241	129	445,280	825	67.92	0.92
10	94,314	2,468	469,485	14,065	57.09	7.79	88,871	201	443,654	1,175	63.14	0.91
15	93,480	3,158	460,887	21,671	52.32	7.66	88,591	269	441,268	2,074	58.30	0.90
20	90,875	5,511	445,622	35,392	47.68	7.45	87,916	561	437,273	3,774	53.57	0.88
25	87,373	8,646	430,242	48,958	43.22	7.11	86,993	949	432,767	5,220	48.92	0.84
30	84,723	10,937	418,689	58,329	38.88	6.63	86,114	1,139	428,369	6,003	44.35	0.79
35	82,752	12,395	410,727	63,431	34.69	6.05	85,234	1,262	423,762	6,503	39.78	0.73
40	81,539	12,978	404,752	65,422	30.58	5.42	84,271	1,339	418,177	6,839	35.24	0.66
45	80,362	13,191	397,736	65,844	26.57	4.77	83,000	1,396	410,917	7,007	30.80	0.59
50	78,732	13,147	387,973	65,323	22.72	4.14	81,367	1,406	400,329	7,060	26.44	0.52
55	76,457	12,983	374,240	63,946	19.00	3.53	78,765	1,418	384,398	7,136	22.30	0.44
60	73,239	12,596	353,982	61,185	15.44	2.93	74,994	1,437	359,649	7,126	18.36	0.37
65	68,353	11,878	320,318	56,273	12.11	2.37	68,865	1,414	321,861	6,749	14.85	0.30
70	59,774	10,631	266,489	48,028	9.25	1.90	59,879	1,286	267,244	5,786	11.80	0.24
75	46,822	8,580	196,464	36,889	6.94	1.55	47,019	1,028	199,165	4,364	9.46	0.18
80	31,764	6,175	116,082	24,326	4.96	1.29	32,648	717	127,532	2,683	7.66	0.13
85+	14,669	3,555	72,043	24,777	3.95	1.36	18,365	356	127,993	1,749	6.84	0.09

of the regional birth cohorts that generated the empirical multiregional population. A simple resolution of the problem is to calculate the multi-regional life table with regional radices set proportional to the regional allocation of births in a stationary multiregional population that corresponds to the empirical population. A convenient approximation is provided by the observed regional allocation of births in the empirical multiregional population. For example, out of a total of 205,010 baby girls born to Yugoslavian women in 1961, 6.9065% were born in Slovenia. Thus an appropriate regional allocation of the total radix of 200,000, which previously was allocated equally among the two regions, is $(0.069065)(200,000) = 13,813$ for Slovenia and $200,000 - 13,813 = 186,187$ for the rest of Yugoslavia.[1] Table 3.9 compares the stationary populations obtained using these new radices with those presented in Table 3.8. Also included are the corresponding results obtained with the single-region model.

The total stationary population in our two-region population system now may be calculated as

$$T(0) = T_1(0) + T_2(0) = \sum_{x=0}^{z} L(x) = 949,483 + \cdots + 254,936$$

$$= 13,337,485.$$

Of this total population,

$$T_1(0) = \sum_{x=0}^{z} L_1(x) = 68,148 + \cdots + 13,207$$

$$= 1,049,810$$

persons (or 7.87% of the total) constitute the stationary population of Slovenia, and the remaining $T_2(0) = 12,287,675$ (or 92.13% of the total) are members of the stationary population of the rest of the Yugoslavia. The crude birthrate in the stationary Slovenian population is

$$b_1 = \frac{13,813}{1,049,810} = 0.0136, \quad \text{or} \quad 13.16 \text{ per thousand.}$$

[1] An alternative approximation is the regional allocation of births in the stable multiregional population corresponding to the empirical population. According to Table 4.4 of Chapter 4, this gives Slovenia a radix allocation of 4.6475%. Yet another possible proportion is the regional allocation of the total empirical population. Out of the total Yugoslavian female population in 1961, 8.7640% resided in Slovenia. Finally, we may find the "correct" radix by considering the continuous projection model of Chapter 4 with the intrinsic rate of growth set at zero. This yields a radix allocation of 4.7210% for Slovenia.

Table 3.9 Two-Region Life Table for Yugoslavian Females, 1961: Alternative Regional Radices and Aggregated Stationary Populations

	Two-Region Model: (1) Slovenia; (2) Rest of Yugoslavia								Single-Region Model	
	$l_1(0) = 100{,}000$	$l_2(0) = 100{,}000$			$l_1(0) = 13{,}813$	$l_2(0) = 186{,}187$				
Age, x	$L_1(x)$	$L_2(x)$	$L(x)$	$e(x)$	$L_1(x)$	$L_2(x)$	$L(x)$	$e(x)$	$L(x)$	$e(x)$
0	489,341	476,565	965,906	69.41	68,148	881,334	949,483	66.69	949,532	66.68
5	475,629	454,913	930,542	69.30	67,120	830,384	897,504	68.90	897,602	68.89
10	470,660	457,719	928,378	64.49	67,036	827,969	895,005	64.12	895,104	64.11
15	462,961	462,939	925,900	59.61	67,525	824,577	892,101	59.26	892,206	59.25
20	449,396	472,665	922,062	54.80	68,580	819,035	887,616	54.50	887,724	54.48
25	435,462	481,725	917,186	50.06	69,148	812,517	881,665	49.81	881,764	49.79
30	424,692	486,698	911,390	45.33	69,011	805,624	874,635	45.17	874,732	45.15
35	417,230	487,193	904,424	40.63	68,842	797,752	866,594	40.53	866,712	40.51
40	411,591	483,599	895,189	35.95	68,641	787,628	856,268	35.91	856,422	35.90
45	404,743	476,761	881,503	31.36	67,986	774,169	842,154	31.38	842,334	31.36
50	395,033	465,652	860,686	26.91	66,736	754,384	821,121	26.94	821,348	26.93
55	381,376	448,344	829,721	22.63	64,980	724,532	789,512	22.72	789,838	22.70
60	361,108	420,834	781,942	18.54	62,163	678,072	740,235	18.71	740,756	18.68
65	327,067	378,134	705,202	14.80	56,812	607,037	663,849	15.10	664,524	15.07
70	272,275	315,272	587,548	11.57	47,583	504,208	551,791	11.97	552,398	11.93
75	200,828	236,054	436,882	9.03	35,262	375,916	411,178	9.56	411,524	9.50
80	118,765	151,858	270,623	6.97	21,030	240,809	261,839	7.67	261,516	7.60
85+	73,792	152,770	226,561	6.13	13,208	241,729	254,936	6.82	250,516	6.73

The corresponding rate for the rest of Yugoslavia is

$$b_2 = \frac{186,187}{12,287,675} = 0.01515, \quad \text{or} \quad 15.15 \text{ per thousand.}$$

3.4 THE COMPUTATION OF SURVIVORSHIP AND OUTMIGRATION PROPORTIONS

A most useful application of the information provided by a multiregional life table is found in multiregional population projection. As in the single-region model, we assume that the survivorship and migration behavior exhibited by the stationary life table population adequately represents survivorship and migration in the empirical population for which the life table was developed.

In the stationary single-region life table population, the survivorship process was expressed by the relationship

$$L(x + 5) = s(x)L(x), \tag{3.19}$$

in which $s(x)$ denoted the proportion of individuals aged x to $x + 4$ who survived to be $x + 5$ to $x + 9$ years old 5 years later. This led to the following definition of $s(x)$, first set out in Equation 2.7:

$$s(x) = \frac{L(x + 5)}{L(x)} = L(x + 5)L(x)^{-1}. \tag{3.20}$$

A parallel approach, applied to a stationary multiregional life table population, begins with

$$L_i(x + 5) = \sum_{j=1}^{m} s_{ji}(x)L_j(x), \tag{3.21}$$

where $s_{ji}(x)$ denotes the proportion of individuals aged x to $x + 4$ in region j who migrate to region i and survive to be included in that region's $x + 5$ to $x + 9$ year-old population 5 years later. Disaggregating each region's stationary population by region of birth gives

$$L_i(x) = \sum_{j=1}^{m} {}_{j0}L_i(x).$$

Consequently (3.21) may be expressed as

$$\sum_{j=1}^{m} {}_{j0}L_i(x + 5) = \sum_{k=1}^{m} s_{ki}(x) \sum_{j=1}^{m} {}_{j0}L_k(x).$$

Since individuals born in region i can never become members of a j-born population, and vice versa, we may break up the foregoing relation into the following m equations:

$$_{j0}L_i(x + 5) = \sum_{k=1}^{m} s_{ki}(x)_{j0}L_k(x), \qquad i, j = 1, 2, \ldots, m$$

or, more compactly,

$$_0L(x + 5) = S(x)_0L(x), \tag{3.22}$$

the matrix version of (3.19), where in the case of a two-region population system, for example,

$$S(x) = \begin{bmatrix} s_{11}(x) & s_{21}(x) \\ s_{12}(x) & s_{22}(x) \end{bmatrix} \quad \text{and} \quad _0L(x) = \begin{bmatrix} _{10}L_1(x) & _{20}L_1(x) \\ _{10}L_2(x) & _{20}L_2(x) \end{bmatrix}.$$

Consequently,[2]

$$S(x) = {}_0L(x + 5)_0L(x)^{-1}, \tag{3.23}$$

which gives, for the two-region population system,

$$s_{ii}(x) = \frac{_{i0}L_i(x + 5)_{j0}L_j(x) - {}_{j0}L_i(x + 5)_{i0}L_j(x)}{_{i0}L_i(x)_{j0}L_j(x) - {}_{j0}L_i(x)_{i0}L_j(x)}$$

and

$$s_{ij}(x) = \frac{_{i0}L_j(x + 5)_{j0}L_j(x) - {}_{j0}L_j(x + 5)_{i0}L_j(x)}{_{i0}L_i(x)_{j0}L_j(x) - {}_{j0}L_i(x)_{i0}L_j(x)}, \qquad i, j = 1, 2.$$

Dividing both numerators and denominators by the product $_{i0}L_j(x)_{j0}L_j(x)$ yields alternative formulas, which more clearly express the independence of these survivorship and outmigration proportions from the regional radices that were used to construct the multiregional life table:

$$s_{ii}(x) = \left[\frac{_{i0}L_i(x + 5)}{_{i0}L_j(x)} - \frac{_{j0}L_i(x + 5)}{_{j0}L_j(x)} \right] \bigg/ \left[\frac{_{i0}L_i(x)}{_{i0}L_j(x)} - \frac{_{j0}L_i(x)}{_{j0}L_j(x)} \right]$$

and

$$s_{ij}(x) = \left[\frac{_{i0}L_j(x + 5)}{_{i0}L_j(x)} - \frac{_{j0}L_j(x + 5)}{_{j0}L_j(x)} \right] \bigg/ \left[\frac{_{i0}L_i(x)}{_{i0}L_j(x)} - \frac{_{j0}L_i(x)}{_{j0}L_j(x)} \right].$$

[2] We may delete the zero subscripts in (3.23) because the relationship described holds true for any residence "cohort" and not just the birth cohort; that is, we could just as easily have disaggregated the population in each region not by place of birth but by place of previous residence at exact age y, $y \le x$. This property is a consequence of the Markovian assumption implicit in (3.13).

Note that as in the case of the formulas for regional expectations of life, any changes in the sizes of regional radices are canceled out. For example, consider the Yugoslavian stationary female populations described in Tables 3.8 and 3.9. The survivorship proportion $s_{11}(0)$ calculated with the first stationary population, in which each regional radix was 100,000, yields

$$s_{11}(0) = \left(\frac{474,804}{3,462} - \frac{825}{473,103}\right) \Big/ \left(\frac{489,019}{3,462} - \frac{322}{473,103}\right) = 0.970925;$$

whereas the second stationary population, in which $l_1(0) = 13,813$ and $l_2(0) = 186,187$, gives

$$s_{11}(0) = \left(\frac{65,585}{478} - \frac{1,535}{880,856}\right) \Big/ \left(\frac{67,548}{478} - \frac{600}{880,856}\right) = 0.970925.$$

Table 3.10 Two-Region Life Table for Yugoslavian Females, 1961: Survivorship and Outmigration Proportions by Age and Region of Residence

Age, x	(1) Slovenia			(2) Rest of Yugoslavia		
	$s_{1.}(x)$	$s_{11}(x)$	$s_{12}(x)$	$s_{2.}(x)$	$s_{22}(x)$	$s_{21}(x)$
0	0.983961	0.970925	0.013035	0.942263	0.941182	0.001082
5	0.998189	0.988779	0.009410	0.997137	0.996330	0.000807
10	0.997988	0.981625	0.016363	0.996655	0.994579	0.002077
15	0.996893	0.966690	0.030203	0.994815	0.990806	0.004009
20	0.996483	0.965201	0.031282	0.993030	0.989424	0.003606
25	0.995874	0.972905	0.022969	0.991699	0.989562	0.002137
30	0.994495	0.980783	0.013711	0.990490	0.989053	0.001437
35	0.992191	0.985294	0.006898	0.987731	0.986714	0.001017
40	0.986414	0.982555	0.003859	0.983264	0.982576	0.000688
45	0.978328	0.975364	0.002965	0.974734	0.974183	0.000550
50	0.967627	0.964466	0.003160	0.960965	0.960149	0.000816
55	0.949334	0.945699	0.003635	0.936531	0.935550	0.000981
60	0.909055	0.904755	0.004300	0.895686	0.894846	0.000840
65	0.835945	0.831858	0.004087	0.830756	0.830223	0.000533
70	0.741291	0.737166	0.004125	0.745535	0.745167	0.000368
75	0.594356	0.590754	0.003602	0.640784	0.640254	0.000530
80+	0.623627	0.620486	0.003141	1.004205	1.003546	0.000659

A more elegant demonstration of the independence of the survivorship and outmigration proportions and the regional radices appears in Equation A.14 of the Appendix to this chapter, where the survivorship and out-migration proportions are shown to be a function only of the probabilities of surviving and outmigrating.

Table 3.10 contains the entire set of survivorship and outmigration proportions associated with the Yugoslavian two-region life table presented earlier in this chapter.

APPENDIX.   ESTIMATING OUTMIGRATION AND DEATH PROBABILITIES

As in the single-region life table, several variations in life table construction methods may be developed for the multiregional model. We consider only two here by way of illustration.

We begin with an examination of a probability estimation method that views migration data in the same way as mortality data, that is, as reported *events*. Following the terminology adopted in Chapter 2, we call this estimation method the Option 1 method. Then we develop a probability estimation method in which migration data are treated as reported changes of regions of residence from those at a fixed prior date. This method is the multiregional analog of the census survival method we called the Option 2 method in Chapter 2. Thus we can demonstrate that the two alternative estimation procedures for obtaining the probabilities necessary to construct a single-region life table may be generalized to the case of many regions by replacing vectors with matrices in the definitions of the two options described in Section 2.5 of Chapter 2:[3]

OPTION 1

$$\text{Given } \hat{M}(x), \text{ find } P(x) \text{ such that } M(x) = \hat{M}(x) \qquad (\text{A.1})$$

OPTION 2

$$\text{Given } \hat{S}(x), \text{ find } P(x) \text{ such that } S(x) = \hat{S}(x) \qquad (\text{A.2})$$

---

[3] In the multiregional situation it is more convenient to deal with probabilities of surviving, $p_{ii}(x)$, instead of the corresponding probabilities of dying $q_i(x)$.

where in the case of a two-region population system and a unit age interval of 5 years, for example, we have

$$P(x) = \begin{bmatrix} p_{11}(x) & p_{21}(x) \\ p_{12}(x) & p_{22}(x) \end{bmatrix} \qquad M(x) = \begin{bmatrix} m_{1\delta}(x) & m_{21}(x) \\ m_{12}(x) & m_{2\delta}(x) \end{bmatrix}$$

$$S(x) = \begin{bmatrix} s_{11}(x) & s_{21}(x) \\ s_{12}(x) & s_{22}(x) \end{bmatrix}.$$

3.A.1   Estimating Outmigration and Death Probabilities: The Option 1 Method

Consider a two-region population system in which of $K_i(x)$ people, at age x and present in region i at the beginning of a year, $K_{ii}(x)$ are present in the same region at the end of the year, $K_{ij}(x)$ are present in region j at the end of the year, and $D_i(x)$ have died before the end of the year. Then

$$K_i(x) = K_{ii}(x) + K_{ij}(x) + D_i(x); \tag{A.3}$$

the corresponding age-specific death probability is

$$q_i(x) = \frac{D_i(x)}{K_i(x)}, \tag{A.4}$$

and its associated annual death rate is

$$M_{i\delta}(x) = \frac{D_i(x)}{P_i(x)}, \tag{A.5}$$

where $P_i(x)$ denotes the total person-years lived in region i, during the age interval, by the $K_i(x)$ people. Therefore

$$P_i(x) = a_{ii}(x)K_{ii}(x) + a_{ij}(x)K_{ij}(x) + a_{i\delta}(x)D_i(x), \tag{A.6}$$

whence, by (A.3),

$$P_i(x) = a_{ii}(x)[K_i(x) - K_{ij}(x) - D_i(x)] + a_{ij}(x)K_{ij}(x) + a_{i\delta}(x)D_i(x) \tag{A.7}$$

and

$$K_i(x) = \frac{1}{a_{ii}(x)} P_i(x) + \left[1 - \frac{a_{ij}(x)}{a_{ii}(x)}\right]K_{ij}(x) + \left[1 - \frac{a_{i\delta}(x)}{a_{ii}(x)}\right]D_i(x). \tag{A.8}$$

Recalling (A.4) and substituting (A.8) for $K_i(x)$, we divide both the numerator and denominator by $P_i(x)$ to obtain

$$q_i(x) = \cfrac{M_{i\delta}(x)}{\cfrac{1}{a_{ii}(x)} + \left[1 - \cfrac{a_{ij}(x)}{a_{ii}(x)}\right]M_{ij}(x) + \left[1 - \cfrac{a_{i\delta}(x)}{a_{ii}(x)}\right]M_{i\delta}(x)}, \qquad (A.9)$$

where

$$M_{ij}(x) = \frac{K_{ij}(x)}{P_i(x)}. \qquad (A.10)$$

An analogous calculation for $p_{ij}(x)$ yields an expression that is identical to the right-hand side of (A.9) but in which $M_{i\delta}(x)$ is replaced by $M_{ij}(x)$ in the numerator:

$$p_{ij}(x) = \cfrac{M_{ij}(x)}{\cfrac{1}{a_{ii}(x)} + \left[1 - \cfrac{a_{ij}(x)}{a_{ii}(x)}\right]M_{ij}(x) + \left[1 - \cfrac{a_{i\delta}(x)}{a_{ii}(x)}\right]M_{i\delta}(x)}. \qquad (A.11)$$

Table 3.A.1 presents the input data that were used to generate the two-region life table for Yugoslavian females in Chapter 3. To obtain that table we begin our computations with the calculation of the regional age-specific outmigration and death rates. For example,

$$M_{12}(0) = \frac{K_{12}(0)}{P_1(0)} = \frac{192}{67,800} = 0.002832$$

and

$$M_{1\delta}(0) = \frac{D_1(0)}{P_1(0)} = \frac{417}{67,800} = 0.006150.$$

Next, assuming that $a_{11}(x) = a_{22}(x) = 5$ and $a_{12}(x) = a_{1\delta}(x) = a_{21}(x) = a_{2\delta}(x) = \frac{5}{2}$, for all x, we compute the associated regional age-specific outmigration and death probabilities. Thus, for example,

$$p_{12}(0) = \frac{5M_{12}(0)}{1 + \frac{5}{2}M_{12}(0) + \frac{5}{2}M_{1\delta}(0)} = \frac{5(0.002832)}{1 + \frac{5}{2}(0.002832) + \frac{5}{2}(0.006150)}$$

$$= 0.013848$$

and

$$q_1(0) = \frac{5M_{1\delta}(0)}{1 + \frac{5}{2}M_{12}(0) + \frac{5}{2}M_{1\delta}(0)} = \frac{5(0.006150)}{1 + \frac{5}{2}(0.002832) + \frac{5}{2}(0.006150)}$$

$$= 0.030077.$$

Table 3.A.1   Two-Region Life Table for Yugoslavian Females, 1961: Input Data

Age, x	(1) Slovenia			(2) Rest of Yugoslavia		
	Popula-tion	Out-migrants	Deaths	Popula-tion	Out-migrants	Deaths
0	67,800	192	417	847,900	231	19,051
5	74,100	170	32	905,200	150	606
10	70,700	105	21	808,100	127	386
15	60,100	310	31	617,400	419	534
20	62,900	451	47	725,500	680	885
25	66,500	368	45	774,000	392	1,227
30	67,100	252	67	728,400	255	1,277
35	62,900	111	77	633,300	143	1,313
40	39,500	40	76	392,400	72	1,127
45	47,900	26	171	437,100	41	1,700
50	51,300	34	268	453,800	59	2,896
55	46,100	29	369	389,300	80	3,743
60	39,600	35	513	325,800	66	5,492
65	29,500	28	763	230,600	36	6,407
70	21,700	19	1,036	180,000	14	8,652
75	14,400	16	1,088	120,900	12	8,715
80	7,100	5	1,041	61,200	12	6,843
85+	3,600	4	733	39,300	3	5,639

Source.   Rogers and McDougall (1968).

The complete set of these probabilities of outmigrating and dying is given in Table 3.1. Applying them to two regional birth cohorts of radix 100,000 each, we obtain the life table statistics summarized in Tables 3.2 through 3.5. Observe that the fundamental rationale of the Option 1 method is satisfied in that the life table outmigration and death rates in Table 3.5 are equal to their empirical counterparts. For example,

$$m_{12}(0) = \frac{l_{12}(0)}{{}_{10}L_1(0)} = \frac{1,385}{489,019} = 0.002832 = M_{12}(0)$$

and

$$m_{1\delta}(0) = \frac{d_1(0)}{{}_{10}L_1(0)} = \frac{3,008}{489,019} = 0.006150 = M_{1\delta}(0).$$

3.A.2   Estimating Outmigration and Death Probabilities:
The Option 2 Method

Our second probability estimation method reflects the choice not to treat migration as a "vital event," since the data do not so report it, but instead to apply an estimation method that seeks the equality of observed and life table survivorship and outmigration proportions. Earlier we called this latter alternative the Option 2 method.

We begin our exposition of the multiregional Option 2 method by developing in matrix form the multiregional analog of the argument set out for the single-region model in Section 2.1.5. First, we recall the expressions for $S(x)$ and $_xL(y)$ that were presented in (3.23) and (3.15), respectively:

$$S(x) = {}_0L(x + 5){}_0L(x)^{-1} \tag{A.12}$$

and

$$_xL(y) = \tfrac{5}{2}[I + P(y)]_x l(y). \tag{A.13}$$

Setting $x = 0$ and $y = x + 5$ in (A.13) gives

$$_0L(x + 5) = \tfrac{5}{2}[I + P(x + 5)]_0 l(x + 5).$$

By definition,

$$_0l(x + 5) = P(x)_0 l(x);$$

hence

$$_0L(x + 5) = \tfrac{5}{2}[I + P(x + 5)]P(x)_0 l(x).$$

Next we express $S(x)$ solely as a function of $P(x + 5)$ and $P(x)$:

$$
\begin{aligned}
S(x) &= {}_0L(x + 5){}_0L(x)^{-1} \\
&= \tfrac{5}{2}[I + P(x + 5)]P(x)_0 l(x)_0 l(x)^{-1}[I + P(x)]^{-1}(\tfrac{2}{5}) \tag{A.14} \\
&= [I + P(x + 5)]P(x)[I + P(x)]^{-1}.
\end{aligned}
$$

Finally, postmultiplying both sides of (A.14) by $[I + P(x)]$ and premultiplying both sides by $[I + P(x + 5)]^{-1}$, we have

$$[I + P(x + 5)]^{-1}S(x)[I + P(x)] = P(x),$$

whence

$$P(x) = [I + P(x + 5) - S(x)]^{-1}S(x), \tag{A.15}$$

where $P(x)$ may be seen to be the matrix version of the corresponding single-region $p(x)$ set out in (2.22).

As in the single-region model, calculations with the Option 2 method must start with the last age group, 85 years and over say, and work backward to find $P(80)$ and, ultimately, $P(0)$. Since the last age interval is open-ended, we assume that $P(85) = \mathbf{0}$ and modify (A.15) for the next-to-last age group, as follows. First we recall that

$$_{80}\mathbf{L}(85) = {}^{\infty}M(85)^{-1}{}_{80}\mathbf{l}(85).$$

Next, we observe that

$$\mathbf{S}(80) = {}_{80}\mathbf{L}(85)_{80}\mathbf{L}(80)^{-1}$$

and

$$_{80}\mathbf{L}(80) = \tfrac{5}{2}[\mathbf{I} + P(80)]_{75}\mathbf{l}(80).$$

Hence

$$\mathbf{S}(80) = {}^{\infty}M(85)^{-1}{}_{80}\mathbf{l}(85)_{75}\mathbf{l}(80)^{-1}[\mathbf{I} + P(80)]^{-1}(\tfrac{2}{5}).$$

But by definition,

$$_{80}\mathbf{l}(85) = P(80)_{75}\mathbf{l}(80).$$

Consequently

$$\mathbf{S}(80) = \tfrac{2}{5}M(85)^{-1}P(80)[\mathbf{I} + P(80)]^{-1},$$

from which we may obtain

$$P(80) = \tfrac{5}{2}[\mathbf{I} - \tfrac{5}{2}M(85)\mathbf{S}(80)]^{-1}M(85)\mathbf{S}(80). \tag{A.16}$$

Note that $P(80)$ is the matrix version of the corresponding single-region expression defined in (2.23).

If migration data come from the census question regarding region of residence at a named previous date, as in the United States, then to use the Option 1 method one must somehow approximate the corresponding annual outmigration data. For example, if the previous date chosen is 5 years ago, one could take one-fifth of the census-reported totals. This of course would understate the actual level of outmigration to the extent that multiple moves and moves by nonsurviving migrants would not be included. Consequently the Option 2 method is conceptually more appealing.

Table 3.A.2 Two-Region Life Table for United States Females, 1968: A Comparison of Alternative Life Table Construction Methods

Method	Age, x	(1) West Virginia				(2) Rest of United States			
		$p_{12}(x)$	$q_1(x)$	$p_{21}(x)$	$q_2(x)$	$_{1x}e_1(x)$	$_{1x}e_2(x)$	$_{2x}e_2(x)$	$_{2x}e_1(x)$
A. Option 2: migration reported as a change of region of residence from that at a fixed prior date (1965–1970)	0	−0.046474	0.113415	0.000519	0.146552	31.23	40.73	70.78	0.22
	5	0.319598	−0.123879	0.001262	−0.146539	28.30	47.64	77.53	0.24
	10	−0.135861	0.109567	−0.000152	0.112584	29.51	33.21	62.97	0.18
	25	0.235179	−0.116516	0.001443	−0.093144	32.41	22.28	54.95	0.13
	40	0.033459	0.134700	0.000104	0.092500	28.05	6.62	36.41	0.03
	55	0.063672	−0.115948	0.000480	−0.024442	22.26	3.44	25.48	0.02
B. Option 1: migration reported as an "event" (1968)	0	0.142958	0.022860	0.001176	0.021389	29.51	44.88	74.11	0.26
	5	0.121507	0.001744	0.000820	0.001833	29.84	41.25	70.71	0.23
	10	0.092229	0.001462	0.000580	0.001508	28.65	37.58	65.86	0.21
	25	0.214805	0.002585	0.001255	0.004327	28.99	22.73	51.41	0.13
	40	0.075480	0.014072	0.000410	0.014133	29.43	8.03	37.35	0.04
	55	0.045619	0.045619	0.000257	0.044789	21.39	3.15	24.38	0.02

Since we do not have actual annual migration data for United States regions, a true test of the two options cannot be carried out on the same data base. However, the results of an illustrative calculation are presented in Table 3.A.2, for which we computed two multiregional life tables using 1965–1970 data for West Virginia and the rest of the United States. In the Option 1 calculations, we used one-fifth of the 5-year outmigration flows as our migration data input and obtained a two-region life table in which the life table and empirical outmigration and death rates are equal. For our Option 2 calculations we used the census-reported 5-year flows and calculated a corresponding two-region life table in which the life table and observed survivorship and outmigration proportions are equal. The results indicate that as in the single-region model, the census-reported survivorship history of an empirical population cannot be used to construct a multiregional life table without considerable data "smoothing." This aspect is taken up in Chapter 6.

CHAPTER
FOUR

The Continuous Model of
Multiregional Demographic Growth

This chapter focuses on the multiregional generalization of Alfred Lotka's fundamental integral equation, which relates the births of one generation to those of the one preceding. Lotka's model deals with a single-region population that is assumed to be undisturbed by migration. In this chapter we show how his arguments can be extended to the case of a multiregional population that experiences internal migration. In so doing we focus on the impact of a multiregional population's fertility, mortality, and migration schedules on its growth, regional shares, and age distributions.

4.1 THE MULTIREGIONAL RENEWAL EQUATION

A continuous model of single-sex population growth may be defined for a multiregional population system by means of a straightforward generalization of the corresponding single-region model. Beginning with the density of female births, say, at time t in each region, $B_i(t)$, we note that women aged x to $x + dx$ in region i at time t were born since time zero and are survivors of those born x years ago anywhere in the multiregional system and now living in region i at age x; that is, $\sum_{j=1}^{m} B_j(t - x)_{j0}p_i(x)\, dx$, where $x \leq t$. At time t, these women give birth to

$$\left[\sum_{j=1}^{m} B_j(t - x)_{j0}p_i(x) \right] m_i(x)\, dx \tag{4.1}$$

baby girls in region i per year. Here $_{j0}p_i(x)$ denotes the probability that a baby girl born in region j will survive to age x in region i, and $m_i(x)\, dx$ is the annual rate at which women aged x to $x + dx$ in region i bear female children.

Integrating (4.1) over all x and adding $G_i(t)$ to include births to women already alive at time zero, we have the fundamental integral equation

$$B_i(t) = G_i(t) + \int_0^t \left[\sum_{j=1}^{m} B_j(t - x)_{j0}p_i(x) \right] m_i(x)\, dx, \tag{4.2}$$

where

$$G_i(t) = \int_0^\beta \left[\sum_{j=1}^{m} k_j(x)_{jx}p_i(x + t) \right] m_i(x + t)\, dx, \tag{4.3}$$

$k_j(x)\, dx$ denoting the number of women alive between ages x and $x + dx$ in region j at time zero.

Expressing (4.2) in matrix form for a system of m regions, we have the multiregional renewal equation

$$\{\mathbf{B}(t)\} = \{\mathbf{G}(t)\} + \int_0^t \mathbf{M}(x)_0\mathbf{P}(x)\{\mathbf{B}(t - x)\}\, dx, \tag{4.4}$$

where $\mathbf{M}(x)$ is a diagonal matrix with diagonal elements $m_i(x)$ and the element in the ith row and jth column of $_0\mathbf{P}(x)$ is $_{j0}p_i(x)$. Note that $\{\mathbf{B}(t)\}$ and $\{\mathbf{G}(t)\}$ are vectors.

When t exceeds β, the last age of childbearing, births among persons surviving from time zero will be zero, that is, $\{\mathbf{G}(t)\} = \{\mathbf{0}\}$, and (4.4) reduces to the homogeneous equation set out by LeBras (1971):

$$\{\mathbf{B}(t)\} = \int_\alpha^\beta \mathbf{M}(x)_0\mathbf{P}(x)\{\mathbf{B}(t - x)\}\, dx. \tag{4.5}$$

As in the single-region model, the solution of the integral equation in (4.4) can be found by first obtaining a solution of (4.5) and then choosing values for the arbitrary constants in that solution such that in addition to satisfying (4.5), $\{\mathbf{B}(t)\}$ also satisfies (4.4).

We begin with the trial solution $\{\mathbf{B}(t)\} = \{\mathbf{Q}\}e^{rt}$. Substituting this solution into (4.5) gives

$$\{\mathbf{Q}\} = \int_{\alpha}^{\beta} e^{-rx}\mathbf{M}(x)_0\mathbf{P}(x)\{\mathbf{Q}\}\,dx$$

$$= \left[\int_{\alpha}^{\beta} e^{-rx}\mathbf{\Phi}(x)\,dx\right]\{\mathbf{Q}\}$$

$$= \mathbf{\Psi}(r)\{\mathbf{Q}\}, \tag{4.6}$$

where $\mathbf{\Phi}(x) = \mathbf{M}(x)_0\mathbf{P}(x)$ is the *multiregional net maternity function* and $\mathbf{\Psi}(r) = \int_{\alpha}^{\beta} e^{-rx}\mathbf{\Phi}(x)\,dx$ is the *multiregional characteristic matrix*.[1]

The problem now has been altered from one of solving the integral equation in (4.5) to that of solving (4.6) which, unlike (4.5), is a function of only a single variable, r.

To solve for r in (4.6), we rewrite that equation as

$$[\mathbf{\Psi}(r) - \mathbf{I}]\{\mathbf{Q}\} = \{\mathbf{0}\}, \tag{4.7}$$

from which we conclude that $\{\mathbf{Q}\}$ is the characteristic vector corresponding to the characteristic root of unity of the multiregional characteristic matrix

$$\mathbf{\Psi}(r) = \int_{\alpha}^{\beta} e^{-rx}\mathbf{M}(x)_0\mathbf{P}(x)\,dx, \tag{4.8}$$

and r is the number that gives $\mathbf{\Psi}(r)$ a characteristic root of unity or, equivalently,

$$|\mathbf{\Psi}(r) - \mathbf{I}| = 0. \tag{4.9}$$

---

[1] The multiregional net maternity function defined in (4.6) is a natural generalization of $\Phi(x)$ in (2.31). However it assumes that inmigrants immediately acquire the fertility schedule of the region into which they move. This assumption may be relaxed somewhat by differentiating the fertility schedule of a region by the region of birth of the parent. Thus in the case of a two-region example we would have

$$\Phi(x) = \begin{bmatrix} {}_{10}p_1(x){}_{10}m_1(x) & {}_{20}p_1(x){}_{20}m_1(x) \\ {}_{10}p_2(x){}_{10}m_2(x) & {}_{20}p_2(x){}_{20}m_2(x) \end{bmatrix}.$$

The analysis of the integral equation in (4.6) remains unaffected.

Alternatively, the solution of (4.6) may be approached in a manner that more clearly resembles the single-region procedure. Premultiplying both sides of (4.6) by the inverse of

$$\mathbf{Q} = \begin{bmatrix} Q_1 & 0 & \cdots & 0 \\ 0 & Q_2 & & \vdots \\ \vdots & & \ddots & \vdots \\ 0 & 0 & \cdots & Q_m \end{bmatrix}$$

gives

$$\{1\} = \mathbf{Q}^{-1} \int_{\alpha}^{\beta} e^{-rx} \mathbf{M}(x)_0 \mathbf{P}(x) \{\mathbf{Q}\} \, dx = \mathbf{Q}^{-1} \mathbf{\Psi}(r) \{\mathbf{Q}\} = \{\mathbf{\Psi}(r)\}. \quad (4.10)$$

Noting that $\mathbf{Q}\{1\} = \{\mathbf{Q}\}$, we may rewrite (4.10) as

$$\{1\} = \mathbf{Q}^{-1} \mathbf{\Psi}(r) \{\mathbf{Q}\} = \mathbf{Q}^{-1} \mathbf{\Psi}(r) \mathbf{Q}\{1\}$$

and observe that

$$[\mathbf{Q}^{-1} \mathbf{\Psi}(r) \mathbf{Q} - \mathbf{I}]\{1\} = \{0\}. \quad (4.11)$$

Thus the solution of (4.10) may be found by determining that value of r for which

$$|\mathbf{Q}^{-1} \mathbf{\Psi}(r) \mathbf{Q} - \mathbf{I}| = 0. \quad (4.12)$$

That the value of r satisfying (4.12) also satisfies (4.9) may be seen by observing that the weights are canceled out in the expansion of the determinant in (4.12).

4.2 MULTIREGIONAL STABLE GROWTH

In the preceding section we have seen that $\{\mathbf{Q}\}e^{rt}$ is a solution to (4.6), provided r is such that:

1. a characteristic root, $\lambda(r)$ of the matrix $\mathbf{\Psi}(r)$ is unity:

    $$\lambda(r) = 1 \quad (4.13)$$

2. $|\mathbf{\Psi}(r) - \mathbf{I}| = 0 \quad (4.14)$

3. $\{\mathbf{\Psi}(r)\} = [\mathbf{Q}^{-1} \mathbf{\Psi}(r) \mathbf{Q}]\{1\} = \{1\}. \quad (4.15)$

Moreover, all three conditions were shown to be equivalent in that a value of r that satisfies any one of them also satisfies the other two.

The matrix $\mathbf{\Psi}(r)$ normally has more than one real characteristic root of unity as r ranges between $-\infty$ and $+\infty$. Consequently (4.13), (4.14), and (4.15) may be satisfied by more than one real value of the root r. However, we are always interested in the largest, or *maximal*, real root, which we denote by r_1 when it is necessary to distinguish it from the submaximal roots. There can be only one such root, and in addition to exceeding the value of all other real roots r of (4.13), (4.14), and (4.15), it also is greater than the real part of any complex root of the same three equations.

In most empirical situations $\mathbf{\Psi}(r)$ is a matrix with only positive elements. Consequently, by the well-known Perron–Frobenius properties of positive matrices [Gantmacher, Vol. II (1959), pp. 53–66]:[2]

1.   The matrix $\mathbf{\Psi}(r)$ has a real and positive maximal characteristic root $\lambda_1(r)$ that is a simple root and is greater than the absolute value of any other characteristic root.
2.   Associated with $\lambda_1(r)$ is a characteristic vector, $\{\mathbf{Q}_1\}$, with all its elements positive. No other such vector of positive elements exists except for multiples of $\{\mathbf{Q}_1\}$.
3.   The maximal root $\lambda_1(r)$ of $\mathbf{\Psi}(r)$ decreases in value when an element of $\mathbf{\Psi}(r)$ is decreased (which, as in the single-region model, occurs when r is increased).

Of the real roots r that satisfy (4.13), (4.14), and (4.15), let r_1 denote the r for which $\lambda_1(r) = 1$ and r_k denote the r for which $\lambda_k(r) = 1$, for $k = 2, 3, \ldots$; that is, $\lambda_1(r_1) = 1$ and $\lambda_k(r_k) = 1$. If $\mathbf{\Psi}(r)$ is a positive matrix, $\lambda_1(r) > \lambda_k(r)$, whence

$$\lambda_1(r_k) > 1. \tag{4.16}$$

Consequently, $r_1 > r_k$. This can be understood by observing that if $r_k > r_1$, then by the third property of positive matrices listed previously $\lambda_1(r_k) < \lambda_1(r_1) = 1$, which is a contradiction of (4.16). Therefore $r_1 > r_k$, for all $k = 2, 3, \ldots$.

The maximal root $\lambda_1(r)$ is in fact a function that assigns to any value of r the maximal characteristic root of the matrix $\mathbf{\Psi}(r)$. This function is continuous and concave upward throughout, and its values decrease monotonically

---

[2] These properties also apply, in slightly weaker form, to nonnegative matrices $\mathbf{\Psi}(r)$ that are irreducible. The matrix $\mathbf{\Psi}(r)$ is nonnegative by definition.

between $+\infty$ to 0 as its argument increases between $-\infty$ and $+\infty$. Consequently $\lambda_1(r) = 1$ can occur only once: when $r = r_1$. Such a function is illustrated in the next section (Figure 4.1) as a graph in which $\lambda_1(r)$ is plotted as the ordinate with r as the abscissa.

As in the single-region model, any complex roots that satisfy (4.13), (4.14), and (4.15), and therefore (4.6), must occur in complex conjugate pairs. Suppose that $u + iv$ is such a root. Then

$$\mathbf{\Psi}(u + iv)\{\mathbf{Q}\} = \{\mathbf{Q}\}, \tag{4.17}$$

where, for example,

$$_i\Psi_j(u + iv) = \int_\alpha^\beta e^{-(u+iv)x}{}_i\Phi_j(x)\,dx$$

$$= \int_\alpha^\beta e^{-ux}[\cos(vx) - i\sin(vx)]_i\Phi_j(x)\,dx.$$

Equating real and imaginary parts in (4.17), we find

$$\left.\begin{array}{c} \displaystyle\sum_{j=1}^m Q_j \int_\alpha^\beta e^{-ux}\cos(vx)_j\Phi_i(x)\,dx = Q_i \\[2em] \displaystyle\sum_{j=1}^m Q_j \int_\alpha^\beta e^{-ux}\sin(vx)_j\Phi_i(x)\,dx = 0 \end{array}\right\}, \qquad i = 1, 2, \ldots, m. \tag{4.18}$$

It follows that $u - iv$ also is a complex root of (4.6), whence

$$\mathbf{\Psi}(u - iv)\{\mathbf{Q}\} = \{\mathbf{Q}\}. \tag{4.19}$$

Moreover, the maximal real root r_1 is greater than u in the complex root $u + iv$. Since $\cos(vx) < 1$ in (4.18) for some values of x within the range of integration,

$$\sum_{j=1}^m Q_j \int_\alpha^\beta e^{-ux}{}_j\Phi_i(x)\,dx > Q_i.$$

But

$$\sum_{j=1}^m Q_j \int_\alpha^\beta e^{-r_1 x}{}_j\Phi_i(x)\,dx = Q_i.$$

Hence $u < r_1$. That is, the maximal real root that satisfies (4.13), (4.14), and (4.15) is larger than the real part of any complex root that also satisfies the same three equations.

Finally, since (4.6) is homogeneous, its solution vectors are additive. Thus if $r_1, r_2, \ldots$, are roots satisfying (4.13), (4.14), and (4.15),

$$\{\mathbf{B}(t)\} = \{\mathbf{Q}_k\}e^{r_k t}, \qquad k = 1, 2, \ldots,$$

are solutions of (4.6), as is the general solution

$$\{\mathbf{B}(t)\} = \{\mathbf{Q}_1\}e^{r_1 t} + \{\mathbf{Q}_2\}e^{r_2 t} + \cdots$$

$$= \{\mathbf{Q}_1\}e^{r_1 t} + \sum_{k=2}^{w} \{\mathbf{Q}_k\}e^{r_k t} + \sum_{s=w+1}^{\infty} \{\mathbf{Q}_s\}e^{u_s t}[\cos(v_s t) + i\sin(v_s t)],$$

$$(4.20)$$

where the vectors $\{\mathbf{Q}_k\}$, $k = 1, 2, \ldots$, may be chosen to satisfy (4.4). As in the single-region model, the birth sequence $\{\mathbf{B}(t)\}$ is increasingly dominated by the maximal real root r_1 as t becomes large. Because $r_1 > \mathrm{Re}(r_k)$ for $k = 2, 3, \ldots$, all terms after the first in (4.20) become negligible compared to the first for large t, and

$$\{\mathbf{B}(t)\} \doteq \{\mathbf{Q}_1\}e^{r_1 t}. \qquad (4.21)$$

In Section 4.5 it is shown that exponential births lead to an exponentially growing population with a stable distribution in which each age-by-region subpopulation maintains a constant proportional relationship to the total population and increases at the same constant rate r_1. The influence of the initial population distribution is forgotten as time goes by, a condition defined in Chapter 2 as ergodicity.

We conclude this section by considering the problem of evaluating the vectors $\{\mathbf{Q}_k\}$, $k = 1, 2, \ldots$, to fit a particular initial condition specified by $\{\mathbf{G}(t)\}$.

The simplest method for deriving the formula for Q_k in the single-region model is by means of Laplace transforms (Keyfitz, 1968, p. 117). Following the same procedure in the multiregional model, we take Laplace transforms of both sides of (4.4), after denoting $\mathbf{M}(x)_0\mathbf{P}(x)$ by $\mathbf{\Phi}(x)$, and obtain

$$\{\mathbf{B}^*(r)\} = \{\mathbf{G}^*(r)\} + \mathbf{\Phi}^*(r)\{\mathbf{B}^*(r)\}, \qquad (4.22)$$

where

$$\{\mathbf{B}^*(r)\} = \int_0^{\infty} e^{-rt}\{\mathbf{B}(t)\}\, dt$$

$$\{\mathbf{G}^*(r)\} = \int_0^{\infty} e^{-rt}\{\mathbf{G}(t)\}\, dt$$

$$\mathbf{\Phi}^*(r) = \int_0^{\infty} e^{-rt}\mathbf{\Phi}(t)\, dt.$$

Consequently[3]

$${\bf \{B^*(r)\} = \sum_{k=1}^{\infty} \frac{\{Q_k\}}{r - r_k},} \qquad (4.23)$$

whence

$${\bf \{B(t)\} = \sum_{k=1}^{\infty} \{Q_k\}e^{r_k t}} \qquad (4.24)$$

Extending the ordinary procedure for obtaining the coefficients of partial fractions, we set $r = r_1 + \varepsilon = 0$ in (4.23) and proceed to the limit $\varepsilon = 0$ to find

$$\lim_{r \to r_1} \frac{[\mathbf{I} - \mathbf{\Phi}^*(r)]}{r - r_1} \{\mathbf{Q}_1\} = \{\mathbf{G}^*(r)\}.$$

A generalization of L'Hospital's rule gives

$$\frac{d}{dr}[\mathbf{I} - \mathbf{\Phi}^*(r)]\{\mathbf{Q}_1\}|_{r=r_1} = \{\mathbf{G}^*(r_1)\},$$

whence

$$-\mathbf{\Psi}'(r_1)\{\mathbf{Q}_1\} + [\mathbf{I} - \mathbf{\Psi}(r_1)]\left\{\frac{d}{dr}\mathbf{Q}_1\right\}_{r=r_1} = \{\mathbf{G}^*(r_1)\},$$

since

$$\mathbf{\Phi}^*(r) = \mathbf{\Psi}(r),$$

and

$$[\mathbf{I} - \mathbf{\Psi}(r_1)]\left\{\frac{d}{dr}\mathbf{Q}_1\right\}_{r=r_1} = \{\mathbf{G}^*(r_1)\} + \mathbf{\Psi}'(r_1)\{\mathbf{Q}_1\}. \qquad (4.25)$$

Because $[\mathbf{I} - \mathbf{\Psi}(r_1)]$ is singular, the derivation of $\{d/dr\ \mathbf{Q}_1\}$ requires the use of generalized inverses (Rogers, 1971, pp. 254–264). Denoting a generalized inverse of $\mathbf{D}$ by $\mathbf{D}^+$, we solve (4.25) for $\{d/dr\ \mathbf{Q}_1\}$ to find

$$\left\{\frac{d}{dr}\mathbf{Q}_1\right\}_{r=r_1} = \mathbf{D}^+[\{\mathbf{G}^*(r_1)\} + \mathbf{\Psi}'(r_1)\{\mathbf{Q}_1\}] + [\mathbf{D}^+\mathbf{D} - \mathbf{I}]\{\mathbf{Z}\}, \quad (4.26)$$

---

[3] The author is grateful to Jacques Ledent for pointing out the errors in an earlier formulation and for suggesting the argument that follows.

where $\{Z\}$ is an arbitrary vector and $D = I - \Psi(r_1)$. Recalling (4.6), we observe that $\{Q_1\}$ is the characteristic vector that satisfies $D\{Q_1\} = \{0\}$, whence

$$\{Q_1\} = D^+\{0\} + (D^+D - I)\{Z\} = (D^+D - I)\{Z\}.$$

Thus (4.26) may be rewritten as

$$\left\{\frac{d}{dr}Q_1\right\}_{r=r_1} = D^+[\{G^*(r_1)\} + \Psi'(r_1)\{Q_1\}] + \{Q_1\}, \qquad (4.27)$$

which when substituted into (4.25) yields

$$DD^+[\{G^*(r_1)\} + \Psi'(r_1)\{Q_1\}] + D\{Q_1\} = \{G^*(r_1)\} + \Psi'(r_1)\{Q_1\},$$

whence

$$[D - (I - DD^+)\Psi'(r_1)]\{Q_1\} = [I - DD^+]\{G^*(r_1)\}, \qquad (4.28)$$

and

$$\{Q_1\} = [D - (I - DD^+)\Psi'(r_1)]^{-1}[I - DD^+]\{V\}, \qquad (4.29)$$

since the matrix $[D - (I - DD^+)\Psi'(r_1)]$ can be shown to be nonsingular and $\{G^*(r_1)\} = \{V\}$, the vector of *regional total reproductive values* (Keyfitz, 1968, p. 264).

Because $D\{Q_1\} = \{0\}$, the first term in (4.28) may be eliminated so that

$$[I - DD^+][\Psi'(r_1)\{Q_1\} + \{G^*(r_1)\}] = \{0\}. \qquad (4.30)$$

Numerical evaluations of $[I - DD^+]$ indicate that the matrix has only one row of nonzero elements. Consequently it appears that (4.30) defines a single linear relationship between the elements of the vector $\{Q_1\}$ which, added to the $m - 1$ independent relationships set out in (4.6), gives $\{Q_1\}$ a unique solution.

4.3   NUMERICAL SOLUTION OF THE MULTIREGIONAL CHARACTERISTIC EQUATION

In the single-region model one normally evaluates $\Psi(r)$ with the numerical approximation

$$\Psi(r) = \sum_{x=\alpha}^{\beta-5} e^{-r(x+2.5)} L(x)F(x), \qquad (4.31)$$

in which the integral $\int_0^5 e^{-r(x+t)} p(x+t) m(x+t)\, dt$ is replaced by the product of $e^{-r(x+2.5)}$, $L(x)$, computed on a unit radix, and $F(x)$. The summation is over ages x, which are multiples of 5.

An analogous approach may be followed in the multiregional model. Replacing the integral $\int_0^5 e^{-r(x+t)} \mathbf{M}(x+t)_0 \mathbf{P}(x+t)\, dt$ by the product of $e^{-r(x+2.5)}$, $\mathbf{F}(x)$, and $_0\mathbf{L}(x)$, where $\mathbf{F}(x)$ is a diagonal matrix with regional birthrates in the diagonal, and the element in the ith row and jth column of $_0\mathbf{L}(x)$ is $_{j0}L_i(x)$, *computed using unit radices for all regions.* Thus the multiregional counterpart of (4.31) is

$$\mathbf{\Psi}(r) = \sum_{x=\alpha}^{\beta-5} e^{-r(x+2.5)} \mathbf{F}(x)_0\mathbf{L}(x), \tag{4.32}$$

which in the case of a two-region system, for example, gives the following numerical approximation to the multiregional characteristic matrix:

$$\mathbf{\Psi}(r) = \begin{bmatrix} \sum_{x=\alpha}^{\beta-5} e^{-r(x+2.5)} {}_{10}L_1(x)F_1(x) & \sum_{x=\alpha}^{\beta-5} e^{-r(x+2.5)} {}_{20}L_1(x)F_1(x) \\ \sum_{x=\alpha}^{\beta-5} e^{-r(x+2.5)} {}_{10}L_2(x)F_2(x) & \sum_{x=\alpha}^{\beta-5} e^{-r(x+2.5)} {}_{20}L_2(x)F_2(x) \end{bmatrix}. \tag{4.33}$$

Table 4.1 presents age-specific birthrates and data from a two-region life table with which we may calculate $\mathbf{\Psi}(r)$ for United States females residing in California and the rest of the United States in 1958. For example, beginning with $r = 0.020$, we obtain

$$\mathbf{\Psi}(0.020) = \begin{bmatrix} 0.721352 & 0.060908 \\ 0.286915 & 0.955783 \end{bmatrix},$$

a matrix with a maximal characteristic root of $\lambda_1(0.020) = 1.015245$. Increasing the argument of $\mathbf{\Psi}(r)$ to 0.025 yields

$$\mathbf{\Psi}(0.025) = \begin{bmatrix} 0.637567 & 0.053311 \\ 0.250884 & 0.841747 \end{bmatrix}$$

and $\lambda_1(0.025) = 0.893921$. Since $\lambda_1(0.020) > 1$ and $\lambda_1(0.025) < 1$, r must lie between 0.020 and 0.025. An average of these two values yields $\lambda_1(0.0225) = 0.952632$. Continuing in this manner we ultimately converge on $r = 0.02059$, for which $\lambda_1(r)$ is unity to four decimal places, thereby satisfying (4.13). At this point

$$\mathbf{\Psi}(r) = \begin{bmatrix} 0.710836 & 0.059950 \\ 0.282371 & 0.941447 \end{bmatrix}.$$

Table 4.1 The Multiregional Net Maternity Function for United States Females, 1958: Two-Region Model of California and the Rest of the United States

Region	Age, x	$F_1(x)$	$_{10}L_1(x)$	$_{20}L_1(x)$	$_1\Phi_1(x)$	$_2\Phi_1(x)$
(1) California	10	0.00032	4.16220	0.14050	0.00134	0.00004
	15	0.04959	3.92220	0.18953	0.19451	0.00940
	20	0.12323	3.65597	0.25690	0.45052	0.03166
	25	0.08945	3.33854	0.33460	0.29862	0.02993
	30	0.05262	3.06113	0.39018	0.16109	0.02053
	35	0.02387	2.86151	0.42907	0.06831	0.01024
	40	0.00606	2.70519	0.45559	0.01640	0.00276
	45	0.00030	2.57330	0.47038	0.00078	0.00014
	50	0.00002	2.44204	0.47586	0.00004	0.00001
		$F_2(x)$	$_{10}L_2(x)$	$_{20}L_2(x)$	$_1\Phi_2(x)$	$_2\Phi_2(x)$
(2) Rest of	10	0.00048	0.69909	4.70382	0.00034	0.00225
United	15	0.04584	0.92960	4.64493	0.04261	0.21291
States	20	0.12567	1.18150	4.56260	0.14848	0.57338
	25	0.09311	1.48124	4.46573	0.13792	0.41582
	30	0.05477	1.73468	4.38419	0.09502	0.24014
	35	0.02825	1.90037	4.30997	0.05369	0.12177
	40	0.00819	2.00486	4.22927	0.01642	0.03463
	45	0.00048	2.05530	4.12971	0.00100	0.00200
	50	0.00001	2.06703	4.00307	0.00003	0.00005

Note that (4.14) and (4.15) are also satisfied:

$$(0.710836 - 1)(0.941447 - 1) - (0.282371)(0.059950) = 0$$

and

$$\begin{bmatrix} 0.710836 & \dfrac{Q_2}{Q_1}(0.059950) \\[2mm] \dfrac{Q_1}{Q_2}(0.282371) & 0.941447 \end{bmatrix} \begin{Bmatrix} 1 \\ 1 \end{Bmatrix} = \begin{Bmatrix} 1 \\ 1 \end{Bmatrix},$$

where

$$\frac{Q_2}{Q_1} = \frac{1 - 0.710836}{0.059950} = 4.82322 \quad \text{and} \quad \frac{Q_1}{Q_2} = \frac{1 - 0.941447}{0.282371} = 0.20733.$$

Table 4.2 and Figure 4.1 illustrate the behavior of $\lambda_1(r)$ as a function of r. Also detailed are the functions $|\Psi(r) - I|$ and $\{\Psi(r)\}$.'

Table 4.2 Values of $\lambda(r)$, $|\Psi(r) - \mathbf{I}|$ and $\{\Psi(r)\}$ for a Two-Region Model of United States Females, 1958: (1) California and (2) Rest of the United States[a]

r	$\lambda_1(r)$	$\|\Psi(r) - \mathbf{I}\|$	$\{\Psi(r)\}$ $\sum_{j=1}^{m}\dfrac{Q_j}{Q_1}\,_j\Psi_1(r)$	$\sum_{j=1}^{m}\dfrac{Q_j}{Q_2}\,_j\Psi_2(r)$	$\lambda_2(r)$
0.000	1.704195	0.063645	1.696689	1.705700	1.090379
0.001	1.660048	0.041696	1.653113	1.661438	1.063171
0.002	1.617105	0.022633	1.610714	1.618387	1.036676
0.003	1.575331	0.006257	1.569459	1.576510	1.010875
0.0032	1.567114	0.003287	1.561342	1.568272	1.005796
0.0034	1.558942	0.000416	1.553270	1.560080	1.000745
0.0036	1.550815	−0.002358	1.545242	1.551934	0.995720
0.0038	1.542732	−0.005036	1.537257	1.543831	0.990721
0.004	1.534694	−0.007620	1.529315	1.535774	0.985749
0.005	1.495160	−0.019173	1.490252	1.496147	0.961279
0.006	1.456699	−0.028568	1.452238	1.457596	0.937448
0.007	1.419280	−0.035959	1.415243	1.420092	0.914238
0.008	1.382872	−0.041492	1.379240	1.383603	0.891631
0.009	1.347448	−0.045303	1.344199	1.348102	0.869612
0.010	1.312978	−0.047522	1.310095	1.313559	0.848164
0.011	1.279437	−0.048267	1.276901	1.279948	0.827272
0.012	1.246798	−0.047652	1.244591	1.247243	0.806920
0.013	1.215035	−0.045782	1.213140	1.215418	0.787094
0.014	1.184124	−0.042757	1.182525	1.184447	0.767780
0.015	1.154041	−0.038670	1.152723	1.154307	0.748964
0.016	1.124761	−0.033607	1.123710	1.124974	0.730632
0.017	1.096264	−0.027650	1.095464	1.096425	0.712771
0.018	1.068526	−0.020875	1.067965	1.068639	0.695369
0.019	1.041526	−0.013354	1.041191	1.041594	0.678412
0.020	1.015245	−0.005154	1.015123	1.015269	0.661890
0.020592	1.000016	−0.000006	1.000015	1.000016	0.652309
0.020593	0.999990	0.000003	0.999990	0.999991	0.652293
0.020594	0.999965	0.000012	0.999964	0.999965	0.652277
0.021	0.989661	0.003662	0.989741	0.989645	0.645790
0.022	0.964755	0.013037	0.965025	0.964700	0.630102
0.023	0.940508	0.022915	0.940958	0.940417	0.614813
0.024	0.916903	0.033246	0.917522	0.916777	0.599914
0.025	0.893921	0.043981	0.894700	0.893762	0.585393
0.026	0.871544	0.055077	0.872473	0.871355	0.571242
0.027	0.849756	0.066491	0.850827	0.849539	0.557449
0.028	0.828542	0.078184	0.829745	0.828297	0.544006
0.029	0.807884	0.090121	0.809211	0.807614	0.530902
0.030	0.787768	0.102268	0.789212	0.787474	0.518130

[a] The weights used for the computations: $Q_2/Q_1 = 4.82322$ and $Q_1/Q_2 = 0.20733$, are derived in Section 4.3, where they are shown to be associated with the maximal root $r = 0.020593$.

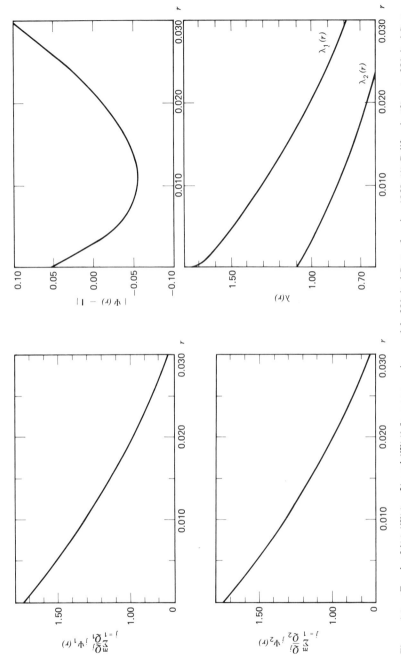

Figure 4.1 Graph of $\lambda(r)$, $|\Psi(r) - I|$, and $\{\Psi(r)\}$ for a two-region model of United States females, 1958: (1) California, (2) rest of United States. *Source.* Table 4.2.

Equations 4.13 and 4.14 both lead naturally to iterative procedures for establishing the value of r. The first requires the derivation of the maximal characteristic root of an $m \times m$ matrix at each iteration. The second instead requires the calculation of the determinant of an $m \times m$ matrix. By means of standard single-region methods, (4.15) yields an approximation of r that is consistent with the system of weights defined by the ratios Q_j/Q_i, for $i, j = 1, 2, \ldots, m$.[4] However, since these ratios cannot be determined until one finds r, they must be approximated along with r by iteration. As an initial approximation, the ratios may all be set equal to unity, say, and the corresponding initial approximation of r then may be obtained by a standard single-region method, such as the method of *functional iteration* described by Keyfitz (1968, p. 111). In the case of the two-region system of California and the rest of the United States, we find for $Q_2/Q_1 = Q_1/Q_2 = 1$, an initial approximation of $r(1) = 0.01021$ with the equation relating to California and $r(1) = 0.02846$ with the equation for the rest of the United States. With an initial approximation of r, an improved approximation of Q_2/Q_1 and Q_1/Q_2 may be obtained by solving for these two unknowns in (4.15) to find

$$\frac{Q_2}{Q_1} = \frac{1 - \sum_{x=\alpha}^{\beta-5} e^{-r(x+2.5)} {}_{10}L_1(x)F_1(x)}{\sum_{x=\alpha}^{\beta-5} e^{-r(x+2.5)} {}_{20}L_1(x)F_1(x)} \tag{4.34}$$

$$\frac{Q_1}{Q_2} = \frac{1 - \sum_{x=\alpha}^{\beta-5} e^{-r(x+2.5)} {}_{20}L_2(x)F_2(x)}{\sum_{x=\alpha}^{\beta-5} e^{-r(x+2.5)} {}_{10}L_2(x)F_2(x)} \tag{4.35}$$

and computing their values with r set equal to either of the two alternative initial approximations or, preferably, to their average:

$$r(2) = \frac{0.01021 + 0.02846}{2} = 0.01934.$$

Entering these improved approximations of Q_2/Q_1 and Q_1/Q_2 into (4.15) gives an improved approximation of r. Repeating this iterative procedure

---

[4] The fundamental multiregional analog to (4.31) becomes

$$\Psi_i(r) = \sum_{j=1}^{m} \frac{Q_j}{Q_i} {}_j\Psi_i(r) = \sum_{x=\alpha}^{\beta-5} e^{-r(x+2.5)} \sum_{j=1}^{m} \frac{Q_j}{Q_i} {}_{j0}L_i(x)F_i(x)$$

for each region $i = 1, 2, \ldots, m$.

until two consecutive approximations of r differ by less than a fixed small amount, we find $r = 0.02059$ as before.[5]

Turning to the multiregional characteristic equation in (4.6), we solve it with $r = 0.02059$ and find that the characteristic vector $\{Q_1\}$ is proportional to

$$\begin{Bmatrix} 0.1767 \\ 0.8233 \end{Bmatrix}.$$

The precise values of $\{Q_1\}$ that fit the initial conditions may be found by numerically evaluating (4.29).

Calculation of $\{Q_1\}$ in (4.29) requires a finite form by which $\{V\} = \{G^*(r_1)\}$ can be numerically evaluated from multiregional data on, say, the observed population, the life table stationary population, and observed fertility rates, all in 5-year age groups. Recalling the definition of $\{G(t)\}$:

$$\{G(t)\} = \int_0^\beta M(x + t)l(x + t)l(x)^{-1}\{k(x)\}\,dx, \qquad t < \beta, \tag{4.36}$$

where the ith element of the vector $\{k(x)\}$ denotes the number of individuals in region i at age x at time zero, we evaluate $\{G(t)\}$ numerically as

$$\{G(t)\} = \sum_{x=0}^{\beta-5} F(x + t)_0 L(x + t)_0 L(x)^{-1}\{K(x)\},$$

where $\{K(x)\} = \int_0^5 \{k(x + t)\}\,dt$, and generalizing the single-region argument of Keyfitz (1968, p. 264), we conclude that

$$\{V\} = \{G^*(r_1)\} = \sum_{t=0}^\beta \tfrac{5}{2}[e^{-rt}\{G(t)\} + e^{-r(t+5)}\{G(t+5)\}]$$

$$= \tfrac{5}{2}\sum_{x=0}^{\beta-5} F(x)\{K(x)\} + 5\sum_{x=0}^{\beta-5}\sum_{t=5}^{\beta-x-5} e^{-rt}F(x + t)_0 L(x + t)_0 L(x)^{-1}\{K(x)\}. \tag{4.37}$$

Premultiplying (4.37) by the corresponding numerical evaluation of

$$[D - (I - DD^+)\Psi'(r_1)]^{-1}[I - DD^+],$$

---

[5] Care must be exercised to ensure that the iterative procedure converges to the *maximal* real root and not merely a real root that satisfies(4.6). In practice this danger can be minimized by setting r equal to an estimate of the single-region solution for the entire multiregional system and using (4.34) and (4.35) to obtain an initial approximation of Q_2/Q_1 and Q_1/Q_2.

gives $\{\mathbf{Q}_1\}$. By way of illustration, the California–rest of the United States data of Table 4.1 yield

$$\{\mathbf{V}\} = \begin{Bmatrix} 5,173,439 \\ 46,671,636 \end{Bmatrix}$$

and

$$\{\mathbf{Q}_1\} = \begin{Bmatrix} 349,465 \\ 1,685,559 \end{Bmatrix}.$$

The corresponding results for the same data in consolidated single-region form are $V = 51,842,875$ and $Q = 2,029,909$, respectively.

4.4 THE MULTIREGIONAL NET MATERNITY FUNCTION

We now take up the multiregional generalization of several concepts related to the multiregional net maternity function defined in (4.6). Let the nth moment matrix of the multiregional net maternity function be

$$\mathbf{R}(n) = \int_{\alpha}^{\beta} x^n \mathbf{\Phi}(x)\, dx = \int_{\alpha}^{\beta} x^n \mathbf{M}(x)_0 \mathbf{P}(x)\, dx. \tag{4.38}$$

Observe that $\mathbf{\Psi}(0) = \mathbf{R}(0)$, a matrix we call the *net reproduction matrix*. Its typical element $_j R_i(0)$ gives the number of children expected to be born in region i to a baby now born in region j, under the current regime of fertility, mortality, and migration.

Next, generalizing two other conventional measures in the single-region model, define the matrices $\mathbf{\mu}$ and $\mathbf{\sigma}^2$, with elements

$$_j\mu_i = \frac{\int_{\alpha}^{\beta} x\, _j\Phi_i(x)\, dx}{\int_{\alpha}^{\beta} {}_j\Phi_i(x)\, dx} = \frac{_jR_i(1)}{_jR_i(0)} \tag{4.39}$$

and

$$_j\sigma_i^{\,2} = \frac{\int_{\alpha}^{\beta} (x - {}_j\mu_i)^2\, _j\Phi_i(x)\, dx}{\int_{\alpha}^{\beta} {}_j\Phi_i(x)\, dx} = \frac{_jR_i(2)}{_jR_i(0)} - {}_j\mu_i^{\,2}, \text{ respectively,} \tag{4.40}$$

where $_j\mu_i$ is the mean age of childbearing among j-born persons who are members of the stationary population of region i, and $_j\sigma_i^{\,2}$ is the associated variance.

Using the empirical multiregional net maternity function set out in Table 4.1, we may calculate the matrices $\mathbf{R}(0)$, $\mathbf{\mu}$, and $\mathbf{\sigma}^2$ that are presented

Table 4.3 Net Reproduction Rates and the Means and Variances of the Multiregional Net Maternity Function for United States Females, 1958: Two-Region Model of (1) California and (2) Rest of the United States

	R(0)	μ	σ^2

1. Multiregional model

$$\begin{bmatrix} 1.192 & 0.105 \\ 0.495 & 1.603 \end{bmatrix} \quad \begin{bmatrix} 25.430 & 27.468 \\ 27.713 & 26.221 \end{bmatrix} \quad \begin{bmatrix} 34.234 & 37.837 \\ 40.122 & 37.629 \end{bmatrix}$$

2. Separate single-region models (no internal migration)

$$\begin{bmatrix} 1.664 & \\ & 1.712 \end{bmatrix} \quad \begin{bmatrix} 25.967 & \\ & 26.325 \end{bmatrix} \quad \begin{bmatrix} 36.092 & \\ & 37.921 \end{bmatrix}$$

3. Consolidated single-region model

$$1.708 \qquad\qquad 26.295 \qquad\qquad 37.767$$

at the top of Table 4.3.[6] Their interpretation is straightforward. For example, under the 1958 regime of growth, a woman born in California is expected to be replaced by $1.192 + 0.495 = 1.687$ girl children, of whom 0.495 will be born in the rest of the United States. The mean age of childbearing of the stationary *native* California population is 25.430 years, with a variance of 34.234 years. This may be contrasted with 25.967 years, which is the same measure computed with the single-region model, under the assumption of no internal migration. In turn, this may be compared with the 26.295 years, which the single-region model yields when applied to the consolidated data, that is, the United States female population.

In Chapter 2 we saw that Lotka's method for numerically evaluating the intrinsic rate of growth in the single-region model revolved around the solution of the quadratic equation in (2.49):

$$\tfrac{1}{2}\sigma^2 r^2 - \mu r + \ln R(0) = 0,$$

[6] Numerical evaluation of these matrices follows a straightforward generalization of the single-region formulas. For example,

$$\mathbf{R}(n) = \sum_{x=\alpha}^{\beta-5} (x + 2.5)^n \mathbf{F}(x)_0 \mathbf{L}(x).$$

which may be solved iteratively as

$$r = \ln R(0) \bigg/ \left(\mu - \frac{\sigma^2 r}{2}\right),$$

where the r on the left-hand side is regarded as an improved approximation of the r on the right-hand side. A parallel argument for the multiregional model leads to the solution of the regional quadratic equations in

$$\tfrac{1}{2}\{\sigma^2\}r^2 - \{\mu\}r + \ln\{\mathbf{R}(0)\} = \{\mathbf{0}\}, \tag{4.41}$$

where

$$\{\mathbf{R}(n)\} = \mathbf{Q}^{-1}\mathbf{R}(n)\{\mathbf{Q}\}, \tag{4.42}$$

and $\{\mu\}$ and $\{\sigma^2\}$ are vectors composed of elements

$$\mu_i = \frac{R_i(1)}{R_i(0)} \tag{4.43}$$

and

$$\sigma_i^2 = \frac{R_i(2)}{R_i(0)} - \mu_i^2, \tag{4.44}$$

respectively.

The quadratic equations in (4.41) may be solved iteratively with standard single-region methods. However, as in the case of (4.15), the Q_j/Q_i ratios consistent with the solution value of r must be approximated along with r at each iteration. Thus, for example, we may begin the iterative solution method by setting $\mathbf{Q}$ equal to the identity matrix $\mathbf{I}$. Solving the m quadratic equations in (4.41) gives m separate approximations of r. If these differ by more than a specified small amount, the iterative solution procedure must continue, because at stability all regional populations of a multiregional population system grow at the same intrinsic rate of growth. That is, we obtain improved approximations of the Q_j/Q_i ratios and recompute r. By iterating back and forth in this way, we converge, as in Section 4.3, to the maximal root. Thus we have yet a fourth method for solving (4.6). As in the single-region model, this method of normal fit yields an approximation for r that is slightly higher than the value found by the other three methods.

A numerical illustration at this point may help to clarify the iterative solution method. Consider the two-region data in Table 4.3. Setting $Q_1 = Q_2 = 1$, we begin by calculating

$$\{\mathbf{R}(n)\} = \mathbf{Q}^{-1}\mathbf{R}(n)\{\mathbf{Q}\}, \qquad \text{for} \quad n = 0, 1, 2,$$

the ith element of which is $R_i(n)$, for $i = 1, 2$. This gives, for example,

$$\{R(0)\} = \begin{Bmatrix} 1.296 \\ 2.098 \end{Bmatrix} \qquad \{R(1)\} = \begin{Bmatrix} 33.179 \\ 55.762 \end{Bmatrix} \qquad \{R(2)\} = \begin{Bmatrix} 894.359 \\ 1562.811 \end{Bmatrix}$$

and

$$\{\mu\} = \begin{Bmatrix} 25.595 \\ 26.573 \end{Bmatrix} \qquad \{\sigma^2\} = \begin{Bmatrix} 34.833 \\ 38.619 \end{Bmatrix}.$$

Substituting these values into (4.41) yields $r(1) = 0.01021$ and $r(2) = 0.02848$. Taking their average as our initial approximation of r, we proceed to compute an improved approximation of Q_2/Q_1 and Q_1/Q_2 using (4.34) and (4.35). These in turn lead to improved approximations of $\{R(n)\}$, and thereby of r. Repeating this iterative procedure, we converge to the values $r = 0.02060$ and $Q_2/Q_1 = 4.823$. At this point,

$$\{R(0)\} = \begin{Bmatrix} 1.697 \\ 1.706 \end{Bmatrix} \qquad \{\mu\} = \begin{Bmatrix} 26.037 \\ 26.311 \end{Bmatrix} \qquad \{\sigma^2\} = \begin{Bmatrix} 36.175 \\ 37.904 \end{Bmatrix}.$$

4.5   RELATIONS UNDER STABILITY

Let $k_i(x, t)$ denote the density of persons at age x in region i at time t. These individuals are survivors in region i of births that may have occurred in any of the m regions in the multiregional population system. Hence if $B_j(t - x)$ is the density of births in region j at time $t - x$, the survivors of these births x years later in region i will be $B_j(t - x)_{j0}p_i(x)$, whence

$$k_i(x, t) = \sum_{j=1}^{m} B_j(t - x)_{j0}p_i(x).$$

Integrating this quantity over all ages of life gives the total female population in region i at time t

$$K_i(t) = \int_0^\infty k_i(x, t)\, dx,$$

and the proportion of this regional population which is at age x at time t is of density

$$c_i(x, t) = \frac{k_i(x, t)}{\int_0^\infty k_i(x, t)\, dx} = \frac{\sum_{j=1}^{m} B_j(t - x)_{j0}p_i(x)}{\int_0^\infty \sum_{j=1}^{m} B_j(t - x)_{j0}p_i(x)\, dx}. \qquad (4.45)$$

If $c_i(x, t)\, dx$ is the proportion of females in region i who are aged x to $x + dx$ at time t, the consolidated or "crude" annual death rate at time t of this population is

$$d_i(t) = \int_0^\omega c_i(x, t)\mu_i(x)\, dx,$$

and its crude annual birthrate at time t is

$$b_i(t) = \int_0^\omega c_i(x, t)m_i(x)\, dx,$$

where $\mu_i(x)$ is the instantaneous annual force of mortality in region i and $m_i(x)$ is the instantaneous annual force of fertility in the same region. The crude birthrate in region i at time t also may be found by setting $x = 0$ in the numerator of (4.45):

$$b_i(t) = c_i(0, t) = \frac{B_i(t)}{\int_0^\omega \sum_{j=1}^m B_j(t - x)_{j0}p_i(x)\, dx} = \frac{B_i(t)}{K_i(t)}.$$

Recall that at stability births in each region will be increasing exponentially at the rate r, for example, $B_i(t) = Q_i e^{rt}$. Consequently

$$c_i(x, t) = \frac{e^{-rx}\sum_{j=1}^m Q_j {}_{j0}p_i(x)}{\int_0^\omega e^{-rx}\sum_{j=1}^m Q_j {}_{j0}p_i(x)\, dx} = c_i(x),$$

an expression for $c_i(x, t)$ that does not contain t. It follows, therefore, that the intrinsic birthrate in region i at stability will be

$$b_i = c_i(0) = \frac{Q_i}{\displaystyle\int_0^\omega e^{-rx}\sum_{j=1}^m Q_j {}_{j0}p_i(x)\, dx} = \frac{1}{\displaystyle\int_0^\omega e^{-rx}\sum_{j=1}^m \frac{Q_j}{Q_i} {}_{j0}p_i(x)\, dx}, \qquad (4.46)$$

whence

$$c_i(x) = b_i e^{-rx}\sum_{j=1}^m \frac{Q_j}{Q_i} {}_{j0}p_i(x) = \sum_{j=1}^m \frac{Q_j}{Q_i} {}_jc_i(x), \qquad (4.47)$$

where $_jc_i(x) = b_i e^{-rx} {}_{j0}p_i(x)$.

Equation 4.46 in its single-region form has been used to infer the birthrate and intrinsic rate of increase from a reliable census age distribution and an appropriate life table (Keyfitz, 1968, p. 184). Starting with the relation

$$\frac{c(x)}{p(x)} = be^{-rx},$$

we may take natural logarithms to obtain

$$\ln \frac{c(x)}{p(x)} = \ln b - rx. \tag{4.48}$$

Fitting a straight line $y = \alpha + \beta x$ through the observed points $y = \ln[c(x)/p(x)]$, gives

$$b = e^{\alpha}$$
$$r = -\beta.$$

We may generalize the foregoing to the multiregional case by starting with (4.47) in the form of

$$c_i(x) \bigg/ \sum_{j=1}^{m} \frac{Q_j}{Q_i} \, {}_{j0}p_i(x) = b_i e^{-rx}, \qquad i, j = 1, 2, \ldots, m$$

and taking natural logarithms of both sides:

$$\ln \bigg(c_i(x) \bigg/ \sum_{j=1}^{m} \frac{Q_j}{Q_i} \, {}_{j0}p_i(x) \bigg) = \ln b_i - rx, \qquad i, j = 1, 2, \ldots, m,$$

which is the multiregional counterpart of (4.48).

Having found r and b_j, for example, we may obtain $\Delta_j = d_j + o_j - i_j$ as a residual, since

$$r = b_j - d_j - o_j + i_j = b_j - \Delta_j, \tag{4.49}$$

where Δ_j may be defined to be the intrinsic net "absence" rate in region j, the absences being the result of deaths and migration. Introducing $v_{ji}(x)$, the instantaneous annual force of outmigration from region j to region i, we also may define

$$o_j = \int_0^{\infty} c_j(x) \sum_{\substack{i=1 \\ i \neq j}}^{m} v_{ji}(x) \, dx$$

and obtain

$$i_j = r - b_j + d_j + o_j$$

as a residual, and with it, the intrinsic net migration rate

$$n_j = i_j - o_j.$$

As in the single-region model, the total population of each region increases exponentially at stability. For example,

$$K_i(t) = \int_0^\omega k_i(x, t)\, dx = \int_0^\omega \sum_{j=1}^m B_j(t - x)_{j0}p_i(x)\, dx = \int_0^\omega e^{r(t - x)} \sum_{j=1}^m Q_{j\,j0}p_i(x)\, dx$$

$$= e^{rt} \int_0^\omega e^{-rx} \sum_{j=1}^m Q_{j\,j0}p_i(x)\, dx = \left(\frac{Q_i}{b_i}\right) e^{rt} = Y_i e^{rt}, \tag{4.50}$$

where Y_i is the *stable equivalent* of region i. Thus the *stable regional share* of the total multiregional population allocated to region i is

$$(\%)_i = \frac{Y_i}{\sum_{j=1}^m Y_j}. \tag{4.51}$$

According to (4.50), each generation in a stable population is a multiple e^{rt} of the one before. Since the net reproduction rate in region i is a measure of the level of intergenerational increase, we conclude that

$$e^{rT_i} = R_i(0),$$

where $R_i(0) = \sum_{j=1}^m Q_j/Q_{i\,j}R_i(0)$, and T_i is the *mean length of generation in region i*. Taking natural logarithms of both sides and simplifying, we find

$$T_i = \frac{1}{r} \ln R_i(0). \tag{4.52}$$

Continuing our consideration of relations under stability, we define the matrix

$$\bar{\mathbf{R}}^r(n) = \int_\alpha^\beta x^n e^{-rx} \mathbf{\Phi}(x)\, dx, \tag{4.53}$$

which is the stable population analog of $\mathbf{R}(n)$ and consists of elements such as

$$_j\bar{R}_i^r(n) = \int_\alpha^\beta x^n e^{-rx} {}_{j0}p_i(x)m_i(x)\, dx = \int_\alpha^\beta x^n e^{-rx} {}_j\Phi_i(x)\, dx.$$

We can then proceed to develop the stable population analog of $\boldsymbol{\mu}$ by defining the matrix $\mathbf{A}$ with elements such as

$$_jA_i = \frac{_j\bar{R}_i^r(1)}{_j\bar{R}_i^r(0)}, \tag{4.54}$$

which represents *the mean age of childbearing among j-born persons in the stable population of region i.* It follows that

$$A_i = \frac{\bar{R}_i^r(1)}{\bar{R}_i^r(0)} = \bar{R}_i^r(1),$$ (4.55)

where

$$\bar{R}_i^r(n) = \sum_{j=1}^m \frac{Q_j}{Q_i} \, {}_j\bar{R}_i^r(n) \qquad \text{and} \qquad \bar{R}_i^r(0) = \int_\alpha^\beta e^{-rx} \sum_{j=1}^m \frac{Q_j}{Q_i} \, {}_{j0}P_i(x)m_i(x)dx = 1.$$

Similarly, we may define the matrix **a** with elements such as

$$_ja_i = \frac{\int_0^\omega xe^{-rx} \, {}_{j0}P_i(x)\,dx}{\int_0^\omega e^{-rx} \, {}_{j0}P_i(x)\,dx},$$ (4.56)

to be the matrix of mean ages in the regional stable populations. Whence

$$a_i = \frac{\int_0^\omega xe^{-rx} \sum_{j=1}^m (Q_j/Q_i)_{j0}P_i(x)\,dx}{\int_0^\omega e^{-rx} \sum_{j=1}^m (Q_j/Q_i)_{j0}P_i(x)\,dx}$$

$$= \int_0^\omega x \sum_{j=1}^m \frac{Q_j}{Q_i} \, {}_jc_i(x)\,dx = \int_0^\omega xc_i(x)\,dx.$$ (4.57)

Finally, the proportion of the total stable population in region *i* that is aged *x* to *x* + 4 is

$$C_i(x) = \sum_{j=1}^m \frac{Q_j}{Q_i} \, {}_jC_i(x) = \sum_{j=1}^m \frac{Q_j}{Q_i} \int_x^{x+5} {}_jc_i(a)\,da,$$ (4.58)

where

$$_jc_i(a) = b_i e^{-ra} \, {}_{j0}P_i(a).$$

On defining **b** to be a diagonal matrix with regional intrinsic birthrates along the diagonal, we may collect the foregoing elements into matrices (with transposed subscripting as before), to establish the following results:

$$\mathbf{c}(x) = \mathbf{b}e^{-rx} \, {}_0\mathbf{P}(x)$$ (4.59)

$$\{\mathbf{c}(x)\} = \mathbf{Q}^{-1}\mathbf{c}(x)\{\mathbf{Q}\}$$ (4.60)

$$\mathbf{C}(x) = \int_x^{x+5} \mathbf{c}(a)\,da$$ (4.61)

$$\{\mathbf{C}(x)\} = \mathbf{Q}^{-1}\mathbf{C}(x)\{\mathbf{Q}\}.$$ (4.62)

Table 4.4 Relations Under Stability: Female Populations of Yugoslavia and the United States

Two-Region Model

Parameter	Yugoslavia, 1961		United States, 1958				United States, 1968			
	(1) Slovenia	(2) Rest of Yugoslavia	(1) California	(2) Rest of U.S.	(1) West Virginia	(2) Rest of U.S.	(1) California	(2) Rest of U.S.	(1) West Virginia	(2) Rest of U.S.
r	0.00610		0.02059		0.02067		0.00569		0.00572	
b	0.01545	0.01901	0.02648	0.02741	0.02520	0.02736	0.01521	0.01685	0.01604	0.01670
Δ	0.00935	0.01291	0.00589	0.00682	0.00453	0.00669	0.00952	0.01116	0.01032	0.01098
V	383,154	5,145,911	5,173,439	46,671,636	430,516	51,408,075	5,002,198	45,929,485	361,952	50,553,908
Q	9,374	192,313	349,465	1,685,559	8,565	2,020,415	214,176	1,747,181	10,763	1,947,603
Q_2/Q_1	20.516		4.823		235.892		8.158		180.954	
$Y = Q/b$	606,861	10,118,816	13,195,129	61,483,555	339,899	73,850,447	14,076,821	103,702,457	670,920	116,647,358
$\% = Y/\Sigma Y$	0.0566	0.9434	0.1767	0.8233	0.0046	0.9954	0.1195	0.8805	0.0057	0.9943
A	27.648	27.116	25.319	25.560	25.517	25.545	26.066	25.987	25.871	25.999
a	36.776	35.043	29.165	28.292	28.586	28.369	37.721	36.088	35.985	36.225
T	27.767	27.251	25.673	25.930	25.919	25.915	26.169	26.088	25.980	26.101

Single-Region Model

Parameter	Yugoslavia, 1961	United States, 1958	United States, 1968
r	0.00599	0.02065	0.00572
b	0.01869	0.02734	0.01669
d	0.01271	0.00669	0.01098
V	5,535,772	51,842,875	50,916,901
Q	203,863	2,029,909	1,958,470
A	27.154	25.540	25.998
a	35.195	28.376	36.225
T	27.284	25.905	26.100

The numerical evaluation of the various stable growth measures defined previously is straightforward and follows from the numerical approximations set out in Section 2.3. Thus, for example,

$$b_i = \frac{1}{\sum_{x=0}^{z} e^{-r(x+2.5)} \sum_{j=1}^{m} (Q_j/Q_i)_{j0} L_i(x)}, \tag{4.63}$$

and with this result we may obtain

$$C(x) = b e^{-r(x+2.5)} {}_0 L(x). \tag{4.64}$$

Similarly,

$$_j \bar{R}_i^r(n) = \sum_{x=\alpha}^{\beta-5} (x + 2.5)^n e^{-r(x+2.5)} {}_{j0} L_i(x) F_i(x), \tag{4.65}$$

which leads to the numerical evaluation of $_j A_i$ [and $_j R_i(n)$ when r is zero]. The numerical evaluation of $_j a_i$ follows by an analogous argument.

To illustrate several numerical calculations carried out using data on Yugoslavian and United States females, we present in Table 4.4 several summary measures describing relations under stability in these two-region female population systems. Note the sharp decline in the United States intrinsic rate of growth over the decade 1958–1968 and the corresponding decline in the share of the total national female population that is allocated to California at stability. Observe also that the two-region results are consistent with those found using single-region model calculations.

CHAPTER
FIVE
_____

The Discrete Model of
Multiregional Demographic Growth

This chapter considers the multiregional generalization of the single-region matrix cohort survival population projection process. We extend the discrete model of demographic growth described in Chapter 2 by introducing migration into the projection matrix, while simultaneously disaggregating the population by region of residence. As with the continuous model, we examine the influence of a multiregional population's fertility, mortality, and migration patterns on its growth and regional age distributions. We also treat the problem of aggregation and identify the consistency between the continuous and discrete models of multiregional demographic growth.

5.1 THE MULTIREGIONAL PROJECTION PROCESS

The projection of a multiregional population of a given sex forward through time may be carried out by calculating the region- and age-specific survivors of that population and adding to this total the new births that survive to the end of the unit time interval. This growth process may be described by the

117

following system of equations:

$$K_i^{(t+1)}(0) = \sum_{x=\alpha}^{\beta-5} \sum_{j=1}^{m} b_{ji}(x)K_j^{(t)}(x), \qquad \begin{matrix} \alpha - 5 \le x \le \beta - 5, \\ i, j = 1, 2, \ldots, m \end{matrix}$$

$$K_i^{(t+1)}(x+5) = \sum_{j=1}^{m} s_{ji}(x)K_j^{(t)}(x), \qquad x = 0, 5, 10, \ldots, z-5 \qquad (5.1)$$

where henceforth we assume a time and age interval of 5 years, and

$b_{ij}(x)$ = average number of babies born during the unit time interval and alive in region j at end of that interval, per x- to $(x + 4)$-year-old resident of region i at beginning of that interval

$s_{ij}(x)$ = proportion of x- to $(x + 4)$-year-old residents of region i at time t who are alive and $x + 5$ to $x + 9$ years old in region j 5 years later at time $t + 1$

$K_i^{(t)}(x)$ = x- to $(x + 4)$-year-old population in region i at time t

α = first age of childbearing

β = last age of childbearing.

5.1.1 Survivorship and Migration

Consider an m-region population system with $k_i(x)$ individuals at age x in region i. As in the life table population,

$$k_i(x) = \sum_{j=1}^{m} {}_{j0}k_i(x), \qquad i = 1, 2, \ldots, m, \qquad (5.2)$$

where ${}_{j0}k_i(x)$ denotes the number of j-born individuals who are in region i at age x. The expected survivors of the multiregional population after 5 years are

$$k_j(x+5) = \sum_{i=1}^{m} k_i(x)p_{ij}(x), \qquad j = 1, 2, \ldots, m,$$

where $p_{ij}(x)$ is the probability that an individual in region i at age x will be in region j at age $x + 5$. Substituting the definitional relationship of (5.2) into the equation just given and utilizing the fact that i-born individuals can never become members of a j-born population (and vice versa), we have

$$_{j0}k_i(x+5) = \sum_{s=1}^{m} {}_{j0}k_s(x)p_{si}(x), \qquad i, j = 1, 2, \ldots, m \qquad (5.3)$$

or, in matrix form,

$$_0\mathbf{k}(x + 5) = P(x)_0\mathbf{k}(x);$$

whence

$$P(x) = {}_0\mathbf{k}(x + 5)_0\mathbf{k}(x)^{-1}, \tag{5.4}$$

where, for example, in a two-region system

$$_0\mathbf{k}(x) = \begin{bmatrix} {}_{10}k_1(x) & {}_{20}k_1(x) \\ {}_{10}k_2(x) & {}_{20}k_2(x) \end{bmatrix} \quad P(x) = \begin{bmatrix} p_{11}(x) & p_{21}(x) \\ p_{12}(x) & p_{22}(x) \end{bmatrix}.$$

The expected survivors of this multiregional population aged x to $x + dx$, $_0\mathbf{k}(x)\, dx$, say, after 5 years are

$$_0\mathbf{k}(x + 5)\, dx = P(x)_0\mathbf{k}(x)\, dx,$$

and those between ages x and $x + 5$ expected to survive 5 years are

$$_0\mathbf{K}(x + 5) = \int_0^5 {}_0\mathbf{k}(x + 5 + t)\, dt = \int_0^5 P(x + t)_0\mathbf{k}(x + t)\, dt. \tag{5.5}$$

As in the single-region model, we assume that the survivorship and migration behavior of the stationary life table population adequately represents that of the empirical population. Substituting the life table matrix product $_0\mathbf{l}(x + 5)_0\mathbf{l}(x)^{-1}$ for $P(x)$ in (5.5) gives

$$_0\mathbf{K}(x + 5) = \int_0^5 {}_0\mathbf{l}(x + 5 + t)_0\mathbf{l}(x + t)^{-1}{}_0\mathbf{k}(x + t)\, dt. \tag{5.6}$$

And the multiregional analog of the numerical approximation to the integral in (5.6) that is normally used in the single-region model yields

$$_0\mathbf{K}(x + 5) = \int_0^5 {}_0\mathbf{l}(x + 5 + t)\, dt \left[\int_0^5 {}_0\mathbf{l}(x + t)\, dt \right]^{-1} \int_0^5 {}_0\mathbf{k}(x + t)\, dt$$

$$= {}_0\mathbf{L}(x + 5)_0\mathbf{L}(x)^{-1}{}_0\mathbf{K}(x)$$

$$= \mathbf{S}(x)_0\mathbf{K}(x), \tag{5.7}$$

where

$$\mathbf{S}(x) = {}_0\mathbf{L}(x + 5)_0\mathbf{L}(x)^{-1} \tag{5.8}$$

as in Chapter 3.

Generally population projections do not call for population totals disaggregated by place of birth. Hence we may consolidate the matrix $_0K(x)$ into the vector

$$\{\overline{\mathbf{K}}^{(t)}(x)\} = {}_0\mathbf{K}^{(t)}(x)\{\mathbf{1}\},$$

and postmultiply both sides of (5.7) by $\{\mathbf{1}\}$ to find

$$\{\overline{\mathbf{K}}^{(t+1)}(x + 5)\} = \mathbf{S}(x)\{\overline{\mathbf{K}}^{(t)}(x)\}. \tag{5.9}$$

We have added a superscript t to denote time and have placed a bar over the vector to distinguish it from the vector $\{\mathbf{K}^{(t)}\}$, to which a somewhat different structure is ascribed below.

In Yugoslavia an estimated $62,900[= K_1^{(t)}(20)]$ and $725,500[= K_2^{(t)}(20)]$ women, aged 20 to 24 at last birthday, were living in Slovenia and in the rest of Yugoslavia, respectively, at midyear of 1961. Recalling the life table survivorship and outmigration proportions for these two regions that appeared in Table 3.10, we find, for example, that

$$s_{11}(20) = 0.96520$$

$$s_{21}(20) = 0.00361.$$

The sum of the two products $s_{11}(20)K_1(20)$ and $s_{21}(20)K_2(20)$ gives the expected number of women aged 25 to 29 in Slovenia in 1966:

$$K_1^{(t+1)}(25) = (0.96520)(62,900) + (0.00361)(725,500)$$

$$= 63,327.$$

5.1.2 Fertility

The multiregional population projection is not complete without an estimate of the total number of surviving births during the unit time interval. Denoting the age-region-specific annual birthrate by $F_i(x)$ and multiplying it by the arithmetic mean of the initial and final populations aged x to $x + 4$ in region i gives

$$\frac{K_i^{(t)}(x) + K_i^{(t+1)}(x)}{2} = \frac{1}{2}\left[K_i^{(t)}(x) + \sum_{j=1}^{m} s_{ji}(x - 5)K_j^{(t)}(x - 5) \right], \tag{5.10}$$

and since this number is exposed for 5 years, we multiply it by 5. The women in region i aged x to $x + 4$ together with those aged $x + 5$ to $x + 9$ at last birthday will contribute, during the 5-year time interval, a total of

$$\tfrac{5}{2}\{K_i^{(t)}(x) + K_i^{(t+1)}(x)\}F_i(x) + \tfrac{5}{2}\{K_i^{(t)}(x+5) + K_i^{(t+1)}(x+5)\}F_i(x+5)$$

births. Of these, a proportion $[_{i0}L_j(0)]/[5l_i(0)]$ will be surviving residents of region j at the end of the time interval. Adding through all ages of childbearing α through β, rearranging, and adopting the more compact notation of matrix algebra, we have the multiregional counterpart to (2.76):

$$\{\overline{\mathbf{K}}^{(t+1)}(0)\} = \sum_{x=\alpha-5}^{\beta-5} \tfrac{1}{2}{}_0\mathbf{L}(0)\mathbf{l}(0)^{-1}[\mathbf{F}(x) + \mathbf{F}(x+5)\mathbf{S}(x)]\{\overline{\mathbf{K}}^{(t)}(x)\} \quad (5.11)$$

$$= \sum_{x=\alpha-5}^{\beta-5} \mathbf{B}(x)\{\overline{\mathbf{K}}^{(t)}(x)\}, \text{ say,} \quad (5.12)$$

where $\mathbf{l}(0)$ is a diagonal matrix with regional radices set out along its principal diagonal, and the element in the ith row and jth column of $\mathbf{B}(x)$ is

$$b_{ji}(x) = \tfrac{1}{2}\left[\frac{{}_{j0}L_i(0)}{l_j(0)} F_j(x) + \sum_{k=1}^{m} s_{jk}(x) \frac{{}_{k0}L_i(0)}{l_k(0)} F_k(x+5) \right]. \quad (5.13)$$

The contribution made to the first age group in Slovenia at time $t + 1$ by surviving female children of 20- to 24-year-old women residents of the rest of Yugoslavia at time t is

$$b_{21}(20) = \tfrac{1}{2}[(0.00322)F_2(20) + (0.00361)(4.89019)F_1(25) \\ + (0.98942)(0.00322)F_2(25)],$$

into which we may substitute $F_2(20) = 0.08798$, $F_2(25) = 0.07426$, and $F_1(25) = 0.06322$ to find

$$b_{21}(20) = 0.00082.$$

Table 5.1 presents all such positive fertility elements together with the corresponding survivorship and outmigration proportions for our Slovenia–rest of Yugoslavia population system.

Table 5.1   The Positive Elements of the Two-Region Projection Matrix: Yugoslavian Females, 1961

Age, x	(1) Slovenia				(2) Rest of Yugoslavia			
	$s_{11}(x)$	$b_{11}(x)$	$s_{12}(x)$	$b_{12}(x)$	$s_{22}(x)$	$b_{22}(x)$	$s_{21}(x)$	$b_{21}(x)$
0	0.97093	—	0.01304	—	0.94118	—	0.00108	—
5	0.98878	0.00017	0.00941	0.00000	0.99633	0.00016	0.00081	0.00000
10	0.98163	0.03823	0.01636	0.00129	0.99458	0.06241	0.00208	0.00012
15	0.96669	0.20577	0.03020	0.00774	0.99081	0.26879	0.00401	0.00088
20	0.96520	0.32195	0.03128	0.00777	0.98942	0.38192	0.00361	0.00082
25	0.97290	0.25235	0.02297	0.00419	0.98956	0.27934	0.00214	0.00041
30	0.98078	0.15533	0.01371	0.00186	0.98905	0.15983	0.00144	0.00019
35	0.98529	0.07468	0.00690	0.00073	0.98671	0.08380	0.00102	0.00008
40	0.98256	0.02077	0.00386	0.00017	0.98258	0.03351	0.00069	0.00002
45	0.97536	0.00243	0.00296	0.00002	0.97418	0.00673	0.00055	0.00000
50	0.96447	0.00071	0.00316	0.00001	0.96015	0.00169	0.00082	0.00000
55	0.94570	—	0.00363	—	0.93555	—	0.00098	—
60	0.90475	—	0.00430	—	0.89485	—	0.00084	—
65	0.83186	—	0.00409	—	0.83022	—	0.00053	—
70	0.73717	—	0.00413	—	0.74517	—	0.00037	—
75	0.59075	—	0.00360	—	0.64025	—	0.00053	—
80+	0.62049	—	0.00314	—	1.00355	—	0.00066	—

5.1.3   The Multiregional Projection Matrix

The multiregional growth and distribution process we have defined enables us to express the relation between the population at times t and $t + 1$ as a set of linear, first-order, homogeneous difference equations with constant coefficients. These can be expressed compactly in matrix form. Two of the most logical formulations use alternative generalizations of the so-called Leslie matrix for the single-region case. The arrangement of elements in Rogers (1966) was of the form

$$\mathbf{G} = \begin{bmatrix} \mathbf{G}_{11} & \mathbf{G}_{21} & \cdots & \mathbf{G}_{m1} \\ \mathbf{G}_{12} & \mathbf{G}_{22} & \cdots & \mathbf{G}_{m2} \\ \vdots & \vdots & \ddots & \vdots \\ \mathbf{G}_{1m} & \mathbf{G}_{2m} & \cdots & \mathbf{G}_{mm} \end{bmatrix}, \tag{5.14}$$

where

$$\mathbf{G}_{ij} = \begin{bmatrix} 0 & 0 & b_{ij}(\alpha - 5) \cdots b_{ij}(\beta - 5) & 0 & \cdots & 0 \\ s_{ij}(0) & & & & & \vdots \\ & s_{ij}(5) & & \ddots & & \\ & & & & s_{ij}(z - 5) & 0 \end{bmatrix}. \quad (5.15)$$

An alternative arrangement is the one suggested by Feeney (1970):

$$\mathbf{H} = \begin{bmatrix} \mathbf{0} & \mathbf{0} & \mathbf{B}(\alpha - 5) \cdots \mathbf{B}(\beta - 5) & \mathbf{0} & \cdots & \mathbf{0} \\ \mathbf{S}(0) & & & & & \vdots \\ & \mathbf{S}(5) & & \ddots & & \\ & & & & \mathbf{S}(z - 5) & \mathbf{0} \end{bmatrix}.$$

We follow Feeney's designations of **G** as the *multiregional matrix growth operator* and **H** as the *generalized Leslie matrix*. The matrix expression of the multiregional growth process using the multiregional matrix growth operator is

$$\{\mathbf{K}^{(t+1)}\} = \mathbf{G}\{\mathbf{K}^{(t)}\}, \quad (5.16)$$

where

$$\{\mathbf{K}^{(t)}\} = \begin{Bmatrix} \mathbf{K}_1^{(t)} \\ \mathbf{K}_2^{(t)} \\ \vdots \\ \mathbf{K}_m^{(t)} \end{Bmatrix} \quad \text{and} \quad \{\mathbf{K}_i^{(t)}\} = \begin{Bmatrix} K_i^{(t)}(0) \\ K_i^{(t)}(5) \\ \vdots \\ K_i^{(t)}(z) \end{Bmatrix}, \quad i = 1, 2, \ldots, m.$$

The same growth process expressed with the generalized Leslie matrix is

$$\{\overline{\mathbf{K}}^{(t+1)}\} = \mathbf{H}\{\overline{\mathbf{K}}^{(t)}\}, \quad (5.17)$$

where

$$\{\overline{\mathbf{K}}^{(t)}\} = \begin{Bmatrix} \overline{\mathbf{K}}^{(t)}(0) \\ \overline{\mathbf{K}}^{(t)}(5) \\ \vdots \\ \overline{\mathbf{K}}^{(t)}(z) \end{Bmatrix} \quad \text{and} \quad \{\overline{\mathbf{K}}^{(t)}(x)\} = \begin{Bmatrix} K_1^{(t)}(x) \\ K_2^{(t)}(x) \\ \vdots \\ K_m^{(t)}(x) \end{Bmatrix}.$$

5.2 MULTIREGIONAL STABLE GROWTH

In Chapter 2 it was established that if a regional population closed to migration is subjected to an unchanging regime of fertility and mortality, it ultimately will achieve a stable age composition that increases at a constant intrinsic rate of growth. Here we once again demonstrate that this property obtains region by region in the case of a system of regions whose totality is closed to migration and is subjected to an unchanging multiregional schedule of fertility, mortality, and internal migration. We proceed by extending the arguments of Sykes (1969) on discrete stable population theory to the multiregional case, drawing on the recent proofs suggested by LeBras (1971) and Feeney (1971).

Following the usual practice of considering only female individuals up to the highest age of reproduction, β say, we partition each growth submatrix $\mathbf{G}_{ij}$, in (5.15) as follows:

$$\mathbf{G}_{ij} = \begin{bmatrix} \mathbf{W}_{ij} & \mathbf{0} \\ \mathbf{U}_{ij} & \mathbf{Z}_{ij} \end{bmatrix},$$

where

$$\mathbf{W}_{ij} = \begin{bmatrix} 0 & 0 & b_{ij}(\alpha - 5) & \cdots & b_{ij}(\beta - 5) \\ s_{ij}(0) & & & & \vdots \\ & s_{ij}(5) & & & \\ & & \ddots & & \\ & & & s_{ij}(\beta - 10) & 0 \end{bmatrix}.$$

Next we partition each age vector $\{\mathbf{K}_i^{(t)}\}$ at the same highest age of reproduction:

$$\{\mathbf{K}_i^{(t)}\} = \begin{Bmatrix} \mathbf{X}_i^{(t)} \\ \mathbf{D}_i^{(t)} \end{Bmatrix} \tag{5.18}$$

and define

$$\{\tilde{\mathbf{K}}^{(t)}\} = \begin{Bmatrix} \mathbf{X}^{(t)} \\ \mathbf{D}^{(t)} \end{Bmatrix} = \begin{Bmatrix} \mathbf{X}_1^{(t)} \\ \mathbf{X}_2^{(t)} \\ \vdots \\ \mathbf{X}_m^{(t)} \\ \mathbf{D}_1^{(t)} \\ \mathbf{D}_2^{(t)} \\ \vdots \\ \mathbf{D}_m^{(t)} \end{Bmatrix}. \tag{5.19}$$

Then we permute the rows and columns of **G** to form

$$\tilde{\mathbf{G}} = \mathbf{PGP}^{-1} = \begin{bmatrix} \mathbf{W} & \mathbf{0} \\ \mathbf{U} & \mathbf{Z} \end{bmatrix}, \tag{5.20}$$

where

$$\mathbf{W} = \begin{Bmatrix} \mathbf{W}_{11} & \mathbf{W}_{21} & \cdots & \mathbf{W}_{m1} \\ \mathbf{W}_{12} & \mathbf{W}_{22} & \cdots & \mathbf{W}_{m2} \\ \vdots & \vdots & \ddots & \vdots \\ \mathbf{W}_{1m} & \mathbf{W}_{2m} & \cdots & \mathbf{W}_{mm} \end{Bmatrix}, \tag{5.21}$$

U and **Z** are defined analogously, and **P** is the product of appropriately defined permutation matrices. Note that (5.16) may be expressed in permuted form, as follows:

$$\{\tilde{\mathbf{K}}^{(t+1)}\} = \mathbf{P}\{\mathbf{K}^{(t+1)}\} = \mathbf{PG}\{\mathbf{K}^{(t)}\} = \mathbf{PGP}^{-1}\mathbf{P}\{\mathbf{K}^{(t)}\} = \tilde{\mathbf{G}}\{\tilde{\mathbf{K}}^{(t)}\} \tag{5.22}$$

Hence

$$\{\tilde{\mathbf{K}}^{(t+n)}\} = \tilde{\mathbf{G}}^{n}\{\tilde{\mathbf{K}}^{(t)}\} = \begin{bmatrix} \mathbf{W}^{n} & \mathbf{0} \\ \mathbf{U}_{n} & \mathbf{Z}^{n} \end{bmatrix} \begin{Bmatrix} \mathbf{X}^{(t)} \\ \mathbf{D}^{(t)} \end{Bmatrix}$$

$$= \begin{Bmatrix} \mathbf{W}^{n}\mathbf{X}^{(t)} \\ \mathbf{U}_{n}\mathbf{X}^{(t)} + \mathbf{Z}^{n}\mathbf{D}^{(t)} \end{Bmatrix} = \begin{Bmatrix} \mathbf{X}^{(t+n)} \\ \mathbf{D}^{(t+n)} \end{Bmatrix}, \tag{5.23}$$

from which it is clear that **U**, **Z**, and **D** never affect the ages younger than the highest age of reproduction β.

It is evident from (5.20) that $\tilde{\mathbf{G}}$ and **G** are similar matrices. Consequently they have the same characteristic roots, and the characteristic vectors of $\tilde{\mathbf{G}}$ are related to those of **G** by

$$\{\tilde{\mathbf{K}}\} = \mathbf{P}\{\mathbf{K}\},$$

where $\{\mathbf{K}\}$ is the characteristic vector for which

$$\mathbf{G}\{\mathbf{K}\} = \lambda\{\mathbf{K}\} \tag{5.24}$$

and λ is a characteristic root of **G**; whence

$$\tilde{\mathbf{G}}\{\tilde{\mathbf{K}}\} = \mathbf{PGP}^{-1}\mathbf{P}\{\mathbf{K}\} = \lambda\mathbf{P}\{\mathbf{K}\}. \tag{5.25}$$

We conclude, therefore, that the characteristic roots of the submatrix **W** completely determine those of $\tilde{\mathbf{G}}$ (Parlett, 1970, p. 194).

Table 5.2 Two-Region Population Projection to Stability: Yugoslavian Females, 1961

A. Base Year Population, 1961

Age, x	(1) Slovenia Population			Single-Region Model (1 + 2)	(2) Rest of Yugoslavia Proportion			Single-Region Model (1 + 2)
	1	2	1 + 2	(1 + 2)	1	2	1 + 2	(1 + 2)
0	67,800	847,900	915,700	915,700	0.0814	0.0978	0.0964	0.0964
5	74,100	905,200	979,300	979,300	0.0890	0.1044	0.1031	0.1031
10	70,700	808,100	878,800	878,800	0.0849	0.0932	0.0925	0.0925
15	60,100	617,400	677,500	677,500	0.0722	0.0712	0.0713	0.0713
20	62,900	725,500	788,400	788,400	0.0755	0.0837	0.0830	0.0830
25	66,500	774,000	840,500	840,500	0.0799	0.0893	0.0884	0.0884
30	67,100	728,400	795,500	795,500	0.0806	0.0840	0.0837	0.0837
35	62,900	633,300	696,200	696,200	0.0755	0.0730	0.0733	0.0733
40	39,500	392,400	431,900	431,900	0.0474	0.0453	0.0454	0.0454
45	47,900	437,100	485,000	485,000	0.0575	0.0504	0.0510	0.0510
50	51,300	453,800	505,100	505,100	0.0616	0.0523	0.0532	0.0532
55	46,100	389,300	435,400	435,400	0.0544	0.0449	0.0458	0.0458
60	39,600	325,800	365,400	365,400	0.0476	0.0376	0.0385	0.0385
65	29,500	230,600	260,100	260,100	0.0354	0.0266	0.0274	0.0274
70	21,700	180,000	201,700	201,700	0.0261	0.0208	0.0212	0.0212
75	14,400	120,900	135,300	135,300	0.0173	0.0139	0.0142	0.0142
80	7,100	61,200	68,300	68,300	0.0085	0.0071	0.0072	0.0072
85+	3,600	39,300	42,900	42,900	0.0043	0.0045	0.0045	0.0045
Total	832,800	8,670,200	9,503,000	9,503,000	1.0000	1.0000	1.0000	1.0000

From here on we may follow the sequence of arguments used in the single-region theory. First the primitivity of **W** may be established under certain conditions regarding the positioning of positive fertility elements in that matrix. The well-known Perron–Frobenius properties of primitive, non-negative matrices then may be used to prove the existence of a unique, real, positive, dominant characteristic root and associated positive characteristic vector. Finally, it can be shown that successive powers of **W** converge to a limiting form with proportional columns; consequently the effects of the

Table 5.2   (*continued*)

B.   Stable Equivalent Population

	(1) Slovenia				(2) Rest of Yugoslavia			
	Population				Proportion			
Age, x	1	2	1 + 2	Single-Region Model (1 + 2)	1	2	1 + 2	Single-Region Model (1 + 2)
0	45,762	896,447	942,209	953,526	0.0754	0.0886	0.0879	0.0874
5	44,038	818,954	862,992	874,777	0.0726	0.0809	0.0805	0.0802
10	42,876	791,842	834,718	846,599	0.0707	0.0783	0.0778	0.0776
15	42,419	764,573	806,992	818,957	0.0699	0.0756	0.0752	0.0751
20	42,748	736,032	778,779	790,795	0.0704	0.0727	0.0726	0.0725
25	42,595	707,669	750,264	762,306	0.0702	0.0699	0.0700	0.0699
30	41,663	680,197	721,860	733,911	0.0687	0.0672	0.0673	0.0673
35	40,583	653,097	693,680	705,722	0.0669	0.0645	0.0647	0.0647
40	39,430	625,334	664,764	676,765	0.0650	0.0618	0.0620	0.0621
45	37,996	596,130	634,125	645,989	0.0626	0.0589	0.0591	0.0592
50	36,264	563,405	599,669	611,307	0.0598	0.0557	0.0559	0.0561
55	34,371	524,815	559,186	570,506	0.0566	0.0519	0.0521	0.0523
60	32,028	476,363	508,391	519,264	0.0528	0.0471	0.0474	0.0476
65	28,495	413,601	442,096	452,080	0.0470	0.0409	0.0412	0.0415
70	23,206	333,180	356,385	364,709	0.0382	0.0329	0.0332	0.0334
75	16,712	240,910	257,621	263,683	0.0275	0.0238	0.0240	0.0242
80	9,700	149,669	159,368	162,620	0.0160	0.0148	0.0149	0.0149
85+	5,933	145,717	151,651	151,183	0.0098	0.0144	0.0141	0.0139
Total	606,820	10,117,932	10,724,752	10,904,697	1.0000	1.0000	1.0000	1.0000

initial population distribution on those at future points in time diminish as
time increases and ultimately disappear entirely as the population assumes
the stable distribution. This feature of the projection process usually is established by diagonalizing **W** on the assumption that its characteristic roots are
distinct (Chapter 2, Section 2.3.4).

The sequence of arguments just outlined hinges on the establishment of
conditions under which **W** is primitive. One such condition in the single-
region theory is that at least two adjacent fertility elements in the first row be

positive (Pollard, 1973, pp. 46–47). A natural generalization of this condition to the multiregional case is, of course, that two adjacent fertility elements be positive in each and every submatrix $\mathbf{W}_{ij}$ of the $\mathbf{W}$ defined in (5.21). However, as in the single-region case, this condition can be shown to be unnecessarily restrictive.

Let $\mathbf{C}$ be an $m \times m$ matrix where $c_{ij} = 1$ if $i = j$ ($i, j = 1, 2, \ldots, m$) or if $\mathbf{W}_{ij}$ has at least a single positive element, and $c_{ij} = 0$ otherwise. If the matrix $\mathbf{C}$ is indecomposable *and* if the diagonal submatrices $\mathbf{W}_{ii}$ of $\mathbf{W}$ all are primitive, $\mathbf{W}$ will also be a primitive matrix (LeBras, 1971; Feeney, 1971). We have then the following sufficient conditions for establishing the primitivity of $\mathbf{W}$ (Sykes, 1969):

THEOREM

Given the growth process $\{\mathbf{X}^{(t+1)}\} = \mathbf{W}\{\mathbf{X}^{(t)}\}$, $\mathbf{W}$ is primitive if for each $i = 1, 2, \ldots, m$ the greatest common divisor of the arguments y of the positive elements $b_{ii}(y)$, where $y = (x + 5)/5$, in the first row of $\mathbf{W}_{ii}$ is 1 *and* if the matrix $\mathbf{C}$ defined earlier, is indecomposable.

If $\mathbf{W}$ is primitive, it has a positive, unique, real dominant characteristic root λ_1, such that

$$\mathbf{W}\{\mathbf{X}_1\} = \lambda_1\{\mathbf{X}_1\},$$

where $\{\mathbf{X}_1\}$ is the associated characteristic vector with all its elements positive and scaled to sum to unity, say. Since the roots of $\mathbf{W}$ completely determine those of $\tilde{\mathbf{G}}$ and $\mathbf{G}$, their dominant root also is λ_1. Equations 5.24 and 5.25 reflect this observation.

Repeating the single-region argument presented in Chapter 2, we may reestablish the relationship set out in (2.88):

$$\{\mathbf{X}^{(t+n)}\} = \lambda_1{}^n\left[Y_1\{\mathbf{X}_1\} + \left(\frac{\lambda_2}{\lambda_1}\right)^n Y_2\{\mathbf{X}_2\} + \cdots + \left(\frac{\lambda_k}{\lambda_1}\right)^n Y_k\{\mathbf{X}_k\} \right]$$

and conclude that as n approaches infinity, the multiregional growth process defined in the foregoing theorem converges to

$$\lambda_1{}^n Y_1\{\mathbf{X}_1\}$$

and that of (5.23) converges to the *multiregional stable population*

$$\lambda^n Y\{\mathbf{K}\},$$

in which we omit the unit subscripts to simplify the notation.

The projection matrix summarized in Table 5.1, when raised to successively higher powers, ultimately stabilizes and converges to the stable growth ratio $\lambda = 1.030968$ and the stable proportional regional age compositions set out in Table 5.2. Note that the stable equivalent for Slovenia is 5.66% of the total.[1] This is a significant decrease for Slovenia, which in 1961 had 8.76% of the total national female population. Finally, as a check on our computations, we include for the total system the stable age composition that was obtained using the single-region model. That single-region calculation yields a stable growth ratio of 1.030408 for the same data in consolidated form.

5.3 INTRINSIC RATES

Stone (1968) points out that classical work in stable population theory has ignored migration and therefore has not dealt with the notion of stable migration rates. His proposed formulas for stable *age-specific* migration rates are our starting point for developing the notion of *intrinsic* migration rates for the multiregional theory. Stone defines

$$^5i_j(x) = \frac{\sum_{k=1, k \neq j}^{m} K_k^{(t)}(x)s_{kj}(x)}{K_j^{(t)}(x)}$$

and

$$^5o_j(x) = \sum_{\substack{k=1 \\ k \neq j}}^{m} s_{jk}(x)$$

to be the stable, age-specific inmigration and outmigration rates, respectively, of a regional population experiencing stable growth. Analogously,

$$^5d_j(x) = 1 - \sum_{k=1}^{m} s_{jk}(x)$$

---

[1] The calculation of the regional stable equivalents in the multiregional model is carried out with the same formula as in the single-region model, namely,

$$Y = \frac{\{1'\}G^n\{K^{(t)}\}}{\lambda^n},$$

where $\{1'\}$ is a row vector of ones. As in the single-region model, $Y_i = Q_i/b_i$, where Q_i denotes the number of births in the stable population of region i and b_i is that region's intrinsic birthrate.

represents the stable age-specific death rate of the same population. Thus among people aged x to $x + 4$ years in region i at stability, a proportion $^5o_j(x)$ leave the region during a 5-year interval, while simultaneously, a fraction $^5d_j(x)$ die and a total of

$$\sum_{\substack{k=1 \\ k \neq j}}^{m} K_k^{(t)}(x) s_{kj}(x)$$

individuals migrate into the region to give it an inmigration rate of $^5i_j(x)$. But outmigrations, deaths, and inmigrations also occur among babies during the same time interval. For example,

$$\frac{\sum_{k=1, k \neq j}^{m} {}_{j0}L_k(0)}{5l_j(0)}$$

is the proportion of babies born in region j who outmigrate and survive to be members of the first age group outside region j at the start of the next unit time interval. Hence the consolidated "crude" 5-year stable outmigration rate of region j is

$$^5o_j = \frac{\sum_{x=0}^{z} K_j^{(t)}(x) \, {}^5o_j(x)}{\sum_{x=0}^{z} K_j^{(t)}(x)} + {}^5b_j \sum_{\substack{k=1 \\ k \neq j}}^{m} \frac{{}_{j0}L_k(0)}{5l_j(0)}, \tag{5.26}$$

where ^5b_j is the corresponding 5-year stable birthrate:

$$^5b_j = \frac{\frac{5}{2} \sum_{x=\alpha}^{\beta-5} [K_j^{(t)}(x) + K_j^{(t+1)}(x)] F_j(x)}{\sum_{x=0}^{z} K_j^{(t)}(x)}. \tag{5.27}$$

By an analogous argument

$$^5d_j = \frac{\sum_{x=0}^{z} K_j^{(t)}(x) \, {}^5d_j(x)}{\sum_{x=0}^{z} K_j^{(t)}(x)} + {}^5b_j \left(1 - \frac{\sum_{k=1}^{m} {}_{j0}L_k(0)}{5l_j(0)}\right), \tag{5.28}$$

and

$$^5i_j = \frac{\sum_{x=0}^{z} K_j^{(t)}(x) \, {}^5i_j(x)}{\sum_{x=0}^{z} K_j^{(t)}(x)} + \frac{\sum_{\substack{k=1 \\ k \neq j}}^{m} {}^5b_k \left(\sum_{x=0}^{z} K_k^{(t)}(x)\right) \frac{{}_{k0}L_j(0)}{5l_k(0)}}{\sum_{x=0}^{z} K_j^{(t)}(x)}. \tag{5.29}$$

Table 5.3 Intrinsic Rates: Female Populations of Yugoslavia and the United States

Parameter	Yugoslavia, 1961		United States, 1958				United States, 1968			
	(1) Slovenia	(2) Rest of Yugoslavia	(1) California	(2) Rest of U.S.	(1) West Virginia	(2) Rest of U.S.	(1) California	(2) Rest of U.S.	(1) West Virginia	(2) Rest of U.S.
Two-Region Model										
r	0.00610		0.02064		0.02072		0.00570		0.00572	
b	0.01545	0.01901	0.02651	0.02744	0.02523	0.02739	0.01522	0.01685	0.01604	0.01670
Δ	0.00935	0.01291	0.00587	0.00680	0.00451	0.00667	0.00952	0.01115	0.01032	0.01097
d	0.01196	0.01275	0.00657	0.00665	0.00665	0.00666	0.01098	0.01096	0.01081	0.01097
o	0.00241	0.00030	0.01137	0.00259	0.02617	0.00013	0.01350	0.00203	0.02221	0.00013
i	0.00502	0.00014	0.01206	0.00244	0.02831	0.00012	0.01496	0.00183	0.02270	0.00013
n	0.00261	−0.00016	0.00070	−0.00015	0.00214	−0.00001	0.00146	−0.00020	0.00049	−0.00000[a]
Single-Region Model										
r	0.00599		0.02070				0.00572			
b	0.01869		0.02734				0.01669			
d	0.01270		0.00664				0.01097			

[a] $n_2 = -0.000003$.

By definition

$$\lambda = 1 + {}^{5}b_{j} - {}^{5}d_{j} - {}^{5}o_{j} + {}^{5}i_{j} = e^{5r}, \qquad (5.30)$$

where λ is the dominant characteristic root of the projection matrix $\mathbf{G}$, and $r = \frac{1}{5}\ln\lambda$. To transform (5.30) into the corresponding equation for *intrinsic* rates

$$r = b_{j} - d_{j} - o_{j} + i_{j} = b_{j} - d_{j} + n_{j} = b_{j} - \Delta_{j}, \qquad (5.31)$$

we rewrite (5.30) as

$$e^{5r} - 1 = {}^{5}b_{j} - {}^{5}d_{j} - {}^{5}o_{j} + {}^{5}i_{j}$$

and multiply both sides of the equation by $r/(e^{5r} - 1)$ to find (5.31), where

$$b_{j} = \frac{r}{e^{5r} - 1}\,{}^{5}b_{j} \qquad d_{j} = \frac{r}{e^{5r} - 1}\,{}^{5}d_{j}$$

$$o_{j} = \frac{r}{e^{5r} - 1}\,{}^{5}o_{j} \qquad i_{j} = \frac{r}{e^{5r} - 1}\,{}^{5}i_{j}$$

$$n_{j} = i_{j} - o_{j} \qquad \Delta_{j} = d_{j} + o_{j} - i_{j} = d_{j} - n_{j}.$$

Table 5.3 sets out intrinsic rates for several two-region population systems. Note that projections to stability under current growth regimes may produce surprising net migration results. According to Table 5.3 the stable net migration rate into California under the 1968 growth regime is twice as high as the corresponding rate under the 1958 regime, and the stable net migration rate into West Virginia is higher than the same rate into California under the 1958 growth regime but lower than California's under the 1968 regime. Yet precisely the opposite is true of the empirical data that underlie these calculations. The observed net migration rate into California was 0.0158 in 1958 and 0.0044 in 1968. For West Virginia the two corresponding rates were -0.0158 and -0.0090, respectively. Observe that no such surprises appear in the stable outmigration and inmigration rates. These mirror the life table migration levels set out in Table 3.6.

5.4 AGGREGATION

Most demographers are regularly confronted with the need to aggregate data over the three fundamental dimensions of multiregional population systems: space, people, and time. The need for aggregation may arise because of data limitations, or it may be occasioned by budget constraints. In either event, it is important to recognize that the results of the analysis depend on the particular consolidation adopted.

Aggregation and disaggregation operations may be conveniently carried out by simple matrix multiplication. For example, to aggregate a three-dimensional population vector $\{K\}$ into a two-dimensional vector $\{\hat{K}\}$ such that the first element of $\{\hat{K}\}$ is the sum of the first two elements of $\{K\}$, we define the consolidation matrix

$$C = \begin{bmatrix} 1 & 1 & 0 \\ 0 & 0 & 1 \end{bmatrix},$$

which when applied to $\{K\}$ will produce $\{\hat{K}\}$. That is,

$$\{\hat{K}\} = C\{K\} = \begin{bmatrix} 1 & 1 & 0 \\ 0 & 0 & 1 \end{bmatrix} \begin{Bmatrix} K_1 \\ K_2 \\ K_3 \end{Bmatrix} = \begin{Bmatrix} K_1 + K_2 \\ K_3 \end{Bmatrix}.$$

To reverse this aggregation, we may define the deconsolidation matrix

$$D = \begin{bmatrix} d_{11} & 0 \\ d_{12} & 0 \\ 0 & 1 \end{bmatrix}.$$

where

$$d_{11} = \frac{K_1}{K_1 + K_2} \quad \text{and} \quad d_{12} = 1 - d_{11}.$$

$$\{K\} = D\{\hat{K}\} = \begin{bmatrix} \dfrac{K_1}{K_1 + K_2} & 0 \\ \dfrac{K_2}{K_1 + K_2} & 0 \\ 0 & 1 \end{bmatrix} \begin{Bmatrix} K_1 + K_2 \\ K_3 \end{Bmatrix} = \begin{Bmatrix} K_1 \\ K_2 \\ K_3 \end{Bmatrix}.$$

The generalization of the foregoing to more complicated aggregations is straightforward (see, e.g., Rogers, 1969).

Now, consider how these two matrices enter into our basic matrix population model:

$$\{K^{(t+1)}\} = G\{K^{(t)}\}.$$

Observe that

$$\{\hat{\mathbf{K}}^{(t+1)}\} = \mathbf{C}\{\mathbf{K}^{(t+1)}\}$$

and

$$\{\mathbf{K}^{(t)}\} = \mathbf{D}(t)\{\hat{\mathbf{K}}^{(t)}\},$$

where $\mathbf{D}$ now receives as its argument the temporal superscript of the vector to which it is applied, to identify the time at which the proportional weights are computed. Hence by simple substitution we have

$$\{\hat{\mathbf{K}}^{(t+1)}\} = \mathbf{C}\{\mathbf{K}^{(t+1)}\} = \mathbf{C}\mathbf{G}\{\mathbf{K}^{(t)}\} = \mathbf{C}\mathbf{G}\mathbf{D}(t)\{\hat{\mathbf{K}}^{(t)}\}$$

or

$$\{\hat{\mathbf{K}}^{(t+1)}\} = \hat{\mathbf{G}}\{\hat{\mathbf{K}}^{(t)}\},$$

where $\hat{\mathbf{G}} = \mathbf{C}\mathbf{G}\mathbf{D}(t)$.[2]

Let us examine the circumstances that will lead to *perfect* aggregation by considering the conditions under which one can consolidate the population projection model without introducing an error into the projected consolidated population totals.

To identify consolidation schemes that produce perfect aggregation we first observe that both

$$\{\hat{\mathbf{K}}^{(t+n)}\} = \mathbf{C}\{\mathbf{K}^{(t+n)}\} = \mathbf{C}\mathbf{G}^n\{\mathbf{K}^{(t)}\} \tag{5.32}$$

and

$$\{\mathbf{K}^{(t+n)}\} = \mathbf{G}^n\{\mathbf{K}^{(t)}\} = \mathbf{G}^n\mathbf{D}(t)\{\hat{\mathbf{K}}^{(t)}\} \tag{5.33}$$

are outputs of the unconsolidated population model and therefore contain no aggregation error. Corresponding to each of these errorless projections, we also have the potentially erroneous projections produced by the consolidated model:

$$\{\hat{\mathbf{K}}^{(t+n)}\} = \hat{\mathbf{G}}^n\{\hat{\mathbf{K}}^{(t)}\} = \hat{\mathbf{G}}^n\mathbf{C}\{\mathbf{K}^{(t)}\} \tag{5.34}$$

and

$$\{\mathbf{K}^{(t+n)}\} = \mathbf{D}(t+n)\{\hat{\mathbf{K}}^{(t+n)}\} = \mathbf{D}(t+n)\hat{\mathbf{G}}^n\{\hat{\mathbf{K}}^{(t)}\}. \tag{5.35}$$

It follows, therefore, that perfect aggregation occurs if

$$\mathbf{C}\mathbf{G}^n = \hat{\mathbf{G}}^n\mathbf{C} \tag{5.36}$$

or

$$\mathbf{G}^n\mathbf{D}(t) = \mathbf{D}(t+n)\hat{\mathbf{G}}^n. \tag{5.37}$$

---

[2] Note that $\hat{\mathbf{G}}$ depends on t and therefore could be expressed as $\hat{\mathbf{G}}(t)$.

We refer to (5.36) and (5.37) as *sufficient conditions for perfect aggregation* in multiregional population projection—they include temporal consolidations as well as spatial or cohort aggregations. (The expansion of the unit time interval in temporal aggregations is often matched by a comparable expansion of the unit age interval, but this is not a necessary feature of such consolidations.) Finally, (5.36) and (5.37) are not the only sufficient conditions for perfect aggregation. For example, perfect aggregation always is possible in populations that are stable; that is, when $\mathbf{D}(t + n) = \mathbf{D}(t)$ for all n, or when

$$\mathbf{CG} = \hat{\mathbf{G}}\mathbf{C} \tag{5.38}$$

or

$$\mathbf{GD}(t) = \mathbf{D}(t)\hat{\mathbf{G}}. \tag{5.39}$$

The latter two conditions may be derived by recalling (5.32) and (5.34) to redefine the errorless projection as

$$\{\hat{\mathbf{K}}^{(t+n)}\} = \mathbf{CG}^n\mathbf{D}(t)\{\hat{\mathbf{K}}^{(t)}\} = \widehat{\mathbf{G}^n}\{\hat{\mathbf{K}}^{(t)}\} \tag{5.40}$$

and the potentially erroneous one as

$$\{\hat{\mathbf{K}}^{(t+n)}\} = \hat{\mathbf{G}}^n\{\hat{\mathbf{K}}^{(t)}\} \tag{5.41}$$

Equation 5.41 will produce an errorless projection if $\hat{\mathbf{G}}^n = \widehat{\mathbf{G}^n}$, and this equality will be satisfied if either (5.38) or (5.39) is satisfied.[3] For if $\mathbf{CG} = \hat{\mathbf{G}}\mathbf{C}$, then $\mathbf{CG} = \mathbf{CGD}(t)\mathbf{C}$, and

$$\begin{aligned}
\hat{\mathbf{G}}^n &= [\mathbf{CGD}(t)]^n = [\mathbf{CGD}(t)]^{n-2}[\mathbf{CGD}(t)\mathbf{C}]\mathbf{GD}(t) = [\mathbf{CGD}(t)]^{n-2} \\
&\quad \times [\mathbf{CG}]\mathbf{GD}(t) \\
&= [\mathbf{CGD}(t)]^{n-k}\mathbf{CG}^k\mathbf{D}(t) \\
&= \mathbf{CG}^n\mathbf{D}(t) = \mathbf{G}^n.
\end{aligned}$$

Similarly, if $\mathbf{GD}(t) = \mathbf{D}(t)\hat{\mathbf{G}}$, then $\mathbf{GD}(t) = \mathbf{D}(t)\mathbf{CGD}(t)$, and

$$\begin{aligned}
\hat{\mathbf{G}}^n &= [\mathbf{CGD}(t)]^n = \mathbf{CG}[\mathbf{D}(t)\mathbf{CGD}(t)][\mathbf{CGD}(t)]^{n-2} = \mathbf{CG}[\mathbf{GD}(t)] \\
&\quad \times [\mathbf{CGD}(t)]^{n-2} \\
&= \mathbf{CG}^k\mathbf{D}(t)[\mathbf{CGD}(t)]^{n-k} \\
&= \mathbf{CG}^n\mathbf{D}(t) = \widehat{\mathbf{G}^n}.
\end{aligned}$$

---

[3] The author is grateful to a former student of his, Pierre Melut, for suggesting the argument that follows.

A slight modification of an argument concerning economic projection models by Ara (1959) can be used to prove that the dominant root λ_1 is preserved in perfectly aggregated population models. For example, assume that the condition for perfect aggregation set out in (5.38) is satisfied. For simplicity, assume also that the projection matrix G is a nonnegative, primitive matrix. Then it has a positive dominant root λ_1, which is real, and with which one can associate a characteristic vector $\{K_1\}$ with all its elements positive. It follows that

$$G\{K_1\} = \lambda_1\{K_1\} > \{0\}. \tag{5.42}$$

Premultiplying both sides of (5.42) by C, we have

$$CG\{K_1\} = \lambda_1 C\{K_1\},$$

and if the equality in (5.38) is satisfied by the particular consolidation scheme that is used to define $\hat{G}$,

$$CG\{K_1\} = \lambda_1 C\{K_1\} = \hat{G}C\{K_1\}.$$

Since $\{K_1\}$ is a vector with only positive elements, $C\{K_1\}$ is too; therefore, λ_1 is also a characteristic root of $\hat{G}$.

From (5.38) it follows that

$$G'C' = C'\hat{G}',$$

and because a square matrix and its transpose have the same characteristic roots, we have

$$|\beta_i I - \hat{G}| = |\beta_i I - \hat{G}'| = 0,$$

where β_i is any characteristic root of $\hat{G}$. By assumption, $\hat{G}'$ is nonnegative and primitive. It, therefore, has a real, positive dominant characteristic root β_1. Hence

$$\hat{G}'\{X_1\} = \beta_1\{X_1\} > \{0\}, \tag{5.43}$$

where $\{X_1\}$ is the characteristic vector associated with β_1. Premultiplying both sides of (5.43) by C', we have

$$C'\hat{G}'\{X_1\} = \beta_1 C'\{X_1\},$$

and if the equality $G'C' = C'\hat{G}'$ is maintained,

$$C'\hat{G}'\{X_1\} = \beta_1 C'\{X_1\} = G'C'\{X_1\}.$$

Since $\{X_1\} > \{0\}$, $C'\{X_1\} > \{0\}$, therefore β_1 is also a root of G.

Table 5.4 Multiregional and Single-Region Projections to Stability and Associated Parameters: United States Females, 1958

A. Five-Region Projection

	Region of Residence				
Projections and Stable Growth Parameters	1. San Francisco SMSA	2. Los Angeles SMSA	3. San Diego SMSA	4. Rest of California	5. Rest of U.S.
$K(1958)$	1,941,994	3,723,919	446,390	1,283,135	80,844,419
%(1958)	0.0220	0.0422	0.0051	0.0145	0.9162
$K(2008)$	7,561,538	14,488,817	2,334,043	4,634,969	180,567,030
%(2008)	0.0361	0.0691	0.0112	0.0221	0.8615
Y	3,620,347	6,612,727	1,023,696	2,210,093	61,171,949
%	0.0485	0.0886	0.0137	0.0296	0.8196
λ		1.10878			
r		0.02065			
b	0.02593	0.02612	0.02826	0.02780	0.02744
$\Delta = b - r$	0.00528	0.00547	0.00760	0.00714	0.00679
d	0.00652	0.00628	0.00721	0.00676	0.00665
i	0.02242	0.01832	0.03163	0.02920	0.00245
o	0.02117	0.01751	0.03202	0.02958	0.00259
n	0.00125	0.00081	−0.00039	−0.00039	−0.00014

B. Single-Region and Aggregated Multiregional Projections

Projections and Stable Growth Parameters	Single-Region Models			Multiregional Models	
				Two-Region	Five-Region
	Total	Males and Females	Females	Females	Females
$K(1958)$	174,149,000	174,149,000	88,239,857	88,239,857	88,239,857
$K(2008)$	432,441,658	417,656,263	209,416,093	209,491,647	209,586,397
Y	143,715,248	148,319,207	74,172,787	74,609,804	74,638,813
λ	1.11625	1.10905	1.10905	1.10874	1.10878
r	0.02199	0.02070	0.02070	0.02064	0.02065
b	0.02904	0.02871	0.02734	0.02728	0.02727
$\Delta = b - r = d$	0.00704	0.00801	0.00664	0.00663	0.00662

We have shown that the dominant characteristic root λ_1 of **G** is also a characteristic root of $\hat{\mathbf{G}}$, and that the dominant characteristic root β_1 of $\hat{\mathbf{G}}$ is also a characteristic root of **G**. Consequently

$$\lambda_1 = \beta_1.$$

We leave it to the reader to show that a consolidation that satisfies the equality in (5.39) also preserves the dominant characteristic root.

The aggregation problem in its many manifestations appears throughout this book. For example, we have assumed that the same regional age-specific probabilities of outmigrating, dying, and bearing a child apply to all residents of a region irrespective of where they were born or have lived since birth. Another example of aggregation appeared in Table 3.9. There we consolidated the birth cohorts of regions 1 and 2, weighting each one by the size of its regional radix. As a final illustration, consider the population projections in Table 5.4, which indicate the effects of several alternative consolidations carried out on the same data base. Observe that as a consequence of imperfect aggregation, the five-region, two-region, and single-region models all lead to different projected populations and relationships under stability.

5.5 RECONCILIATION OF THE DISCRETE AND CONTINUOUS MODELS

Recall the matrix expression of the discrete model of multiregional demographic growth set out in (5.17):

$$\{\overline{\mathbf{K}}^{(t+1)}\} = \mathbf{H}\{\overline{\mathbf{K}}^{(t)}\}$$

and observe that for each age group,

$$\{\overline{\mathbf{K}}^{(t+1)}(x+5)\} = \mathbf{S}(x)\{\overline{\mathbf{K}}^{(t)}(x)\}.$$

Thus, for example,

$$\{\overline{\mathbf{K}}^{(1)}(5)\} = \mathbf{S}(0)\{\overline{\mathbf{K}}^{(0)}(0)\},$$
$$\{\overline{\mathbf{K}}^{(2)}(10)\} = \mathbf{S}(5)\{\overline{\mathbf{K}}^{(1)}(5)\} = \mathbf{S}(5)\mathbf{S}(0)\{\overline{\mathbf{K}}^{(0)}(0)\},$$

whence for $t = 1, 2, \ldots$, and $x = 5, 10, 15, \ldots, z$

$$\{\overline{\mathbf{K}}^{(t)}(x)\} = [\mathbf{S}(x-5)\cdots\mathbf{S}(5)\mathbf{S}(0)]\{\overline{\mathbf{K}}^{(t-x/5)}(0)\}, \quad \text{if} \quad 0 < x \leq 5t$$

and

$$\{\overline{\mathbf{K}}^{(t)}(u)\} = [\mathbf{S}(u - 5) \cdots \mathbf{S}(u - 5t)]\{\overline{\mathbf{K}}^{(0)}(u - 5t)\}, \quad \text{if} \quad u > 5t,$$

or

$$\{\overline{\mathbf{K}}^{(t)}(x + 5t)\} = [\mathbf{S}(x + 5t - 5) \cdots \mathbf{S}(x)]\{\overline{\mathbf{K}}^{(0)}(x)\}, \quad \begin{aligned} x &= u - 5t > 0 \\ &= 5, 10, \cdots, z. \end{aligned}$$

Next, recalling (5.12):

$$\{\overline{\mathbf{K}}^{(t+1)}(0)\} = \sum_{x=0}^{\beta-5} \mathbf{B}(x)\{\overline{\mathbf{K}}^{(t)}(x)\} = \sum_{x=0}^{5t} \mathbf{B}(x)\{\overline{\mathbf{K}}^{(t)}(x)\} + \sum_{u=5t+5}^{\beta-5} \mathbf{B}(u)\{\overline{\mathbf{K}}^{(t)}(u)\}$$

$$= \sum_{x=0}^{5t} \mathbf{B}(x)\{\overline{\mathbf{K}}^{(t)}(x)\} + \sum_{x=5}^{\beta-5} \mathbf{B}(x + 5t)\{\overline{\mathbf{K}}^{(t)}(x + 5t)\}.$$

Hence we have

$$\{\overline{\mathbf{K}}^{(t+1)}(0)\} = \sum_{x=0}^{5t} \mathbf{B}(x)[\mathbf{S}(x - 5) \cdots \mathbf{S}(5)\mathbf{S}(0)]\{\overline{\mathbf{K}}^{(t-x/5)}(0)\}$$

$$+ \sum_{x=5}^{\beta-5} \mathbf{B}(x + 5t)[\mathbf{S}(x + 5t - 5) \cdots \mathbf{S}(x)]\{\overline{\mathbf{K}}^{(0)}(x)\},$$

where we define $\mathbf{S}(u) = \mathbf{I}$ for $u < 0$. That is,

$$\{\overline{\mathbf{K}}^{(t+1)}(0)\} = \{\mathbf{G}(t)\} + \sum_{x=0}^{5t} \mathbf{B}(x)[\mathbf{S}(x - 5) \cdots \mathbf{S}(5)\mathbf{S}(0)]\{\overline{\mathbf{K}}^{(t-x/5)}(0)\}, \quad (5.44)$$

where

$$\{\mathbf{G}(t)\} = \sum_{x=5}^{\beta-5} \mathbf{B}(x + 5t)[\mathbf{S}(x + 5t - 5) \cdots \mathbf{S}(x)]\{\overline{\mathbf{K}}^{(0)}(x)\}. \quad (5.45)$$

Equation 5.44 is the basic recurrence equation for the discrete model of multiregional demographic growth. Note its similarity to (4.4) in Chapter 4.

Following the argument in Section 4.1, we note that $\mathbf{B}(x) = \mathbf{0}$, for all $x > \beta - 5$. Therefore $\{\mathbf{G}(t)\} = \{\mathbf{0}\}$, for $t > (\beta - 5)/5$, and (5.44) becomes a system of homogeneous linear recurrence equations of order $n = \beta/5$. Using conventional procedures, we adopt a trial solution vector

$$\{\mathbf{K}^{(t)}(0)\} = \lambda^t\{\mathbf{Q}\}.$$

Substituting it into (5.44), we find

$$\lambda^{t+1}\{Q\} = \sum_{x=0}^{\beta-5} B(x)[S(x-5)\cdots S(5)S(0)]\lambda^{t-x/5}\{Q\}.$$

Premultiplying both sides by

$$Q^{-1} = \begin{bmatrix} \dfrac{1}{Q_1} & 0 & \cdots & 0 \\ 0 & \dfrac{1}{Q_2} & \cdots & 0 \\ \vdots & & \ddots & \vdots \\ 0 & 0 & \cdots & \dfrac{1}{Q_m} \end{bmatrix}$$

and rearranging, we have

$$\lambda^{t+1}\{1\} - \sum_{x=0}^{\beta-5} \lambda^{t-x/5} Q^{-1}B(x)[S(x-5)\cdots S(5)S(0)]\{Q\} = \{0\}, \quad (5.46)$$

where, as before, $S(u) = I$ for $u < 0$.

Thus λ is the solution of the characteristic equation of the projection matrix G:

$$\lambda^n\{1\} - \lambda^{n-1}Q^{-1}B(0)\{Q\} - \lambda^{n-2}Q^{-1}B(5)S(0)\{Q\} - \cdots$$
$$- Q^{-1}B(\beta - 5)[S(\beta - 10)\cdots S(5)S(0)]\{Q\} = \{0\}. \quad (5.47)$$

Observe that (5.47) is a natural generalization of its counterpart in the single-region model:

$$\lambda^n - \lambda^{n-1}b(0) - \lambda^{n-2}b(5)s(0) - \cdots - b(\beta - 5)s(\beta - 10)\cdots s(5)s(0) = 0.$$
$$(5.48)$$

However, as in Chapter 4 the multiregional expression includes a "weighting" that reflects ratios of births in the stable population.

To determine the stable growth ratio, λ_1 of the discrete projection model, we solved for the dominant characteristic root of the characteristic equation $|G - \lambda I| = 0$. An equivalent procedure is to derive the dominant characteristic root of the characteristic equation in (5.47), which for $\lambda \neq 0$ may be rewritten as

$$\{f(\lambda)\} = \lambda^{-1}[Q^{-1}B(0)\{Q\}] + \lambda^{-2}[Q^{-1}B(5)S(0)\{Q\}] + \cdots$$
$$+ \lambda^{-n}[Q^{-1}B(\beta - 5)[S(\beta - 10)\cdots S(5)S(0)]\{Q\}] = \{1\}. \quad (5.49)$$

If (but not *only* if) two consecutive matrices $\mathbf{B}(x)$ are positive matrices in (5.49), the elements of $\{\mathbf{f}(\lambda)\}$ decrease monotonically from infinity to zero as λ increases from zero to infinity. Hence there can only be a single real positive root that satisfies each of the equations in (5.49). And by arguments analogous to those used with the continuous model in Chapter 4, it can be established that each of the equations will be satisfied by the same λ_1, where

$$\lambda_1 > |\lambda_j|,$$

λ_j being any other root of (5.49). Thus (5.49) demonstrates that as in Chapter 4, one can combine iteration, weighting, and single-region solution methods to solve multiregional problems.

The correspondence between the discrete and continuous models can be developed further, as Keyfitz (1968, Chapter 8) has shown. We demonstrated in Chapter 4 that the trajectory of births described by the integral equation

$$\{\mathbf{B}(t)\} = \{\mathbf{G}(t)\} + \int_0^t \mathbf{M}(x)_0 \mathbf{P}(x)\{\mathbf{B}(t - x)\} \, dx \qquad (5.50)$$

may be established by means of the solution

$$\{\mathbf{B}(t)\} = \{\mathbf{Q}_1\}e^{r_1 t} + \{\mathbf{Q}_2\}e^{r_2 t} + \cdots, \qquad (5.51)$$

in which the r's are the zeros of the characteristic equation

$$\{\boldsymbol{\Psi}(r)\} - \{\mathbf{1}\} = \int_\alpha^\beta e^{-rx}\mathbf{M}(x)\mathbf{Q}^{-1}{}_0\mathbf{P}(x)\{\mathbf{Q}\} \, dx - \{\mathbf{1}\} = \{\mathbf{0}\}, \qquad (5.52)$$

Using the numerical approximation to $\boldsymbol{\Psi}(r)$ that was given in (4.32), setting $\lambda = e^{5r}$, and multiplying (5.52) through by λ^n, gives, after some rearrangement,

$$\lambda^n\{\mathbf{1}\} - \lambda^{n-1/2}\mathbf{F}(0)\mathbf{Q}^{-1}{}_0\mathbf{L}(0)\{\mathbf{Q}\} - \lambda^{n-3/2}\mathbf{F}(5)\mathbf{Q}^{-1}{}_0\mathbf{L}(5)\{\mathbf{Q}\} - \cdots = \{\mathbf{0}\}.$$
$$(5.53)$$

Equation 5.53 is not the same as (5.47), but a slight generalization of Keyfitz's (1968) argument may be used to prove the asymptotic equivalence of the characteristic roots of the discrete and continuous models of multiregional demographic growth as the interval of time and age is shortened to zero. We confine our attention here, however, to the numerical discrepancies in the maximal roots and related measures derived using the two models.

Consider the relationships between the discrete and continuous population projection methods, which we call methods D and C, respectively. If

Table 5.5   Relations Under Stability in Discrete and Continuous Models of Demographic Growth

A.   Value of 1000r by Discrete and Continuous Models for Six Female Populations

	Method			
	D	C		
Population	$1000r_D$	$1000r_C$	$1000(r_D - r_C)$	$1000(\frac{1}{8}r_D^2)$
Yugoslavia (1961)	6.100	6.095	0.005	0.005
United States (1958)				
4 California Regions — Rest of U.S.	20.652	20.600	0.052	0.053
California — Rest of U.S.	20.645	20.593	0.052	0.053
West Virginia — Rest of U.S.	20.720	20.668	0.052	0.054
United States (1968)				
California — Rest of U.S.	5.695	5.691	0.004	0.004
West Virginia — Rest of U.S.	5.723	5.719	0.004	0.004

applied to an initial population that is stable, an age group starting with $\{\overline{\mathbf{K}}(x)\}$ individuals will end a 5-year unit interval with $e^{5r}\{\overline{\mathbf{K}}(x)\}$ persons. In method D, the observed age-specific fertility rates are applied to the arithmetic mean of the population at the beginning and end of the unit interval:

$$\tfrac{1}{2}[\{\overline{\mathbf{K}}(x)\} + \mathbf{S}(x - 5)\{\overline{\mathbf{K}}(x - 5)\}].$$

Thus the implicit average of method D in the first period is

$$\tfrac{1}{2}[\{\overline{\mathbf{K}}(x)\}(1 + e^{5r})].$$

Method C, however, instead uses the midpoint population $\{\overline{\mathbf{K}}(x)\}e^{5r/2}$. Hence,

$$\frac{\tfrac{1}{2}(1 + e^{5r})}{e^{5r/2}} = \frac{e^{5r/2} + e^{-5r/2}}{2} = 1 + \frac{25}{8}r^2 + \frac{625}{384}r^4 + \cdots$$

is the ratio of the level of method D to that of method C. Therefore, neglecting terms beyond those in r^2, we have

$$\{\boldsymbol{\Psi}_D(r)\} = (1 + \tfrac{25}{8}r^2)\{\boldsymbol{\Psi}_C(r)\} = \{\mathbf{1}\},$$

Table 5.5   (*continued*)

B.   Stable Births, Stable Equivalents, and Stable Equivalent Population Projections: United States Females, 1958

Projections and Stable Growth Parameters	Region of Residence				
	1. San Francisco SMSA	2. Los Angeles SMSA	3. San Diego SMSA	4. Rest of California	5. Rest of U.S.
Discrete Model: Method D					
$Q = bY$	93,872	172,742	28,925	61,433	1,678,680
$Y = Q/b$	3,620,347	6,612,727	1,023,696	2,210,093	61,171,949
Ye^{50r}	10,167,114	18,570,695	2,874,873	6,206,663	171,790,781
Continuous Model: Method C					
$Q = bY$	93,862	172,717	28,920	61,421	1,678,495
$Y = Q/b$	3,623,830	6,619,030	1,024,673	2,212,034	61,228,196
Ye^{50r}	10,150,380	18,539,963	2,870,119	6,195,929	171,500,738

which allows us to conclude like Keyfitz (1968, p. 255), that

$$r_D \doteq r_C + \frac{25}{8}\frac{r_D{}^2}{A} \doteq r_C + \tfrac{1}{8}r_D{}^2,$$

where A, which we have set equal to 25 years as a crude approximation, is the average age of childbearing in the stable population.

Table 5.5A shows for six female populations how the discrepancy between the two methods of calculating the intrinsic rate of growth increases with the square of the rate. Table 5.5B illustrates the corresponding discrepancies in stable births, stable equivalents, and stable equivalent population projections, the latter referring to the projections of the regional populations in which only the maximal root is used, for example,

$$K_i(2008) \doteq Y_i(1958)e^{50r}.$$

The discrepancy between such (discrete model) projections and those set out in Table 5.4 for the same year may be attributed to the persisting influences of the submaximal roots.

CHAPTER SIX

Estimating Basic Multiregional Demographic Measures from Incomplete Data

The state of the art in methods for estimating demographic measures from incomplete data is relatively well developed for single-region population systems. In Chapter 2 we saw that the principal feature of the "United Nations" methods is the use of *model life tables*, in which the regularities exhibited by available mortality data, collected in countries with accurate registration systems, are employed to systematically approximate the mortality of a region for which such data are unavailable. These tables are entered with observed survivorship proportions to obtain the expectation of life at birth that best matches the pattern of mortality implied by these survivorship proportions. The expectation of life then is the parameter that identifies the appropriate model life table.

The UN methods of estimating a single-region life table from incomplete data may be generalized to include the estimation of multiregional life tables that describe the multiregional mortality and migration schedules of a multiregional population system. Such a generalization follows from the introduction of the concept of *model multiregional life tables* and utilizes a set of initial estimates of survivorship and outmigration proportions obtained from two consecutive place of residence by place of birth census age distributions.

6.1 MODEL MULTIREGIONAL LIFE TABLES

A model single-region life table approximates the mortality schedule of a region that is closed to migration by resorting to the mortality experience of other regions with populations and conditions that may be presumed to be similar to the one being studied. Analogously, a model multiregional life table approximates the mortality and migration schedules of a system of regions by resorting to data on the mortality and migration experience in other multiregional systems with populations and conditions that may be presumed to be similar to those being studied.

It has been noted that mortality risks experienced by different age and sex groups of a population are interrelated in that if higher than average death rates prevail among one such segment of a given population, the rates are likely to be higher than average in another segment of the same population, as well. This interrelationship reflects the fact that if health conditions, for example, are good or poor for one group in the population, they also will tend to be good or poor for other groups as well.

An analogous observation may be made regarding migration. Migration risks experienced by different age and sex groups of a population are inter-correlated, and high outmigration rates among one segment of a given population usually imply high outmigration rates for other segments of the same population. This association occurs partly because if economic conditions are good or poor for one segment of the population, they also are likely to be good or poor for other segments.

Demographers have long recognized the persisting regularities that prevail among age-specific outmigration schedules, the most prominent being the high concentration of migration among young adults (Lowry, 1966; Long, 1973). Rates of migration also are high among children, varying from a high during the first year of life to a low at about age 16. From that point, the age profile turns sharply upward to a peak in the neighborhood of 22 years, declining regularly with age except for a slight hump around ages 62 through 65.

The empirical regularities are not surprising. Young adults exhibit the highest migration rates because they are less constrained by ties to their community. Their children generally are not in school, they are more likely to be renters than home owners, and job seniority is not yet an important consideration. Since children ordinarily move only as members of a family, their migration pattern mirrors that of their parents. Consequently, because younger children generally have younger parents, the geographical mobility of infants is higher than that of adolescents. Finally, the small hump in the age profile between ages 62 to 65 describes migration after retirement and reflects, for example, moves made to the sunnier and milder climates of states such as Arizona, California, and Florida.

Figure 6.1 repeats the fundamental age profile of most outmigration schedules but expresses it in terms of age intervals 5 years wide. In consequence, the low rate of migration at age 16 now is aggregated with the substantially higher rates that follow it, thereby shifting the low point among teenagers on the age profile to a lower age group. The rest of the distribution, however, remains essentially the same as before, with peaks occurring in the following age groups: 0 to 4, 20 to 24, and 60 to 64 year olds. Note, however, that in some instances the aggregation produces a younger than normal peak. This seems to be especially true of migration from the Northeast region of the United States.

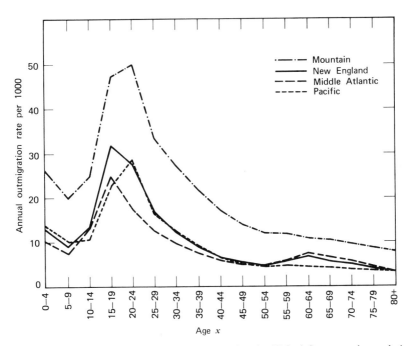

Figure 6.1   Age-specific annual outmigration rates for the United States total population, 1955–1960: various geographic divisions.

Two alternative ways of formally summarizing the above-mentioned regularities in age-specific migration patterns are immediately apparent: (1) a generalization of the procedure used by Coale and Demeny to define a family of basic fertility schedules (Figure 2.2); or (2) an extension of Coale and Demeny's regression equation method. Thus, for example, we may define a measure analogous to the gross reproduction rate called the *migration production rate*, $MPR_{ij}(\bar{m})$, where

$$MPR_{ij}(\bar{m}) = 5 \sum_{x=0}^{z} M_{ij}(x), \qquad (6.1)$$

$\bar{m}$ is the mean age of the migration schedule, and $M_{ij}(x)$ denotes the annual migration rate from region i to region j among individuals aged x to $x + 4$ years. A basic migration schedule with an MPR of 1 could be developed for each of several values of $\bar{m}$, and a given pair of values for $\bar{m}$ and $MPR_{ij}(\bar{m})$ would imply a particular model schedule of age-specific migration rates from region i to region j. Such information for all pairs of regions and a set of model mortality schedules are sufficient input data for the construction of a model multiregional life table.

Alternatively, as in the case of model single-region life tables, the generalized experience of several regions can be summarized by regression equations. Specifically, we may associate the regional probabilities of outmigrating at each age, $p_{ij}(x)$, with the fraction of the expectation of life at birth of persons born in region i that is expected to be lived in region j, that is, the *migration level* $_i\Theta_j = {}_{i0}e_j(0)/{}_{i0}e(0)$.

Consider, for example, the regional migration levels and the probabilities of outmigration within the first 5 years of age that appear in Figure 6.2. A simple linear regression of the 72 probabilities on the associated 72 migration levels yields

$$p_{ij}(0) = -0.0013205 + 0.22075 {}_{i0}e_j(0)/{}_{i0}e(0) = -0.0013205 + 0.22075 {}_i\Theta_j,$$
$$(6.2)$$

and a coefficient of determination (R^2) of 0.82. Thus the probability of outmigrating within the first 5 years of age from one Geographic Division of the United States to another may be approximated by inserting the appropriate $_i\Theta_j$ into (6.2) and solving for $p_{ij}(0)$. Comparable equations may be obtained for all other age groups (Table 6.1A) and the results combined with model mortality schedules, to compute a model multiregional life table.

In developing regression equations such as the one in (6.2) one often finds that the intercept term is negative and may produce negative $p_{ij}(x)$'s for

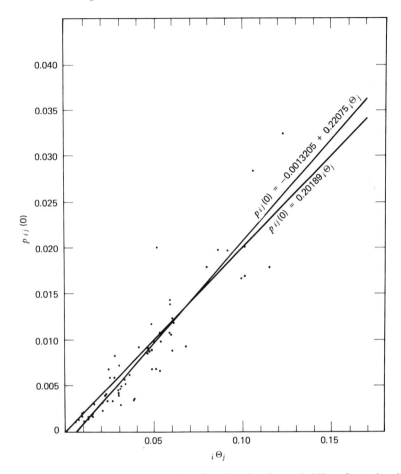

Figure 6.2   Alternative regression equations for obtaining the probability of outmigrating within the first 5 years of age.

sufficiently low ranges of migration levels. It is desirable to ensure that this never happens by forcing the regression equations through the origin. Thus in Table 6.1 B we set out the 17 regression "slope" coefficients of linear regressions which were forced through the origin and fitted to the same data that produced Table 6.1A. Figure 6.3 illustrates graphically the resulting model relationships between age-specific probabilities of outmigrating $p_{ij}(x)$ and various levels of geographical mobility. Note that the fundamental age curve in Figure 6.3 confounds the two distinct age profiles of Figure 6.1,

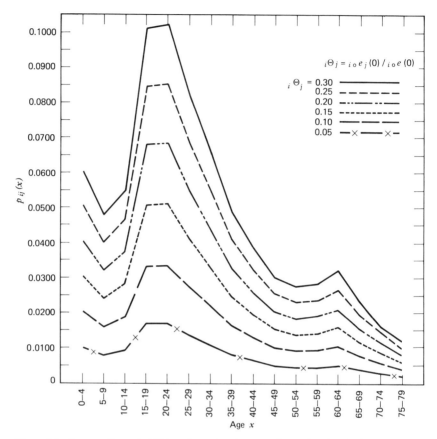

Figure 6.3 Age-specific probabilities of outmigrating at various migration levels.

with the result that the alternative peaks at ages 15 to 19 and 20 to 24 are now "averaged out." This indicates that further study of methods for describing a *family* of alternative migration age profiles is warranted.

The regression coefficients in Table 6.1B were combined with the Coale–Demeny model mortality schedules to compute the specimen model multiregional model life table set out in Table 6.2. The principal steps of that calculation were as follows:

1. Regional probabilities of dying at each age $q_i(x)$ were obtained by interpolation in a consolidated set of model single-region life tables that were developed by aggregating Coale and Demeny's West family of male

Table 6.1 **Regression Coefficients for Obtaining Model Probabilities of Outmigration**

A. With Nonzero Intercept Coefficient

B. With Zero Intercept Coefficient

Age, x	Intercept	Slope	R^2	Age, x	Slope	R^2
0	−0.0013205	0.22075	0.82	0	0.20189	0.82
5	−0.0015022	0.18117	0.82	5	0.15971	0.80
10	−0.0018122	0.21221	0.91	10	0.18633	0.89
15	−0.0010078	0.35212	0.92	15	0.33772	0.91
20	0.0009206	0.32687	0.79	20	0.34002	0.79
25	−0.0017593	0.29788	0.87	25	0.27275	0.86
30	−0.0019062	0.24432	0.83	30	0.21709	0.81
35	−0.0018617	0.18885	0.80	35	0.16226	0.77
40	−0.0019189	0.15569	0.78	40	0.12828	0.74
45	−0.0019471	0.12968	0.77	45	0.10186	0.71
50	−0.0020221	0.12095	0.75	50	0.09207	0.69
55	−0.0021256	0.12499	0.70	55	0.09463	0.64
60	−0.0027736	0.14504	0.57	60	0.10542	0.51
65	−0.0019290	0.10496	0.62	65	0.07741	0.56
70	−0.0013216	0.07698	0.68	70	0.05810	0.62
75	−0.0007652	0.05064	0.77	75	0.03971	0.71
80	−0.0002265	0.02127	0.72	80	0.01804	0.70

and female model life tables. A sex ratio at birth of 1.05 was assumed for the aggregation.

2. Regional probabilities of outmigrating at each age $p_{ij}(x)$ were computed using the regression coefficients given in Table 6.1B.

3. Standard multiregional life table calculations, carried out with the derived values of $q_i(x)$ and $p_{ij}(x)$ as inputs, produced Table 6.2. The life table was closed off by setting the death rates in the terminal age groups equal to those in the consolidated Coale–Demeny tables for the particular regional expectations of life at birth that served as inputs to the regression computations.

In the absence of iteration, these steps do not produce a model multi-regional life table with expectations of life at birth *by place of residence* that exactly match those used as inputs to the regression calculations. This

Table 6.2 Model Multiregional (Two-Region) Life Table

Mortality Levels: $_{10}e(0) = 50$ $_{20}e(0) = 50$
Migration Levels: $_1\Theta_2 = 12/50 = 0.24$ $_2\Theta_1 = 3/50 = 0.06$

Age, x	$p_{11}(x)$	$p_{12}(x)$	$_{10}l_1(x)$	$_{10}l_2(x)$	$_{10}L_1(x)/l_1(0)$	$_{10}L_2(x)/l_1(0)$	$m_{12}(x)$	$m_{1\delta}(x)$	$s_{11}(x)$	$s_{12}(x)$	$_{10}e_1(x)$	$_{10}e_2(x)$
0	0.782129	0.040378	100,000	0	4.19355	0.09501	0.010143	0.037893	0.908538	0.041093	38.00	12.00
5	0.948612	0.031942	78,213	4,038	3.81097	0.26158	0.006557	0.003992	0.948348	0.034562	41.11	14.47
10	0.948048	0.037266	74,226	6,425	3.61639	0.38656	0.007652	0.003016	0.930379	0.051867	37.20	14.43
15	0.911587	0.067544	70,430	9,037	3.36962	0.56226	0.014134	0.004367	0.907947	0.067632	33.20	14.16
20	0.903947	0.068004	64,355	13,453	3.06895	0.76691	0.014287	0.005893	0.908798	0.061623	29.58	13.74
25	0.914298	0.054550	58,403	17,223	2.80087	0.92153	0.011398	0.006509	0.917513	0.049212	26.38	13.12
30	0.921116	0.043418	53,632	19,638	2.58117	1.01737	0.009040	0.007384	0.923663	0.038128	23.40	12.28
35	0.926496	0.032452	49,615	21,057	2.39383	1.06721	0.006738	0.008524	0.926049	0.029132	20.61	11.30
40	0.925597	0.025656	46,139	21,632	2.22458	1.08135	0.005329	0.010126	0.923088	0.023053	17.96	10.20
45	0.920396	0.020372	42,844	21,622	2.05971	1.06816	0.004243	0.012337	0.911678	0.019326	15.43	9.05
50	0.902210	0.018414	39,544	21,104	1.88295	1.02910	0.003872	0.016691	0.889268	0.018521	13.00	7.86
55	0.874921	0.018926	35,774	20,060	1.67922	0.96432	0.004038	0.022647	0.852247	0.019682	10.75	6.69
60	0.826325	0.021084	31,394	18,513	1.43585	0.86912	0.004618	0.033420	0.801165	0.018175	8.66	5.56
65	0.770734	0.015482	26,040	16,252	1.15430	0.73425	0.003497	0.048293	0.731752	0.013348	6.83	4.50
70	0.681184	0.011620	20,133	13,118	0.84711	0.56005	0.002765	0.073090	0.631774	0.009620	5.21	3.52
75	0.559246	0.007942	13,752	9,284	0.53653	0.36601	0.002037	0.111031	0.651765	0.005914	3.85	2.65
80+	0.0	0.0	7,709	5,357	0.35023	0.24335	—	0.220116	—	—	2.68	1.86

Table 6.2 (continued)

Age, x	$p_{22}(x)$	$p_{21}(x)$	$_{20}l_2(x)$	$_{20}l_1(x)$	$_{20}L_2(x)/l_2(0)$	$_{20}L_1(x)/l_2(0)$	$m_{21}(x)$	$m_{2\delta}(x)$	$s_{22}(x)$	$s_{21}(x)$	$_{20}e_2(x)$	$_{20}e_1(x)$
0	0.812413	0.010094	100,000	0	4.26481	0.02375	0.002488	0.037186	0.939357	0.010273	47.00	3.00
5	0.972568	0.007985	81,241	1,009	4.00715	0.06539	0.001619	0.003943	0.974270	0.008641	51.96	3.62
10	0.975998	0.009317	79,045	1,606	3.90631	0.09664	0.001886	0.002973	0.969279	0.012967	48.02	3.61
15	0.962245	0.016886	77,207	2,259	3.79132	0.14056	0.003442	0.004254	0.958671	0.016908	43.82	3.54
20	0.954950	0.017001	74,445	3,363	3.64413	0.19173	0.003479	0.005739	0.955016	0.015406	39.88	3.43
25	0.955210	0.013637	71,320	4,306	3.49202	0.23038	0.002790	0.006373	0.954422	0.012303	36.21	3.28
30	0.953680	0.010855	68,361	4,909	3.34420	0.25434	0.002222	0.007261	0.952259	0.009532	32.61	3.07
35	0.950835	0.008113	65,407	5,264	3.19424	0.26680	0.001663	0.008417	0.947898	0.007283	29.08	2.82
40	0.944839	0.006414	62,362	5,408	3.03559	0.27034	0.001319	0.010026	0.940378	0.005763	25.61	2.55
45	0.935675	0.005093	59,061	5,406	2.86083	0.26704	0.001052	0.012240	0.926172	0.004831	22.22	2.26
50	0.916021	0.004603	55,372	5,276	2.65478	0.25728	0.000961	0.016571	0.903159	0.004630	18.90	1.96
55	0.889116	0.004732	50,819	5,015	2.40246	0.24108	0.001002	0.022477	0.867009	0.004920	15.77	1.67
60	0.842138	0.005271	45,279	4,628	2.08770	0.21728	0.001145	0.033134	0.814796	0.004544	12.83	1.39
65	0.782345	0.003871	38,229	4,063	1.70499	0.18356	0.000869	0.047978	0.741763	0.003337	10.21	1.13
70	0.689899	0.002905	29,971	3,279	1.26715	0.14001	0.000688	0.072713	0.638989	0.002405	7.85	0.88
75	0.565202	0.001986	20,715	2,321	0.81104	0.09150	0.000507	0.110609	0.656200	0.001478	5.83	0.66
80+	0.0	0.0	11,727	1,339	0.53275	0.06084	—	0.220116	—	—	4.08	0.47

also seems to be true of the Coale and Demeny (1966) calculations. The regression coefficients presented in Table XI of their book do not produce a model life table with an expectation of life at age 10 that matches the one used as the input to the regression computations.

6.2   MODEL MULTIREGIONAL STABLE POPULATIONS

The age-specific regional distributions of a multiregional population that is closed to emigration and immigration are determined by the recent regional schedules of fertility, mortality, and migration. If these schedules remain unchanged for a sufficiently long period of time—a century, say—the age-specific regional distributions become fixed and increase at a constant intrinsic annual rate of growth. Recall that in the continuous model such distributions may be expressed, for each age, by the matrix

$$\mathbf{c}(x) = \mathbf{b}e^{-rx}{}_0\mathbf{P}(x) = \mathbf{b}e^{-rx}{}_0\mathbf{l}(x)\mathbf{l}(0)^{-1}, \tag{6.3}$$

where $\mathbf{b}$ is a diagonal matrix of regional intrinsic birthrates, r is the intrinsic rate of growth, $\mathbf{l}(0)$ is a diagonal matrix of regional radices, and $_0\mathbf{l}(x)$ is a multiregional life table matrix of survivors to exact age x. Numerical evaluation of (6.3) over 5-year age groups may be carried out using the approximation

$$\mathbf{C}(x) = \mathbf{b}e^{-r(x+2.5)}{}_0\mathbf{L}(x)\mathbf{l}(0)^{-1} = \mathbf{b}e^{-r(x+2.5)}{}_0\mathbf{L}(x),$$

with the multiregional life table computed on unit radices for all regions ($\mathbf{l}(0) = \mathbf{I}$). But $\mathbf{C}(x)$ is a matrix, and what we seek is the vector $\{\mathbf{C}(x)\}$. Hence as in Chapter 4 the matrix may be consolidated into a vector to define

$$\{\mathbf{C}(x)\} = \mathbf{Q}^{-1}\mathbf{C}(x)\{\mathbf{Q}\} = \mathbf{b}e^{-r(x+2.5)}\mathbf{Q}^{-1}{}_0\mathbf{L}(x)\{\mathbf{Q}\}, \tag{6.4}$$

where a typical diagonal element of $\mathbf{b}$ is

$$b_i = \frac{1}{\displaystyle\sum_{x=0}^{z} e^{-r(x+2.5)} \sum_{j=1}^{m} \frac{Q_j}{Q_i}{}_{j0}L_i(x)},$$

and Q_j/Q_i is the ratio of births in the stable populations of regions j and i; we call this ratio a *stable radix ratio* and denote it by SRR_{ji}.

In numerical calculations carried out with empirical data on an observed population, stable radix ratios are obtained as part of the computed output.[1] For model multiregional stable populations, however, stable radix ratios for all pairs of regions cannot be determined without data on regional fertility schedules. Consequently such radix ratios must be included as an additional input to calculations using the relationship set out in (6.4).

Table 6.3 presents a specimen set of model two-region stable populations generated by combining several intrinsic rates of growth with unit stable radix ratios and the model multiregional stationary population (on unit radix) set out in Table 6.2. Table 6.4 presents the corresponding stable populations that result if the stable radix ratio SRR_{21} is 10 instead of unity. Figure 6.4 displays the regional age compositions that evolve in both instances and contrasts them with those that would arise if migration levels were instead taken to be equal (or zero) in both regions.

Collectively, the numerical results illustrate several interesting properties of multiregional stable populations, some of which are also exhibited by single-region stable populations. First, an unchanging multiregional schedule of growth in which regional fertility, mortality, and migration levels are identical produces identical stable regional populations. Second, higher values of the intrinsic rate of growth create stable regional populations that taper more rapidly with age and, in consequence, include a higher proportion of the population below every age. Third, as in the single-region case, fertility affects the rate of increase of a stable population. In the multiregional case, however, it also affects the stable regional allocations of such populations.[2] For example, in Tables 6.3 and 6.4 we observe that as a stable radix ratio is increased, the stable regional share of the region with the larger number of births also increases. Finally, mortality and migration schedules also affect the form and rate of increase of the stable regional age compositions and shares in an obvious way, and any idiosyncrasies in the age patterns of such schedules will be reflected in the stable regional populations.

Underlying each of the model multiregional stable populations in Tables 6.3 and 6.4 are several multiregional fertility schedules and a single multi-regional mortality-migration schedule. The latter is embodied in the model multiregional life table that forms the basis of these stable populations

---

[1] Given multiregional rates of fertility, mortality, and migration, we compute the numerical values of the matrices $_0L(x)$ and $F(x)$, calculate the multiregional characteristic matrix $\Psi(r)$, determine the r that gives $\Psi(r)$ a dominant characteristic root of unity, and solve for the associated characteristic vector $\{Q\}$.

[2] If we examine the three variable quantities of $\{C(x)\}$ in (6.4), namely, $e^{-r(x+2.5)}$, Q, and $_0L(x)$, it is clear that fertility helps to determine the first two but is not part of the third.

Table 6.3 Model Multiregional (Two-Region) Stable Populations: Equal Regional Stable Radix Ratios

Age, x	Intrinsic Rate of Growth (r)					
	-0.010			0.000		
	Region			Region		
	$1 + 2$	1	2	$1 + 2$	1	2
0	0.0614	0.0753	0.0520	0.0858	0.1028	0.0739
5	0.0613	0.0728	0.0535	0.0815	0.0945	0.0724
10	0.0633	0.0733	0.0566	0.0801	0.0906	0.0728
15	0.0654	0.0728	0.0604	0.0786	0.0856	0.0738
20	0.0670	0.0711	0.0643	0.0767	0.0795	0.0748
25	0.0684	0.0695	0.0676	0.0744	0.0739	0.0748
30	0.0695	0.0684	0.0702	0.0720	0.0692	0.0739
35	0.0703	0.0674	0.0722	0.0692	0.0649	0.0722
40	0.0706	0.0665	0.0733	0.0661	0.0608	0.0698
45	0.0702	0.0652	0.0735	0.0626	0.0567	0.0666
50	0.0687	0.0630	0.0725	0.0582	0.0522	0.0624
55	0.0656	0.0594	0.0696	0.0529	0.0468	0.0571
60	0.0601	0.0538	0.0643	0.0461	0.0403	0.0501
65	0.0518	0.0458	0.0558	0.0378	0.0326	0.0413
70	0.0405	0.0355	0.0439	0.0281	0.0241	0.0310
75	0.0273	0.0237	0.0297	0.0181	0.0153	0.0200
80 +	0.0189	0.0163	0.0206	0.0119	0.0100	0.0132
					Parameters of Multiregional	
Regional share, %	100.00	40.05	59.95	100.00	41.00	59.00
Birthrate, b	0.0140	0.0174	0.0116	0.0200	0.0244	0.0170
Absence rate, Δ	0.0240	0.0274	0.0216	0.0200	0.0244	0.0170
Average age, a	38.40	36.05	39.97	33.64	31.29	35.27

Mortality Levels	$_{10}e(0) = 50$	$_{20}e(0) = 50$
Migration Levels	$_1\Theta_2 = 12/50 = 0.24$	$_2\Theta_1 = 3/50 = 0.06$
Stable Radix Ratios	$SRR_{12} = Q_1/Q_2 = 1$	$SRR_{21} = Q_2/Q_1 = 1$

Intrinsic Rate of Growth (r)

	0.010			0.020			0.030		
		Region			Region			Region	
	1 + 2	1	2	1 + 2	1	2	1 + 2	1	2
	0.1145	0.1342	0.1003	0.1465	0.1681	0.1303	0.1807	0.2034	0.1630
	0.1034	0.1173	0.0934	0.1259	0.1398	0.1155	0.1477	0.1609	0.1374
	0.0967	0.1069	0.0893	0.1120	0.1212	0.1051	0.1249	0.1326	0.1189
	0.0903	0.0961	0.0862	0.0995	0.1036	0.0964	0.1056	0.1079	0.1038
	0.0838	0.0849	0.0831	0.0878	0.0871	0.0884	0.0887	0.0863	0.0905
	0.0774	0.0751	0.0790	0.0771	0.0733	0.0800	0.0741	0.0690	0.0780
	0.0712	0.0668	0.0743	0.0675	0.0620	0.0716	0.0616	0.0556	0.0663
	0.0651	0.0597	0.0691	0.0587	0.0527	0.0633	0.0510	0.0449	0.0558
	0.0592	0.0532	0.0635	0.0507	0.0447	0.0553	0.0419	0.0362	0.0464
	0.0532	0.0472	0.0576	0.0434	0.0377	0.0477	0.0342	0.0291	0.0381
	0.0472	0.0413	0.0514	0.0366	0.0314	0.0405	0.0274	0.0230	0.0307
	0.0407	0.0352	0.0447	0.0301	0.0255	0.0335	0.0214	0.0178	0.0242
	0.0338	0.0289	0.0373	0.0237	0.0198	0.0266	0.0160	0.0132	0.0183
	0.0263	0.0222	0.0293	0.0176	0.0145	0.0199	0.0113	0.0092	0.0130
	0.0187	0.0156	0.0209	0.0119	0.0097	0.0135	0.0073	0.0058	0.0084
	0.0114	0.0094	0.0128	0.0069	0.0056	0.0079	0.0040	0.0032	0.0046
	0.0071	0.0059	0.0080	0.0041	0.0033	0.0047	0.0023	0.0018	0.0026
Stable Populations									
	100.00	41.95	58.05	100.00	42.86	57.14	100.00	43.68	56.32
	0.0274	0.0326	0.0236	0.0359	0.0419	0.0314	0.0454	0.0520	0.0403
	0.0174	0.0226	0.0136	0.0159	0.0219	0.0114	0.0154	0.0220	0.0103
	29.19	26.97	30.80	25.21	23.20	26.73	21.78	20.01	23.15

Table 6.4   Model Multiregional (Two-Region) Stable Populations: Unequal Regional Stable Radix Ratios

Age, x	Intrinsic Rate of Growth (r)					
	−0.010			0.000		
	Region			Region		
	1 + 2	1	2	1 + 2	1	2
0	0.0614	0.0453	0.0637	0.0858	0.0652	0.0887
5	0.0613	0.0480	0.0632	0.0815	0.0657	0.0837
10	0.0633	0.0518	0.0650	0.0801	0.0674	0.0818
15	0.0654	0.0568	0.0666	0.0786	0.0702	0.0798
20	0.0670	0.0623	0.0677	0.0767	0.0733	0.0772
25	0.0684	0.0671	0.0686	0.0744	0.0751	0.0744
30	0.0695	0.0708	0.0693	0.0720	0.0754	0.0715
35	0.0703	0.0735	0.0698	0.0692	0.0744	0.0685
40	0.0706	0.0752	0.0699	0.0661	0.0725	0.0652
45	0.0702	0.0759	0.0693	0.0626	0.0696	0.0616
50	0.0687	0.0752	0.0677	0.0582	0.0655	0.0572
55	0.0656	0.0725	0.0645	0.0529	0.0602	0.0518
60	0.0601	0.0673	0.0590	0.0461	0.0531	0.0451
65	0.0518	0.0586	0.0508	0.0378	0.0440	0.0369
70	0.0405	0.0463	0.0397	0.0281	0.0331	0.0275
75	0.0273	0.0314	0.0267	0.0181	0.0213	0.0176
80+	0.0189	0.0218	0.0185	0.0119	0.0141	0.0116
				Parameters of Multiregional		
Regional share, %	100.00	12.71	87.29	100.00	12.36	87.64
Birthrate, b	0.0140	0.0100	0.0145	0.0200	0.0147	0.0207
Absence rate, Δ	0.0240	0.0200	0.0245	0.0200	0.0147	0.0207
Average age, a	38.40	41.10	38.01	33.64	36.47	33.24

Mortality Levels	$_{10}e(0) = 50$		$_{20}e(0) = 50$	
Migration Levels	$_1\Theta_2 = 12/50 = 0.24$		$_2\Theta_1 = 3/50 = 0.06$	
Stable Radix Ratios	$SRR_{12} = Q_1/Q_2 = 1/10$		$SRR_{21} = Q_2/Q_1 = 10$	

Intrinsic Rate of Growth (r)

0.010			0.020			0.030		
	Region			Region			Region	
1 + 2	1	2	1 + 2	1	2	1 + 2	1	2
0.1145	0.0895	0.1179	0.1465	0.1177	0.1503	0.1807	0.1490	0.1847
0.1034	0.0858	0.1058	0.1259	0.1073	0.1283	0.1477	0.1292	0.1500
0.0967	0.0838	0.0985	0.1120	0.0997	0.1136	0.1249	0.1141	0.1263
0.0903	0.0830	0.0913	0.0995	0.0940	0.1002	0.1056	0.1024	0.1060
0.0838	0.0825	0.0840	0.0878	0.0888	0.0877	0.0887	0.0920	0.0883
0.0774	0.0803	0.0770	0.0771	0.0823	0.0765	0.0741	0.0811	0.0732
0.0712	0.0767	0.0704	0.0675	0.0747	0.0665	0.0616	0.0700	0.0605
0.0651	0.0720	0.0642	0.0587	0.0668	0.0576	0.0510	0.0596	0.0499
0.0592	0.0667	0.0581	0.0507	0.0588	0.0497	0.0419	0.0499	0.0409
0.0532	0.0609	0.0522	0.0434	0.0511	0.0424	0.0342	0.0412	0.0332
0.0472	0.0546	0.0461	0.0366	0.0436	0.0357	0.0274	0.0334	0.0266
0.0407	0.0477	0.0398	0.0301	0.0362	0.0293	0.0214	0.0264	0.0207
0.0338	0.0400	0.0329	0.0237	0.0289	0.0230	0.0160	0.0201	0.0155
0.0263	0.0315	0.0256	0.0176	0.0217	0.0170	0.0113	0.0143	0.0109
0.0187	0.0225	0.0181	0.0119	0.0147	0.0115	0.0073	0.0093	0.0070
0.0114	0.0138	0.0110	0.0069	0.0086	0.0067	0.0040	0.0051	0.0039
0.0071	0.0087	0.0069	0.0041	0.0051	0.0040	0.0023	0.0029	0.0022

Stable Populations

0.010			0.020			0.030		
100.00	12.02	87.98	100.00	11.69	88.31	100.00	11.39	88.61
0.0274	0.0207	0.0283	0.0359	0.0279	0.0370	0.0454	0.0362	0.0466
0.0174	0.0107	0.0183	0.0159	0.0079	0.0170	0.0154	0.0062	0.0166
29.19	32.01	28.81	25.21	27.90	24.86	21.78	24.25	21.46

Figure 6.4 Regional age compositions of multiregional (two-region) stable populations with different intrinsic rates of growth: same regional mortality levels, various regional migration levels and stable radix ratios.

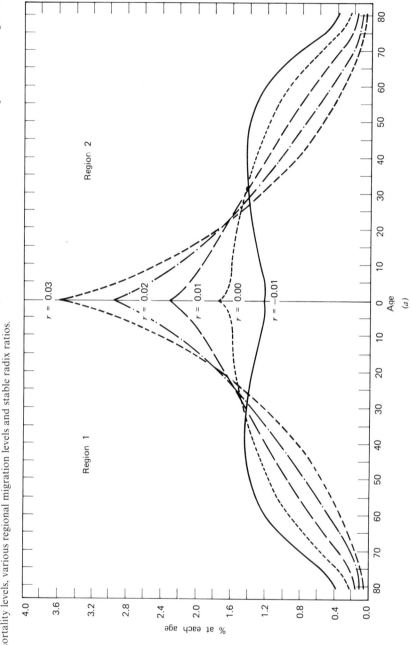

Figure 6.4(a) Same regional mortality levels: $_{10}e(0) = _{20}e(0) = 50$; same regional migration levels: $_1\Theta_2 = _2\Theta_1$; same stable radix ratios: $Q_1/Q_2 = Q_2/Q_1 = 1$.

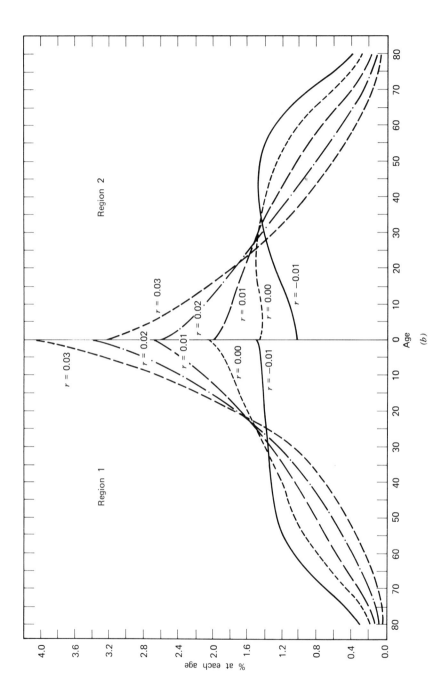

Figure 6.4(b) Same regional mortality levels: $_{10}e(0) = {}_{20}e(0) = 50$; different regional migration levels: $_1\Theta_2 = 12/50 = 0.24$, $_2\Theta_1 = 3/50 = 0.06$; same stable radix ratios: $Q_1/Q_2 = Q_2/Q_1 = 1$.

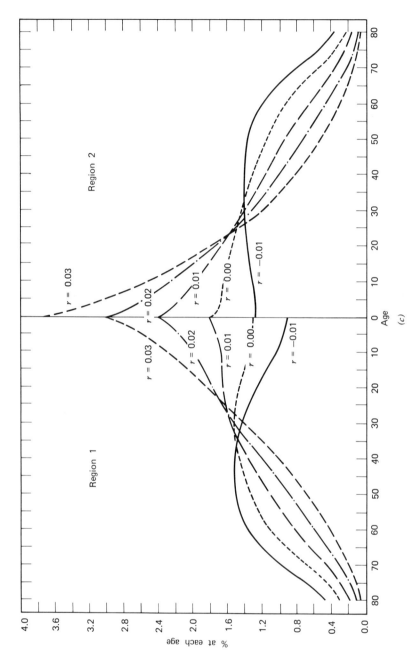

Figure 6.4(*c*) Same regional mortality levels: $_{1,0}e(0) = {_{2,0}}e(0) = 50$; different regional migration levels: $_1\Theta_2 = 12/50 = 0.24$, $_2\Theta_1 = 3/50 = 0.06$; different stable radix ratios: $Q_1/Q_2 = 1/10$, $Q_2/Q_1 = 10/1 = 10$.

(Table 6.2); the fertility schedules are implied by the values taken on by r and the stable radix ratios. Setting out the stable radix ratios as the matrix **SRR**, say,

$$\begin{bmatrix} 1 & SRR_{21} \\ SRR_{12} & 1 \end{bmatrix},$$

where

$$\mathbf{SRR} = \begin{bmatrix} \dfrac{Q_1}{Q_1} & \dfrac{Q_2}{Q_1} \\ \dfrac{Q_1}{Q_2} & \dfrac{Q_2}{Q_2} \end{bmatrix} = \begin{bmatrix} 1 & \dfrac{Q_2}{Q_1} \\ \dfrac{Q_1}{Q_2} & 1 \end{bmatrix}$$

or more generally,

$$\mathbf{SRR} = \mathbf{Q}^{-1}\mathbf{1Q}, \tag{6.5}$$

1 being a matrix of ones, we may express symbolically the dependence of a particular model multiregional stable population on its underlying multiregional model schedules of fertility, mortality, and migration as follows:

$$\text{stable population} = f(_0\mathbf{e}(0), r, \mathbf{SRR}),$$

where the typical element of $_0\mathbf{e}(0)$ is $_{j0}e_i(0)$. For example, the last model stable population in Table 6.4 is a function of

$$_0\mathbf{e}(0) = \begin{bmatrix} 47 & 3 \\ 12 & 38 \end{bmatrix} \qquad r = 0.030 \qquad \mathbf{SRR} = \begin{bmatrix} 1 & 10 \\ \frac{1}{10} & 1 \end{bmatrix}.$$

In the single-region model the relationship between a stable population's fertility schedule and its intrinsic rate of growth is a many-to-one relationship (Section 2.4.2). The same is true, of course, in the multiregional model. That is, a *family* of multiregional fertility schedules in conjunction with a given multiregional life table will produce the same intrinsic growth rate and hence the same multiregional stable population. Thus following Coale and Demeny (1966), we present in Table 6.5 and Figure 6.5, an alternative set of model multiregional stable populations. The basic indices of variation in this second set, the "GRR" set, are the regional gross reproduction rates GRR_1 and GRR_2, both taken at a mean age of fertility of 29 years.[3] Note that

[3] To develop the fertility matrices $\mathbf{F}(x)$ for the *total* (male and female) population that together with the $_0\mathbf{L}(x)$ data in Table 6.2 served as inputs to the computations, we used Coale and Demeny's basic *female* fertility schedule for $\bar{m} = 29$, illustrated in Figure 2.2. The mean age of childbearing in a male fertility schedule, however, is usually several years above that of a female fertility schedule of the same population. And the form of male schedules can be quite different from that of female schedules. Consequently, our GRR stable populations are crude approximations, generated for illustrative purposes only; they should be interpreted with caution.

Table 6.5 Model Multiregional (Two-Region) Stable Populations: Equal Regional Mortality Levels

Age, x	Gross Reproduction Rate (GRR)					
	$GRR_1 = 1, GRR_2 = 1$			$GRR_1 = 1, GRR_2 = 2$		
		Region			Region	
	1 | 2	1	2	1 + 2	1	2
0	0.0599	0.0599	0.0599	0.1201	0.0730	0.1248
5	0.0600	0.0600	0.0600	0.1075	0.0748	0.1108
10	0.0622	0.0622	0.0622	0.0996	0.0760	0.1019
15	0.0645	0.0645	0.0645	0.0922	0.0793	0.0935
20	0.0663	0.0663	0.0663	0.0848	0.0830	0.0850
25	0.0679	0.0679	0.0679	0.0776	0.0837	0.0770
30	0.0692	0.0692	0.0692	0.0707	0.0814	0.0696
35	0.0702	0.0702	0.0702	0.0641	0.0772	0.0628
40	0.0707	0.0707	0.0707	0.0577	0.0718	0.0563
45	0.0706	0.0706	0.0706	0.0515	0.0656	0.0501
50	0.0693	0.0693	0.0693	0.0452	0.0587	0.0438
55	0.0664	0.0664	0.0664	0.0386	0.0511	0.0374
60	0.0610	0.0610	0.0610	0.0318	0.0428	0.0307
65	0.0527	0.0527	0.0527	0.0245	0.0337	0.0236
70	0.0414	0.0414	0.0414	0.0172	0.0240	0.0166
75	0.0280	0.0280	0.0280	0.0104	0.0147	0.0100
80+	0.0194	0.0194	0.0194	0.0065	0.0092	0.0062
				Parameters of Multiregional		
Regional share, %	100.00	20.00	80.00	100.00	8.96	91.04
Birthrate, b	0.0136	0.0136	0.0136	0.0289	0.0162	0.0301
Absence rate, Δ	0.0243	0.0243	0.0243	0.0170	0.0044	0.0183
Growth rate, r	−0.0106	—	—	0.0118	—	—
Average age, a	38.72	38.72	38.72	28.43	33.56	27.92
Radix ratio, SRR_{21}	4.000	—	—	18.885	—	—

Mortality Levels	$_{10}e(0) = 50$			$_{20}e(0) = 50$				
Migration Levels	$_1\Theta_2 = 12/50 = 0.24$			$_2\Theta_1 = 3/50 = 0.06$				

<table>
<tr><td colspan="9" align="center">Gross Reproduction Rate (GRR)</td></tr>
<tr><td colspan="3" align="center">$GRR_1 = 1, GRR_2 = 3$</td><td colspan="3" align="center">$GRR_1 = 2, GRR_2 = 1$</td><td colspan="3" align="center">$GRR_1 = 3, GRR_2 = 1$</td></tr>
<tr><td colspan="3" align="center">Region</td><td colspan="3" align="center">Region</td><td colspan="3" align="center">Region</td></tr>
<tr><td>1 + 2</td><td>1</td><td>2</td><td>1 + 2</td><td>1</td><td>2</td><td>1 + 2</td><td>1</td><td>2</td></tr>
<tr><td>0.1676</td><td>0.0829</td><td>0.1735</td><td>0.0989</td><td>0.1219</td><td>0.0684</td><td>0.1423</td><td>0.1709</td><td>0.0777</td></tr>
<tr><td>0.1396</td><td>0.0883</td><td>0.1432</td><td>0.0917</td><td>0.1087</td><td>0.0692</td><td>0.1230</td><td>0.1417</td><td>0.0809</td></tr>
<tr><td>0.1203</td><td>0.0888</td><td>0.1225</td><td>0.0880</td><td>0.1011</td><td>0.0707</td><td>0.1101</td><td>0.1226</td><td>0.0818</td></tr>
<tr><td>0.1037</td><td>0.0923</td><td>0.1045</td><td>0.0844</td><td>0.0926</td><td>0.0737</td><td>0.0985</td><td>0.1043</td><td>0.0853</td></tr>
<tr><td>0.0887</td><td>0.0955</td><td>0.0882</td><td>0.0805</td><td>0.0830</td><td>0.0771</td><td>0.0875</td><td>0.0868</td><td>0.0890</td></tr>
<tr><td>0.0755</td><td>0.0930</td><td>0.0743</td><td>0.0763</td><td>0.0745</td><td>0.0785</td><td>0.0773</td><td>0.0724</td><td>0.0884</td></tr>
<tr><td>0.0640</td><td>0.0862</td><td>0.0625</td><td>0.0720</td><td>0.0675</td><td>0.0779</td><td>0.0681</td><td>0.0610</td><td>0.0842</td></tr>
<tr><td>0.0540</td><td>0.0773</td><td>0.0524</td><td>0.0676</td><td>0.0614</td><td>0.0758</td><td>0.0596</td><td>0.0516</td><td>0.0778</td></tr>
<tr><td>0.0453</td><td>0.0675</td><td>0.0437</td><td>0.0631</td><td>0.0560</td><td>0.0725</td><td>0.0519</td><td>0.0437</td><td>0.0702</td></tr>
<tr><td>0.0376</td><td>0.0578</td><td>0.0361</td><td>0.0583</td><td>0.0508</td><td>0.0682</td><td>0.0447</td><td>0.0369</td><td>0.0622</td></tr>
<tr><td>0.0307</td><td>0.0484</td><td>0.0294</td><td>0.0530</td><td>0.0454</td><td>0.0630</td><td>0.0379</td><td>0.0308</td><td>0.0539</td></tr>
<tr><td>0.0244</td><td>0.0395</td><td>0.0234</td><td>0.0470</td><td>0.0397</td><td>0.0566</td><td>0.0313</td><td>0.0250</td><td>0.0455</td></tr>
<tr><td>0.0187</td><td>0.0309</td><td>0.0178</td><td>0.0400</td><td>0.0332</td><td>0.0490</td><td>0.0249</td><td>0.0195</td><td>0.0370</td></tr>
<tr><td>0.0134</td><td>0.0227</td><td>0.0128</td><td>0.0320</td><td>0.0262</td><td>0.0397</td><td>0.0186</td><td>0.0143</td><td>0.0282</td></tr>
<tr><td>0.0088</td><td>0.0151</td><td>0.0083</td><td>0.0233</td><td>0.0188</td><td>0.0292</td><td>0.0126</td><td>0.0096</td><td>0.0194</td></tr>
<tr><td>0.0049</td><td>0.0086</td><td>0.0047</td><td>0.0146</td><td>0.0117</td><td>0.0185</td><td>0.0074</td><td>0.0055</td><td>0.0115</td></tr>
<tr><td>0.0028</td><td>0.0050</td><td>0.0027</td><td>0.0094</td><td>0.0074</td><td>0.0119</td><td>0.0044</td><td>0.0033</td><td>0.0069</td></tr>
<tr><td colspan="9">table Populations</td></tr>
<tr><td>100.00</td><td>6.58</td><td>93.42</td><td>100.00</td><td>56.92</td><td>43.08</td><td>100.00</td><td>69.32</td><td>30.68</td></tr>
<tr><td>0.0417</td><td>0.0176</td><td>0.0434</td><td>0.0233</td><td>0.0294</td><td>0.0154</td><td>0.0348</td><td>0.0427</td><td>0.0169</td></tr>
<tr><td>0.0155</td><td>−0.0086</td><td>0.0172</td><td>0.0186</td><td>0.0246</td><td>0.0106</td><td>0.0160</td><td>0.0239</td><td>−0.0018</td></tr>
<tr><td>0.0262</td><td>—</td><td>—</td><td>0.0047</td><td>—</td><td>—</td><td>0.0187</td><td>—</td><td>—</td></tr>
<tr><td>23.01</td><td>30.07</td><td>22.52</td><td>31.48</td><td>28.60</td><td>35.29</td><td>25.69</td><td>22.95</td><td>31.88</td></tr>
<tr><td>34.939</td><td>—</td><td>—</td><td>0.396</td><td>—</td><td>—</td><td>0.176</td><td>—</td><td>—</td></tr>
</table>

Figure 6.5 Regional age compositions of multiregional (two-region) stable populations with various regional gross reproduction rates: same regional mortality levels, different regional migration levels.

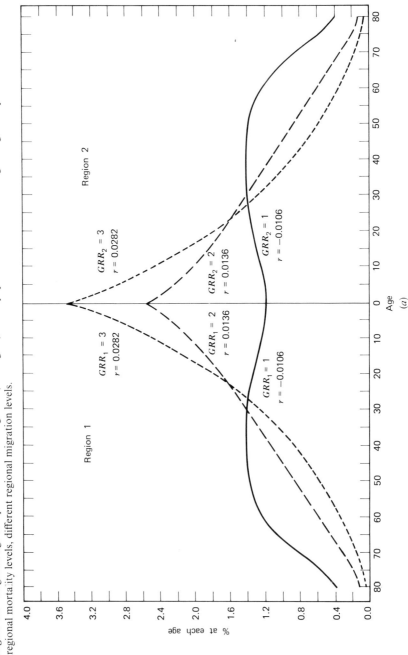

Region 2

$GRR_2 = 3$
$r = 0.0282$

$GRR_2 = 2$
$r = 0.0136$

$GRR_2 = 1$
$r = -0.0106$

Region 1

$GRR_1 = 3$
$r = 0.0282$

$GRR_1 = 2$
$r = 0.0136$

$GRR_1 = 1$
$r = -0.0106$

% at each age

Age

(a)

Figure 6.5(a) Same regional mortality levels: $_{10}e(0) = {}_{20}e(0) = 50$; different regional migration levels: $\Theta_2 = 12/50 = 0.24$; $_2\Theta_1 = 3/50 = 0.06$; same regional fertility levels: $GRR_1 = GRR_2$.

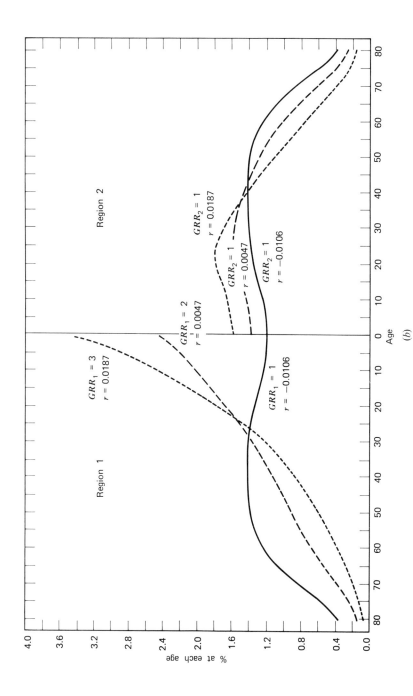

Figure 6.5(b) Same regional mortality levels: $_{10}e(0) = \; _{20}e(0) = 50$; different regional migration levels: $_1\Theta_2 = 12/50 = 0.24$; $_2\Theta_1 = 3/50 = 0.06$; different regional fertility levels: $GRR_1 = 1, 2, 3$; $GRR_2 = 1$.

167

as in the first set, the "growth rate" set, two indices of variation related to fertility are needed to uniquely identify a particular model two-region stable population in each table. Symbolically, we may express the two alternative sets of populations as:

1. Growth Rate Stable Populations: $f(_0\mathbf{e}(0), r, \mathbf{SRR})$
2. GRR Stable Populations: $g(_0\mathbf{e}(0), \mathbf{GRR})$,

where **GRR** is a diagonal matrix with regional gross reproduction rates for its diagonal elements. These symbolic relationships readily show that $m^2 + m$ nonredundant indices of variation will uniquely identify a model m-region stable population. Of these, m pertain to fertility, another m to mortality, and the remaining $m^2 - m$, or $m(m - 1)$, relate to migration. This is a straightforward generalization of Rele's (1967) observation that knowledge of any two nonredundant measures of fertility and mortality is all that is necessary to identify a model single-region stable population and all its characteristics.

Coale and Demeny observe that growth rate stable populations are more convenient for exploring the implications of various recorded intercensal growth rates, whereas GRR stable populations are more useful for studying the effects of different levels of fertility. An analogous observation may be made for the multiregional case. The growth rate multiregional stable populations are useful for analyzing the consequences of different combinations of growth rates and alternative regional allocations of total births in the multiregional population. The GRR multiregional stable populations, on the other hand, are more suitable for examining the impacts of alternative multiregional schedules of fertility, mortality, and migration.

Several of the patterns exhibited by our GRR set of stable populations are repetitions of those identified earlier in the growth rate set. For example, higher fertility levels produce stable populations that have a greater relative slope at every age. Other patterns, obscured in the growth rate populations, now become readily apparent. For example, Figure 6.3a illustrates that regional populations exposed to identical fixed schedules of mortality and fertility, and *arbitrary* combinations of migration levels, will converge to identical age compositions. The stable regional shares, however, do depend on migration and vary inversely with migration levels. That is, $(\%)_j/(\%)_i = {}_i\Theta_j/{}_j\Theta_i$. The first multiregional stable population in Table 6.5 provides an illustration of this property.

Table 6.5 and Figure 6.5*b* exhibit properties of multiregional stable populations that evolve from fixed multiregional schedules of growth in which mortality levels are the same in each region, migration levels are not, and regional fertility levels are allowed to vary in different combinations.[4] A rather surprising finding is the relative insensitivity of the regional age compositions and birthrates to migration behavior. Consider, for example, the cases of $GRR_1 = 1$, $GRR_2 = 3$ and $GRR_1 = 3$, $GRR_2 = 1$. In the first instance the region with the larger (by a factor of 4) outmigration has the lower fertility level; in the second case the situation is reversed. Yet in both cases the region with the higher fertility shows approximately 44% of its population in the 0- to 14-year-old age group and exhibits a birthrate of approximately 43 per 1000. An analogous computation carried out with migration levels set at 10% in each region produced virtually the same numerical values. This insensitivity to migration behavior does not carry over to systemwide measures, however. For example, the intrinsic growth rate and systemwide birthrate are considerably lower in the first case than in the second, and the higher fertility region assumes a stable regional share of 93% in the first case but receives only 69% in the second.

To identify more clearly the interactions between different levels of fertility and migration in model multiregional stable populations, we have so far limited our numerical illustrations to multiregional systems with regional populations that have been exposed to identical schedules of mortality. The mechanics of relaxing this restriction are straightforward operationally, but the confounding of regional differentials in mortality with those of fertility and migration produces complex interactions that generate complex patterns of growth and change. Table 6.6 illustrates several such patterns. First, in a two-region population system with fixed, identical regional schedules of fertility and migration, the regional population with the higher expectation of life at birth (that is, with the lower mortality level) ultimately assumes the higher stable regional share of the total multiregional population and becomes the older population with the lower birthrate. Second, as fertility in the region with the higher life expectancy is increased relative to that in the other region, its population assumes an even higher stable regional share and develops into the younger population with the higher

---

[4] The simpler case of identical regional migration levels produces patterns similar to those exhibited by two stable single-region populations that have been exposed to identical mortality schedules but different levels of fertility. The population of the higher fertility region is younger in average age and larger.

Table 6.6 Model Multiregional (Two-Region) Stable Populations: Unequal Regional Mortality Levels

	Gross Reproduction Rate (*GRR*)					
	$GRR_1 = 1, GRR_2 = 1$			$GRR_1 = 1, GRR_2 = 2$		
		Region			Region	
Age, x	1 + 2	1	2	1 + 2	1	2
0	0.0661	0.0569	0.0669	0.1364	0.0701	0.1388
5	0.0625	0.0589	0.0628	0.1139	0.0739	0.1154
10	0.0639	0.0615	0.0642	0.1034	0.0761	0.1044
15	0.0653	0.0655	0.0653	0.0937	0.0818	0.0941
20	0.0665	0.0700	0.0662	0.0845	0.0884	0.0844
25	0.0674	0.0735	0.0668	0.0760	0.0904	0.0755
30	0.0681	0.0756	0.0674	0.0682	0.0880	0.0674
35	0.0686	0.0764	0.0679	0.0609	0.0824	0.0601
40	0.0687	0.0758	0.0681	0.0542	0.0748	0.0534
45	0.0683	0.0740	0.0677	0.0477	0.0663	0.0471
50	0.0668	0.0707	0.0665	0.0415	0.0573	0.0409
55	0.0640	0.0655	0.0639	0.0353	0.0480	0.0348
60	0.0591	0.0580	0.0592	0.0290	0.0385	0.0286
65	0.0517	0.0478	0.0521	0.0225	0.0287	0.0223
70	0.0414	0.0352	0.0420	0.0160	0.0191	0.0159
75	0.0289	0.0219	0.0296	0.0099	0.0107	0.0099
80+	0.0225	0.0129	0.0234	0.0069	0.0056	0.0070
				Parameters of Multiregiona		
Regional share, %	100.00	8.48	91.52	100.00	3.51	96.49
Birthrate, b	0.0135	0.0146	0.0134	0.0291	0.0173	0.0295
Absence rate, Δ	0.0201	0.0212	0.0200	0.0114	−0.0003	0.0118
Growth rate, r	−0.0066	—	—	0.0176	—	—
Average age, a	38.35	37.79	38.41	27.22	32.65	27.03
Radix ratio, SRR_{21}	9.889	—	—	46.838	—	—

Mortality Levels	$_{10}e(0) = 40$		$_{20}e(0) = 60$					
Migration Levels	$_1\Theta_2 = 1/40 = 0.025$		$_2\Theta_1 = 1.5/60 = 0.025$					

Gross Reproduction Rate (GRR)								
$GRR_1 = 1, GRR_2 = 3$			$GRR_1 = 2, GRR_2 = 1$			$GRR_1 = 3, GRR_2 = 1$		
	Region			Region			Region	
1 + 2	1	2	1 + 2	1	2	1 + 2	1	2
0.1881	0.0800	0.1909	0.1106	0.1134	0.0740	0.1566	0.1593	0.0836
0.1459	0.0872	0.1475	0.1025	0.1050	0.0701	0.1351	0.1371	0.0818
0.1230	0.0891	0.1239	0.0967	0.0987	0.0704	0.1185	0.1199	0.0810
0.1036	0.0951	0.1039	0.0912	0.0926	0.0720	0.1038	0.1046	0.0828
0.0869	0.1010	0.0865	0.0851	0.0860	0.0740	0.0902	0.0903	0.0855
0.0726	0.0995	0.0719	0.0789	0.0792	0.0749	0.0777	0.0774	0.0849
0.0606	0.0918	0.0597	0.0728	0.0726	0.0745	0.0665	0.0660	0.0813
0.0503	0.0810	0.0495	0.0666	0.0661	0.0728	0.0566	0.0558	0.0757
0.0416	0.0690	0.0408	0.0604	0.0597	0.0702	0.0477	0.0469	0.0690
0.0341	0.0572	0.0334	0.0542	0.0533	0.0667	0.0397	0.0389	0.0617
0.0275	0.0462	0.0270	0.0478	0.0467	0.0623	0.0325	0.0317	0.0541
0.0217	0.0361	0.0214	0.0409	0.0397	0.0569	0.0258	0.0251	0.0463
0.0166	0.0271	0.0163	0.0334	0.0321	0.0502	0.0196	0.0189	0.0383
0.0120	0.0189	0.0118	0.0254	0.0242	0.0419	0.0138	0.0132	0.0300
0.0079	0.0117	0.0078	0.0174	0.0163	0.0320	0.0088	0.0083	0.0214
0.0046	0.0061	0.0045	0.0102	0.0093	0.0212	0.0047	0.0044	0.0133
0.0030	0.0030	0.0030	0.0058	0.0051	0.0158	0.0025	0.0022	0.0092

table Populations

100.00	2.57	97.43	100.00	92.88	7.12	100.00	96.37	3.63
0.0415	0.0186	0.0421	0.0298	0.0309	0.0148	0.0440	0.0451	0.0164
0.0092	−0.0137	0.0098	0.0235	0.0246	0.0084	0.0232	0.0242	−0.0045
0.0323	—	—	0.0063	—	—	0.0208	—	—
21.82	29.35	21.63	29.14	28.64	35.66	23.62	23.29	32.15
85.397	—	—	0.037	—	—	0.0137	—	—

birthrate. However, if the increase in relative fertility occurs instead in the region with the lower life expectancy, this pattern is reversed and the regional population with the higher mortality level becomes the population with the higher stable regional share, the lower average age, and the higher birthrate. Finally, if regional fertility, mortality, and migration levels all are allowed to vary, the patterns of growth and change that arise depend very much on the particular combinations of levels that are assumed. Nevertheless, the following conclusion still persists: *the growth impacts of differential regional migration levels are relatively minor when compared with those of fertility and mortality, but their distributive effects can be substantial and appear as changes in stable regional shares.*

6.3   ESTIMATING REGIONAL SURVIVORSHIP AND OUTMIGRATION PROPORTIONS USING PLACE OF RESIDENCE BY PLACE OF BIRTH DATA: THE PRPB METHOD

The UN method of obtaining initial age-specific estimates of 10-year survivorship proportions from two consecutive decennial census-enumerated age distributions may be generalized to multiregional population systems if age-specific place of residence by place of birth (PRPB) data are available for both census years.[5] This easily may be demonstrated by expressing the single-region procedure in algebraic form and reverting to matrix algebra to define the corresponding multiregional method. First observe that the single-region procedure for estimating $s(x)$ may be expressed as follows:

$$^{10}\hat{s}(x) = \frac{K^{(t+1)}(x+10)}{K^{(t)}(x)} = K^{(t+1)}(x+10)K^{(t)}(x)^{-1}, \qquad (6.6)$$

where $K^{(t)}(x)$ denotes the number of persons aged x to $x + 9$ years at time t. Next recall the multiregional model of (5.6), which projects populations disaggregated by place of residence and place of birth:

$$_0\mathbf{K}(x+5) = \mathbf{S}(x)_0\mathbf{K}(x). \qquad (6.7)$$

In Chapter 5 our interest in this model centered on the determination of $_0\mathbf{K}(x+5)$, given particular numerical values for $\mathbf{S}(x)$ and $_0\mathbf{K}(x)$. Now

---

[5] If the population is stable, then as in the single-region case, one census distribution and the stable growth rate are sufficient; for if the multiregional population is stable, so are its place of residence by place of birth age distributions.

Table 6.7 Female White Population Born in Conterminous United States on or Before April 1, 1950, and Living in Conterminous United States at the Census Dates by Age and Region of Birth and Residence, 1950 and 1960

| | 1950 | | | | 1960 | | | |
| | Born in East North Central Division | | Born in Rest of United States | | Born in East North Central Division | | Born in Rest of United States | |
Age in 1960	Residing in East North Central Division	Residing in Rest of United States	Residing in East North Central Division	Residing in Rest of United States	Residing in East North Central Division	Residing in Rest of United States	Residing in East North Central Division	Residing in Rest of United States
10–19	2,483,713	147,837	155,891	9,801,238	2,346,843	292,440	297,300	9,698,003
20–29	1,756,764	143,976	160,694	7,273,574	1,559,712	323,966	393,358	6,909,415
30–39	1,825,243	294,603	376,239	7,894,787	1,713,942	415,994	469,111	7,829,246
40–49	1,704,199	318,651	401,567	7,448,640	1,599,395	377,096	425,929	7,254,277
50–59	1,326,919	297,010	328,338	5,807,428	1,231,036	328,082	320,020	5,596,271
60–69	1,053,964	281,900	225,735	4,306,682	922,722	294,099	191,696	3,930,453
70+	1,291,687	494,154	233,062	4,927,497	736,288	297,892	134,143	2,986,742

Source: U.S. Census of Population: 1950 and 1960, *State of Birth*. Adjusted.

consider the application of (6.7) to derive $S(x)$ given numerical values for $_0K(x)$ and $_0K(x + 5)$. Clearly,

$$\hat{S}(x) = {_0K}(x + 5) {_0K}(x)^{-1},$$

and for a 10-year age and time interval,

$${^{10}\hat{S}}(x) = {_0K}^{(t + 1)}(x + 10) {_0K}^{(t)}(x)^{-1}. \tag{6.8}$$

Observe that (6.8) is the matrix expression of (6.6); moreover, it is precisely the relationship used in Chapters 3 and 5 to obtain life table survivorship and outmigration proportions from the multiregional region of residence by region of birth stationary population.

To illustrate the application of the PRPB method, we now consider some empirical results using United States data. Table 6.7 sets out place of residence by place of birth data for white females in the two-region system of East North Central Division and the rest of the United States in 1950 and 1960.[6] The application of the estimation method to these data produces the estimates set out in Figure 6.6. Applying this projection matrix to the 1950 data, we find that it projects *exactly* the 1960 observed data (Table 6.8). Table 6.9 presents the estimated inmigration, outmigration, and net migration flows for the decade.

The PRPB estimation method appears to be consistent with another procedure that has been suggested for estimating interregional migration from place of residence by place of birth data. In a recent study, Eldridge and Kim (1968) describe their Division of Birth (DOB) method for estimating *net* migration from the same data. The method proceeds as follows:

1. DOB-specific survivorship proportions are estimated and applied to the respective components of the observed 1950 population of each residence division to yield the expected 1960 population, by place of residence, that would have resulted if net migration were zero for each division of residence by division of birth component.

2. Differences between the observed and the expected 1960 population components are viewed as estimates of the net migration for each place of residence, cross-classified by division of birth, over the 10-year period preceding 1960.

---

[6] Since the model assumes a multiregional system that is closed to the rest of the world, adjustments were made to eliminate the impact of emigration and immigration, following the procedure described in Eldridge and Kim (1968).

$$
\begin{bmatrix}
0 & 0 & 0 & 0 & 0 & 0 & 0 & 0 & 0 & 0 & 0 & 0 & 0 & 0 & 0 & 0 \\
0.9440 & 0 & 0 & 0 & 0 & 0 & 0 & 0 & 0.0153 & 0 & 0 & 0 & 0 & 0 & 0 & 0 \\
0 & 0.8850 & 0 & 0 & 0 & 0 & 0 & 0 & 0 & 0.0345 & 0 & 0 & 0 & 0 & 0 & 0 \\
0 & 0 & 0.9366 & 0 & 0 & 0 & 0 & 0 & 0 & 0 & 0.0148 & 0 & 0 & 0 & 0 & 0 \\
0 & 0 & 0 & 0.9373 & 0 & 0 & 0 & 0 & 0 & 0 & 0 & 0.0067 & 0 & 0 & 0 & 0 \\
0 & 0 & 0 & 0 & 0.9271 & 0 & 0 & 0 & 0 & 0 & 0 & 0 & 0.0027 & 0 & 0 & 0 \\
0 & 0 & 0 & 0 & 0 & 0.8759 & 0 & 0 & 0 & 0 & 0 & 0 & 0 & -0.0014 & 0 & 0 \\
0 & 0 & 0 & 0 & 0 & 0 & 0.5699 & 0 & 0 & 0 & 0 & 0 & 0 & 0 & 0.0003 & 0 \\
0 & 0 & 0 & 0 & 0 & 0 & 0 & 0 & 0 & 0 & 0 & 0 & 0 & 0 & 0 & 0 \\
0.0589 & 0 & 0 & 0 & 0 & 0 & 0 & 0 & 0.9885 & 0 & 0 & 0 & 0 & 0 & 0 & 0 \\
0 & 0.1068 & 0 & 0 & 0 & 0 & 0 & 0 & 0 & 0.9476 & 0 & 0 & 0 & 0 & 0 & 0 \\
0 & 0 & 0.0684 & 0 & 0 & 0 & 0 & 0 & 0 & 0 & 0.9884 & 0 & 0 & 0 & 0 & 0 \\
0 & 0 & 0 & 0.0396 & 0 & 0 & 0 & 0 & 0 & 0 & 0 & 0.9718 & 0 & 0 & 0 & 0 \\
0 & 0 & 0 & 0 & 0.0320 & 0 & 0 & 0 & 0 & 0 & 0 & 0 & 0.9618 & 0 & 0 & 0 \\
0 & 0 & 0 & 0 & 0 & 0.0354 & 0 & 0 & 0 & 0 & 0 & 0 & 0 & 0.9108 & 0 & 0 \\
0 & 0 & 0 & 0 & 0 & 0 & -0.0013 & 0 & 0 & 0 & 0 & 0 & 0 & 0 & 0.6062 & 0
\end{bmatrix}
$$

Figure 6.6 Estimated multiregional projection matrix for white females: East North Central Division and rest of the conterminous United States, 1950–1960.

Table 6.8   Observed and Projected White Female Age Distributions: East North Central Division and Rest of the Conterminous United States, 1950–1960

| | | Female Population | | |
| | | Observed | | Projected |
Region	Age in 1960	1950	1960	1960
East North Central	10–19	2,639,604	2,644,143	2,644,143
Division	20–29	1,917,458	1,953,070	1,953,070
	30–39	2,201,482	2,183,053	2,183,053
	40–49	2,105,766	2,025,324	2,025,324
	50–59	1,655,257	1,551,056	1,551,056
	60–69	1,279,699	1,114,418	1,114,418
	70+	1,524,749	870,431	870,431
Rest of United States	10–19	9,949,075	9,990,443	9,990,443
	20–29	7,417,550	7,233,381	7,233,381
	30–39	8,189,390	8,245,240	8,245,240
	40–49	7,767,291	7,631,373	7,631,373
	50–59	6,104,438	5,924,353	5,924,353
	60–69	4,588,582	4,224,552	4,224,552
	70+	5,421,651	3,284,634	3,284,634

Table 6.9   Estimated Migration of White Females: East North Central Division, 1950–1960

Age in 1960	Inmigration	Outmigration	Net Migration
10–19	152,406	155,481	−3,075
20–29	256,115	204,692	51,422
30–39	121,068	150,521	−29,454
40–49	51,677	83,331	−31,654
50–59	16,403	52,901	−36,498
60–69	−6,408	45,349	−51,757
70+	1,449	−1,964	3,412
Total	592,710	690,312	−97,602

In comparing the DOB and the PRPB estimation methods, we first consider the two-region results appearing in Figure 6.6 and Tables 6.8 and 6.9. We may compare them with the results that Eldridge and Kim's DOB method would have produced by focusing on the net migration rates that are generated by each method. These data are displayed in Table 6.10 and in Figure 6.7. Note that for purposes of comparability the inmigration and outmigration rates in Table 6.10 have been given a common denominator and therefore may be combined to yield the net migration rate, as in Eldridge and Kim (1968).

A quick glance at Table 6.10 and Figure 6.7 reveals that the two sets of net migration rates are remarkably similar. Thus it appears that the PRPB

Table 6.10   Rates of Migration of Native White Females, 10 Years Old and over, by Age, as Derived by DOB and PRPB Methods: Two-Region Division of the Conterminous United States, 1950–1960

Residence and Age in 1960	Rates per 1000 Average Population		Net Migration	
	Inmigration, PRPB	Outmigration, PRPB	PRPB	DOB
East North Central Division				
10–19	57.7	58.8	−1.2	−1.3
20–29	132.3	105.8	26.6	28.0
30–39	55.2	68.7	−13.4	−12.9
40–49	25.0	40.3	−15.3	−15.8
50–59	10.2	33.0	−22.8	−24.6
60–69	−5.4	37.9	−43.2	−42.5
70+	1.2	−1.6	2.8	−15.5
Total, 10+	46.2	53.8	−7.6	−9.3
Rest of United States				
10–19	15.6	15.3	0.3	0.3
20–29	27.9	35.0	−7.0	−7.4
30–39	18.3	14.7	3.6	3.4
40–49	10.8	6.7	4.1	4.2
50–59	8.8	2.7	6.1	6.6
60–69	10.3	1.4	11.8	11.6
70+	−0.4	0.3	−0.8	4.3
Total, 10+	14.4	12.4	2.0	2.5

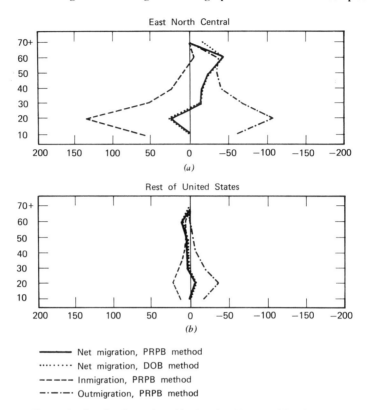

Figure 6.7 Rates of migration for native white females, 10 years old and over. (*a*) East North Central Division; (*b*) rest of United States.

and the DOB methods produce almost identical estimates of net migration in all age groups except the last. (The differences in the last age group are a consequence of the negative elements in the projection matrix.) However, the PRPB method in addition provides estimates of interregional migration streams.

A two-region population system does not permit a convincing comparison of the PRPB and DOB methods because of insufficient data observations. Hence to carry out a more extensive comparison of the two estimation methods, we now expand our two-region system to Eldridge and Kim's nine-region division of the conterminous United States.

Table 6.11 and Figure 6.8 summarize the results for the nine-region population system and correspond directly to the results for the two-region

Table 6.11 Rates of Migration of Native White Females, 10 Years Old and over, by Age, as Derived by DOB and PRPB Methods: Geographic Divisions of the Conterminous United States, 1950–1960

Residence and Age in 1960	Rates per 1000 Average Population			
	Inmigration, PRPB	Outmigration, PRPB	Net Migration	
			PRPB	DOB
New England Division				
10–19	40.9	58.4	−17.5	−17.8
20–29	82.8	131.8	−49.0	−49.0
30–39	32.9	72.1	−39.2	−40.5
40–49	13.2	39.9	−26.7	−24.7
50–59	7.6	21.8	−14.2	−13.3
60–69	4.6	26.4	−21.8	−22.8
70+	2.6	8.4	−5.9	−10.3
Total 10+	30.3	56.8	−26.5	−26.8
Middle Atlantic Division				
10–19	19.0	58.9	−39.9	−39.6
20–29	52.8	107.5	−54.8	−54.8
30–39	18.7	61.7	−43.0	−42.4
40–49	5.4	34.4	−29.0	−31.5
50–59	−0.7	25.9	−26.6	−29.2
60–69	−4.0	34.7	−38.7	−41.4
70+	1.0	8.0	−6.9	−17.5
Total 10+	15.3	51.3	−36.1	−37.8
East North Central Division				
10–19	57.7	58.9	−1.2	−1.1
20–29	132.0	105.3	26.7	28.4
30–39	54.8	67.9	−13.1	−12.6
40–49	24.6	38.6	−13.9	−15.4
50–59	10.0	31.6	−21.7	−24.5
60–69	−5.3	36.6	−41.9	−42.5
70+	1.5	−14.0	15.6	−15.2
Total, 10+	46.0	51.9	−5.9	−9.0

Table 6.11 (*continued*)

Residence and Age in 1960	Rates per 1000 Average Population			
	Inmigration, PRPB	Outmigration, PRPB	Net Migration	
			PRPB	DOB
West North Central Division				
10–19	38.7	94.3	−55.6	−57.5
20–29	84.3	201.3	−117.0	−120.4
30–39	28.1	124.2	−96.2	−96.8
40–49	9.3	55.5	−46.2	−53.5
50–59	0.2	39.2	−39.0	−35.8
60–69	−6.0	33.9	−39.9	−40.4
70+	−37.8	36.8	−74.7	−51.9
Total, 10+	21.3	89.4	−68.0	−67.2
South Atlantic Division				
10–19	92.2	51.4	40.8	41.1
20–29	165.4	117.9	47.5	47.8
30–39	97.8	48.4	49.5	47.7
40–49	68.0	19.6	48.4	47.3
50–59	71.2	6.7	64.5	66.5
60–69	110.2	−0.3	110.6	109.1
70+	65.3	−3.3	68.6	66.4
Total, 10+	97.6	41.5	56.2	55.7
East South Central Division				
10–19	31.9	124.5	−92.6	−94.3
20–29	76.7	272.6	−195.8	−201.1
30–39	30.0	133.4	−103.4	−109.6
40–49	11.8	69.0	−57.2	−60.4
50–59	1.2	33.8	−32.6	−36.4
60–69	0.3	15.1	−14.8	−16.1
70+	0.7	−11.7	12.5	−8.3
Total, 10+	26.6	108.8	−82.3	−87.5

Table 6.11 *(continued)*

| Residence and Age in 1960 | Rates per 1000 Average Population | | Net Migration | |
	Inmigration, PRPB	Outmigration, PRPB	PRPB	DOB
West South Central Division				
10–19	42.6	80.2	−37.7	−36.9
20–29	102.0	147.0	−45.0	−45.0
30–39	42.2	69.9	−27.7	−27.1
40–49	16.4	32.4	−16.0	−17.7
50–59	3.4	17.3	−13.9	−12.6
60–69	−1.2	8.4	−9.6	−2.4
70+	−30.8	14.9	−45.8	−13.2
Total, 10+	32.8	61.9	−29.1	−25.4
Mountain Division				
10–19	171.4	98.5	72.8	73.4
20–29	278.2	188.2	90.0	86.9
30–39	201.7	89.0	112.7	120.6
40–49	117.5	23.2	94.2	87.8
50–59	72.9	9.4	63.5	68.2
60–69	70.1	3.7	66.4	44.6
70+	−6.1	71.4	−77.5	33.8
Total, 10+	153.7	80.7	73.0	80.1
Pacific Division				
10–19	176.2	28.9	147.3	148.3
20–29	319.7	49.4	270.3	274.6
30–39	204.4	11.2	193.2	194.9
40–49	97.6	2.8	94.8	114.0
50–59	71.1	−4.0	75.1	79.2
60–69	71.9	−3.5	75.4	85.8
70+	41.4	−0.6	42.0	53.9
Total, 10+	153.8	14.7	139.1	146.0

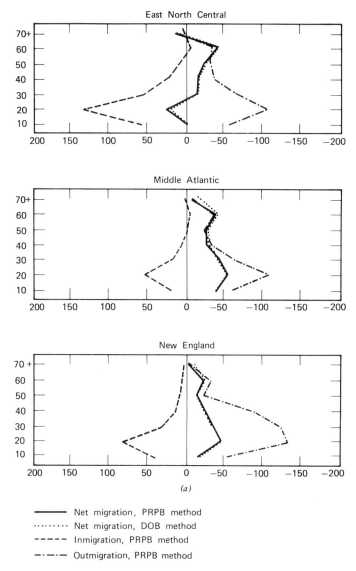

Figure 6.8(*a*)   Rates of migration for native white females, 10 years old and over.

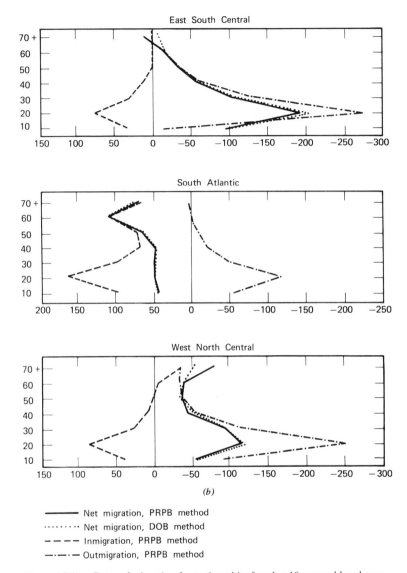

East South Central

South Atlantic

West North Central

(b)

——————— Net migration, PRPB method
············· Net migration, DOB method
— — — — Inmigration, PRPB method
—·—·— Outmigration, PRPB method

Figure 6.8(*b*)   Rates of migration for native white females, 10 years old and over.

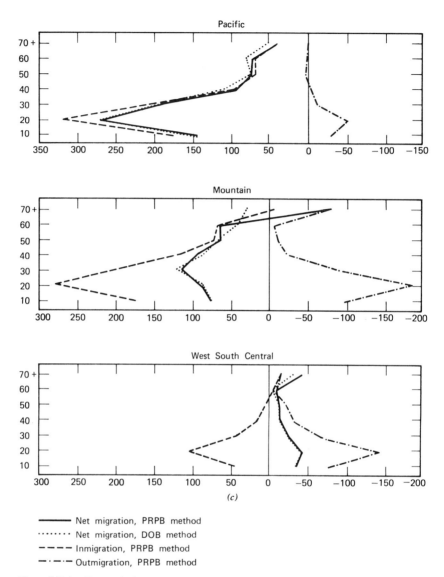

Figure 6.8(c)   Rates of migration for native white females, 10 years old and over.

system that appeared in Table 6.10 and Figure 6.7, respectively. Once again the principal finding is that both methods generate almost the same net migration rates in all age groups except the last.

6.4 SELECTING THE APPROPRIATE MODEL MULTIREGIONAL LIFE TABLE

Having found crude initial estimates of the various regional survivorship and outmigration proportions by means of the PRPB method, we may apply the Option 2 method of life table construction to obtain the regional expectations of life at birth that are implied by these proportions. Then, as in the single-region case, we may "adjust" our initial estimates of probabilities of outmigration and death by interpolating in an appropriate set of model multiregional life tables.

Table 6.12 **Population of Brazil by Age, Region of Residence, and Region of Birth: 1960**

Age, x	Population of the North–Center–West Region (1) by Age and Place of Birth		Population of the Rest of Brazil Region (2) by Age and Place of Birth	
	$_{10}K_1(x)$	$_{20}K_1(x)$	$_{20}K_2(x)$	$_{10}K_2(x)$
0–9	1,744,056	85,968	20,223,841	24,809
10–19	1,149,119	147,639	14,222,226	48,101
20–29	711,678	181,535	10,358,410	56,594
30–39	477,518	148,407	7,802,457	43,118
40–49	327,265	102,808	5,597,277	34,199
50–59	172,883	67,416	3,859,941	18,903
60–69	84,431	45,983	2,144,336	9,739
70+	37,804	24,788	1,008,938	4,999
Totals	4,704,754	804,544	65,217,426	240,462

Source. Special tabulation for the Brazilian Ministry of Planning expanded proportionately from a 1.5% sample to the total population reported in the Brazilian census of 1960.

To illustrate this process, we present the 1960 total population of Brazil, disaggregated by age, region of residence, and region of birth (see Table 6.12). Since comparable data for 1950 are unavailable, we assume that the population was stable and obtain the corresponding 1950 "data" by multiplying each element in Table 6.12 by 0.731935, the reciprocal of the observed 10-year growth ratio. Applying (6.8) to these sets of age distributions, we obtain the initial age-specific estimates of the 10-year survivorship and outmigration proportions that appear in Table 6.13. (Observe that one of the survivorship proportions exceeds unity and that two outmigration proportions are negative.) Entering these estimated proportions into the Option 2 life table

Table 6.13 Initial Estimates of the Age-Specific 10-Year Survivorship and Outmigration Proportions: North–Center–West Region (1) and Rest of Brazil Region (2)

Age, x	$^{10}\hat{s}_{11}(x)$	$^{10}\hat{s}_{12}(x)$	$^{10}\hat{s}_{22}(x)$	$^{10}\hat{s}_{21}(x)$
0	0.9001	0.0240	0.9607	0.0061
10	0.8458	0.0256	0.9948	0.0087
20	0.9164	0.0009	1.0291	0.0035
30	0.9363	0.0094	0.9799	0.0002
40	0.7214	−0.0196	0.9425	0.0032
50	0.6667	−0.0060	0.7591	0.0046
60	0.6114	0.0068	0.6427	0.0027

Table 6.14 Model Life Table Age-Specific 10-Year Survivorship and Outmigration Proportions: North–Center–West Region (1) and Rest of Brazil Region (2)

Age, x	$^{10}s_{11}(x)$	$^{10}s_{12}(x)$	$^{10}s_{22}(x)$	$^{10}s_{21}(x)$
0	0.9221	0.0066	0.9412	0.0024
10	0.9210	0.0098	0.9534	0.0036
20	0.8967	0.0077	0.9372	0.0029
30	0.8708	0.0046	0.9170	0.0017
40	0.8185	0.0030	0.8707	0.0011
50	0.6996	0.0026	0.7641	0.0010
60	0.4910	0.0016	0.5615	0.0006
70	0.2130	0.0004	0.2673	0.0001

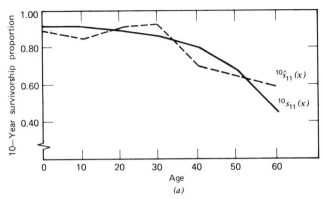

Figure 6.9(a)   Age-specific 10-year survivorship and outmigration proportions: observed and model life table values.

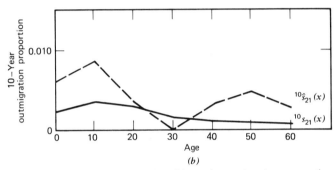

Figure 6.9(b)   Age-specific 10-year survivorship and outmigration proportions: observed and model life table values.

construction method described in the Appendix to Chapter 3, we find[7]

$$_{10}e(0) = 41.06 \qquad _{10}e_1(0) = 40.00 \qquad _{10}e_2(0) = 1.06$$
$$_{20}e(0) = 52.15 \qquad _{20}e_2(0) = 51.74 \qquad _{20}e_1(0) = 0.41$$

With these estimates we now may construct a model multiregional life table by following the procedures outlined in Section 6.1. This table leads to the smoothed *10-year* survivorship and outmigration proportions set out in Table 6.14. Figure 6.9 illustrates the differences between the initial crude proportions in Table 6.13 and their "smoothed" equivalents in Table 6.14.

[7] The Option 2 method of constructing a multiregional life table requires as an input the regional death rates in the terminal age groups. As in Chapter 2, we assume that $_{i0}e(70) = 10$, whence

$$m_{i\delta}(70) = \tfrac{1}{10}, \qquad i = 1, 2.$$

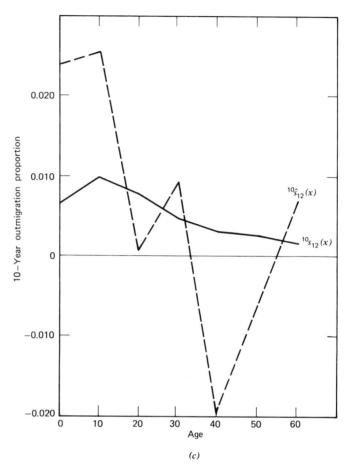

Figure 6.9(*c*)   Age-specific 10-year survivorship and outmigration proportions: observed and model life table values.

With an appropriate model multiregional life table, we may proceed, as in the single-region case, to develop estimates of regional birthrates. First we average the two census age distributions and apply to this average the appropriate age-specific model life table outmigration and death rates to find, after aggregation across age groups, an estimated number of *total annual* outmigrants O_j and deaths D_j for each region. Subtracting these totals from the corresponding total regional population of the average age distribution, K_j, and adding total inmigration, I_j, we obtain a quantity which,

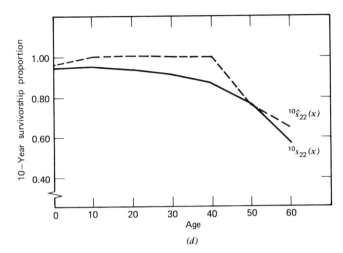

Figure 6.9(d)   Age-specific 10-year survivorship and outmigration proportions: observed and model life table values.

if subtracted from $e^r K_j$, gives the total number of births B_j. That is, for each region j

$$e^r K_j = K_j - O_j - D_j + I_j + B_j,$$

whence

$$B_j = (e^r - 1)K_j + O_j + D_j - I_j,$$

and B_j/K_j is the crude annual regional birthrate in region j. Disaggregating the total regional births according to a model fertility schedule (analogous to those illustrated in Figure 2.2), we may develop crude estimates of age-specific fertility rates $F_j(x)$, thereby completing the input data requirements necessary to calculate a multiregional projection matrix and develop a population projection.

CHAPTER
SEVEN

Conclusion

Population projections work out the numerical consequences to an initial population of a particular set of assumptions about future fertility, mortality, and migration. The mechanics of such projections for single-region populations are well established and typically involve three steps. The first ascertains the starting age distribution and the age-specific schedules of fertility, mortality, and *net* migration to which this population has been subject during a past period. The second adopts a set of assumptions about the future behavior of such schedules. And the third derives the consequences of applying these specified schedules to the initial population.

Most existing population projection models manifest a dynamic but essentially nonspatial structure. That is, they project regional populations over time but not over space. Spatial considerations are accommodated by repeating the projection over as many areal units as comprise the multiregional population system being studied. In consequence, a multiregional population system is analyzed one region at a time.

During the past decade, the need to consider space and time jointly in population studies has produced several efforts that introduce explicitly the interregional dimension into mathematical demographic analysis; as a result, we now have the beginnings of a truly *multiregional* mathematical demography. This book has brought together some of the more fundamental contributions and has linked them in a way that shows their consistency and continuity with conventional single-region theory. Indeed, we have demonstrated that a judicious definition or structuring of a multiregional problem often makes possible a solution with a "weighted" single-region solution method, in which the weights reflect conditions that should prevail under stability. Such methods must of course rely on iterative solution procedures, because the conditions prevailing under stability are part of the solution we seek.

Four major themes in mathematical demography have formed the central focus of this study: the life table, the continuous and the discrete models of population growth, and the estimation of demographic measures using model life tables and stable populations. Thus we began in Chapter 3, with the notion of a multiregional life table and showed how one may develop a multiregional stationary population by applying in the appropriate sequence a set of probabilities of surviving and outmigrating to regional radices of arbitrary size:

$$\mathbf{l}(5) = \mathbf{P}(0)\mathbf{l}(0)$$
$$\vdots \quad \vdots \quad \vdots$$
$$\mathbf{l}(x + 5) = \mathbf{P}(x)\mathbf{l}(x).$$

Integrating these over 5-year age intervals to find

$$\mathbf{L}(x) = \int_0^5 \mathbf{l}(x + t)\, dt,$$

we used the linear approximation

$$\mathbf{L}(x) = \tfrac{5}{2}[\mathbf{l}(x) + \mathbf{l}(x + 5)],$$

with which we calculated the matrix of survivorship and outmigration proportions

$$\mathbf{S}(x) = \mathbf{L}(x + 5)\mathbf{L}(x)^{-1}.$$

In Chapter 4 we adopted the multiregional expression of Lotka's continuous model of demographic growth set out by LeBras (1971):

$$\{\mathbf{B}(t)\} = \int_\alpha^\beta \mathbf{M}(x)_0\mathbf{P}(x)\{\mathbf{B}(t - x)\}\, dx$$

and proceeded to develop its stable growth properties, such as the intrinsic regional birthrates $\mathbf{b}$ and the stable age by region distributions $\mathbf{c}(x) = \mathbf{b}e^{-rx}{}_0\mathbf{P}(x)$. Numerical evaluation of these quantities and the intrinsic rate of growth was carried out using the conventional approximation to the integral

$$\int_0^5 e^{-r(x+t)}\mathbf{M}(x + t)_0\mathbf{P}(x + t)\,dt.$$

in which the integral of the triple product was replaced by the product of $e^{-r(x+2.5)}$, $\mathbf{F}(x)$, and ${}_0\mathbf{L}(x)$, the matrix ${}_0\mathbf{L}(x)$ having been computed on unit radices for all regions.

Chapter 5 developed the discrete model of multiregional demographic growth, marrying the author's earlier matrix model (Rogers, 1966) with the survivorship and outmigration proportions of the multiregional life table of Chapter 3, at the same time reconciling the numerical results with those generated by the continuous model of Chapter 4. The fundamental multiregional projection model

$$\{\mathbf{K}^{(t+1)}\} = \mathbf{G}\{\mathbf{K}^{(t)}\}$$

was shown to converge ultimately to a stable region by age distribution that increases by a ratio of λ after every unit interval of time. It also was demonstrated that this stable growth ratio is preserved under perfect aggregation.

In Chapter 6 we generalized current methods for estimating demographic measures from incomplete data by introducing the notion of model multiregional life tables and stable populations. The conventional procedure for obtaining initial age-specific estimates of survivorship and outmigration proportions from two consecutive census-enumerated age distributions was extended to multiregional population systems by applying the relationship

$$\mathbf{S}(x) = {}_0\mathbf{L}(x + 5)_0\mathbf{L}(x)^{-1}$$

to an empirical population, that is,

$$\hat{\mathbf{S}}(x) = {}_0\mathbf{K}(x + 5)_0\mathbf{K}(x)^{-1}.$$

These census survivorship and outmigration proportions were used to create a multiregional life table, and the resulting regional expectations of life at birth by region of residence were then employed to generate a model multiregional life table that best reflected the observed patterns of mortality and migration.

It is perhaps appropriate to conclude this book by identifying several important themes in multiregional mathematical demography that have not been examined. First, our generalization of classical population mathematics to multiregional population systems has focused on models that are essentially linear in structure. We have not explored the appropriateness of nonlinear functional relationships largely because of the intractable mathematics that such an examination involves (Feeney, 1973). Second, all the models of demographic growth considered here are fundamentally deterministic and unisexual. We have left to others the development of the corresponding stochastic theory (Ginsberg, 1973; Pollard, 1973) and the resolution of the two-sex problem (Feeney, 1972; Keyfitz, 1972). The same is true of the intricacies of competing risks and similar conundrums present in the actuarial domain of multiple decrement-increment life table construction (Chiang, 1972; Hoem, 1969). We have skirted these issues by a judicious choice of assumptions that need to be examined further. Finally, demography, like economics, has both a mathematical dimension (Keyfitz, 1968) and a statistical dimension (Adelman, 1963; Muth, 1972). In economics these two major bodies of thought are called mathematical economics and econometrics, respectively. In demography, one might refer to them as mathematical demography and, perhaps, "demosmetrics." Only the former has been considered in this book, although the latter clearly merits further examination at this time and will undoubtedly assume an increasingly important role in the development of multiregional demographic analysis.

BIBLIOGRAPHY

Adelman, I. "An econometric analysis of population growth," *American Economic Review*, **53** (1963), 314–339.

Ara, K. "The aggregation problem in input–output analysis," *Econometrica*, **26** (1959), 257–262.

Bernardelli, H. "Population waves," *Journal of the Burma Research Society*, **31** (1941), 1–18.

Chiang, C. L. *Introduction to Stochastic Processes in Biostatistics*, Wiley, New York, 1968.

——— "A general migration process," in *Population Dynamics*, T. N. E. Greville, ed., Academic Press, New York, 1972, pp. 333–355.

Coale, A. J. *The Growth and Structure of Human Populations: A Mathematical Investigation*, Princeton University Press, Princeton, N.J., 1972.

——— and P. Demeny. *Regional Model Life Tables and Stable Populations*, Princeton University Press, Princeton, N.J., 1966.

Eldridge, H. T. and Y. Kim. *The Estimation of Intercensal Migration from Birth–Residence Statistics: A Study of Data for the United States, 1950 and 1960*, Population Studies Center, University of Pennsylvania, Philadelphia, 1968.

Feeney, G. M. "Stable age by region distributions," *Demography*, **6**(1970), 341–348.

——— "Comment on a proposition of H. LeBras," *Theoretical Population Biology*, **2**(1971), 122–123.

——— "Marriage rates and population growth: The two-sex problem in demography," Ph.D. dissertation, University of California, Berkeley, 1972.

——— "Two models for multiregional population dynamics," *Environment and Planning*, **5**(1973), 31–43.

Gantmacher, F. R. *The Theory of Matrices*, K. A. Hirsch, trans., vol. 2, Chelsea, New York, 1959.

Ginsberg, R. B. "Semi-Markov processes and mobility," *The Journal of Mathematical Sociology*, **1**(1971), 233–262.

Graunt. J. *Natural and Political Observations Mentioned in a Following Index, and Made upon the Bills of Mortality, with Reference to the Government, Religion, Trade, Growth, Air, Diseases, and the Several Changes of the Said City*, John Martyn, London, 1662.

Hoem, J. M. "Purged and partial Markov chains," *Skandinavisk Aktuarietidskrift*, **52**(1969), 147–155.

Keyfitz, N. *Introduction to the Mathematics of Population*, Addison-Wesley, Reading, Mass., 1968.

———— "Age distribution and the stable equivalent," *Demography*, **6**(1969), 261–269.

———— "Finding probabilities from observed rates or how to make a life table," *The American Statistician*, **24**(1970), 28–33.

———— "The mathematics of sex and marriage," *Proceedings of the Sixth Berkeley Symposium on Mathematical Statistics and Probability*, vol. 4, University of California Press, Berkeley, 1972, pp. 89–108.

———— and W. Flieger. *Population: Facts and Methods of Demography*, Freeman, San Francisco, 1971.

LeBras, H. "Équilibre et croissance de populations soumises à des migrations," *Theoretical Population Biology*, **2**(1971), 100–121.

Ledent, J. and A. Rogers. *An Interpolative–Iterative Procedure for Constructing a Multiregional Life Table*, MGMP Working Paper No. 9, Department of Civil Engineering, Northwestern University, Evanston, Ill., 1972.

Leslie, P. H. "On the use of matrices in certain population mathematics," *Biometrika*, **33**(1945), 183–212.

———— "Some further notes on the use of matrices in population mathematics," *Biometrika*, **35**(1948), 213–245.

Lewis, E. G. "On the generation and growth of a population," *Sankhya*, **6**(1942), 93–96.

Long, L. H. "New estimates of migration expectancy in the United States," *Journal of the American Statistical Association*, **68**(1973), 37–43.

Lopez, A. *Problems in Stable Population Theory*, Office of Population Research, Princeton, N.J., 1961.

Lotka, A. J. "Mode of growth of material aggregates," *American Journal of Science*, **24**(1907), 199–216.

Lowry, I. S. *Migration and Metropolitan Growth: Two Analytical Models*, Chandler, San Francisco, 1966.

McFarland, D. D. "On the theory of stable population; a new and elementary proof of the theorems under weaker assumptions," *Demography*, **6**(1969), 301–322.

Muth, R. F. "Migration: Chicken or egg?" *The Southern Economic Journal*, **37**(1971), 295–306.

Parlett, B. "Ergodic properties of population. I: The one-sex model," *Theoretical Population Biology*, **1**(1970), 191–207.

Pollard, J. H. *Mathematical Models for the Growth of Human Populations*, Cambridge University Press, London, 1973.

Rele, J. R. *Fertility Analysis Through Extension of Stable Population Concepts*, Institute of International Studies, University of California, Berkeley, 1967.

Rogers, A. "The multiregional matrix growth operator and the stable interregional age structure," *Demography*, **3**(1966), 537–544.

——— *Matrix Analysis of Interregional Population Growth and Distribution*, University of California Press, Berkeley, 1968.

——— "On perfect aggregation in the matrix cohort–survival model of interregional population growth," *Journal of Regional Science*, **9**(1969), 417–424.

——— *Matrix Methods in Urban and Regional Analysis*, Holden-Day, San Francisco, 1971.

——— "The multiregional life table," *The Journal of Mathematical Sociology*, **3**(1973), 127–137.

——— "Estimating internal migration from incomplete data using model multiregional life tables," *Demography*, **10**(1973), 277–287.

——— "The mathematics of multiregional demographic growth," *Environment and Planning*, **5**(1973), 3–29.

——— "The multiregional net maternity function and multiregional stable growth," *Demography*, **11**(1974), 473–481.

——— and S. McDougall. *An Analysis of Population Growth and Change in Slovenia and the Rest of Yugoslavia*, Working Paper No. 81, Center for Planning and Development Research, University of California, Berkeley, 1968.

——— and B. von Rabenau. "Estimation of interregional migration streams from place-of-birth-by-residence data," *Demography*, **8**(1971), 185–194.

Sharpe, F. R. and A. J. Lotka, "A problem in age-distribution," *Philosophical Magazine*, Ser. 6, **21**(1911), 435–438.

Stone, L. O. "Stable migration rates from the multiregional growth matrix operator," *Demography*, **5**(1968), 439–442.

Sykes, Z. M. "On discrete stable population theory," *Biometrics*, **25**(1969), 285–293.

United Nations. *Age and Sex Patterns of Mortality: Model Life Tables for Underdeveloped Countries*, New York, 1955.

——— *Methods of Estimating Basic Demographic Measures from Incomplete Data*, New York, 1967.

——— *Methods of Measuring Internal Migration*, New York, 1970.

INDEX

Adelman, I., 194
Age composition, *see* Stable age composition
Age distribution, *see* Stable age distribution
Aggregation, 132–138
Ara, K., 136
Average age, *see* Mean age
Average years lived in interval, by nonmigrant survivors, 59
by outmigrants, 59
by those dying, 11, 59

Bernardelli, H., 7
Birth rate, in observed population, 22, 31, 100, 120
in stable population, *see* Intrinsic rate, of birth
in stationary (life table) population, 74, 76

Characteristic equation, 19, 140, 141
for integral equation, 141
numerical solution of, 21–24, 99–106
for projection matrix, 140

Characteristic matrix, 93, 100
Characteristic roots, dominant, *see* Projection matrix, dominant characteristic root of
of characteristic matrix, 94–96
of projection matrix, 37, 125
Characteristic vectors, of characteristic matrix, 93–99
of projection matrix, 37–38, 125, 128
Chiang, C. L., 60, 194
Coale, A. J., 7, 42, 43, 44, 45, 48, 52, 54, 148, 150, 151, 154, 163, 168
Cohort, 8, 12, 29, 60, 73
Cohort survival projection, 117
Complex roots, 19–20, 96–97
Continuous model of growth, 18–28, 91–115, 138–143

Death probability, *see* Probability, of dying
Death rate, in observed population, 11, 82
in stable population, *see* Intrinsic rate, of death
in stationary population, 11, 84
Decrement, 10

201